'Provocative, timely and incisive, *The New Economics* exposes the failures of conventional economic thinking with humour and wisdom, and sets out the essentials of a vibrant new economy for a just and sustainable 21st century.'
Oliver Tickell, author, *Kyoto2*

'Through the use of engaging stories and analysis, *The New Economics* shows how we can, and must, look at the world in a very different way centred on people, not profit, if we are to create a sustainable future for us all.'
Jessica Fries, Project Director, Accounting for Sustainability, The Household of TRH The Prince of Wales and The Duchess of Cornwall

'By twisting together the green shoots of economic unorthodoxy, *The New Economics* points the way to a more sensible way of doing things... I enjoyed it immensely.'
Christian Hunt, lead author of the Climate Safety report and Managing Director of Cheatneutral

The New Economics

The New Economics

A Bigger Picture

David Boyle and Andrew Simms

publishing for a sustainable future

London • Sterling, VA

First published by Earthscan in the UK and USA in 2009

ISBN: 978-1-84407-675-8

Typeset by MapSet Ltd, Gateshead, UK
Cover design by Rob Watts

For a full list of publications please contact:

Earthscan
Dunstan House
14a St Cross Street
London EC1N 8XA, UK
Tel:+44 (0)20 7841 1930
Fax: +44 (0)20 7242 1474
Email: earthinfo@earthscan.co.uk
Web: **www.earthscan.co.uk**

22883 Quicksilver Drive, Sterling, VA 20166-2012, USA

Earthscan publishes in association with the International Institute
for Environment and Development

A catalogue record for this book is available from the British Library

Library of Congress Cataloging-in-Publication Data

Boyle, David, 1958–
The new economics : a bigger picture / David Boyle and Andrew Simms.
    p. cm.
  Includes bibliographical references and index.
  ISBN 978-1-84407-675-8 (hardback)
  1. Economics–Psychological aspects. 2. Well-being. 3. Sustainable development.
I. Simms, Andrew, 1865– II. Title.
  HB74.P8B65 2009
  330–dc22

                                                                2009022798

At Earthscan we strive to minimize our environmental impacts and carbon footprint
through reducing waste, recycling and offsetting our CO_2 emissions, including those
created through publication of this book. For more details of our environmental policy,
see www.earthscan.co.uk.

This book was printed in the UK by MPG Books,
an ISO 14001 accredited company.
The paper used is FSC certified.

Mixed Sources
Product group from well-managed
forests and other controlled sources
www.fsc.org Cert no. SA-COC-1565
© 1996 Forest Stewardship Council

FSC

There is no wealth but life.
John Ruskin, *Unto This Last*

Contents

Acknowledgements   *ix*
List of Acronyms and Abbreviations   *xi*

1   The Economic Problem   1

2   No Wealth but Life: A Brief History of the New Economics   17

3   Measurement: Why Did an Apparently Poor Pacific Island Hit the
    Top of the Happy Planet Index?   31

4   Money: Why did China Pay for the Iraq War?   49

5   Markets: Why has London Traffic Always Travelled at 12mph?   65

6   Life: Why do Modern Britons Work Harder than Medieval Peasants?   77

7   Resources: Why are Cuban Mechanics the Best in the World?   95

8   Trade: Why Does Britain Import the Same Number of Chocolate Waffles
    as it Exports?   109

9   Community: Why do Fewer People Vote when there is a Wal-Mart
    Nearby?   123

10 Debt: Why are Malawi Villagers Paying the Mortgages of Surbiton
    Stockbrokers?   135

11 The Future   151

*Appendix A From the Ashes of the Crash: 20 First Steps from
New Economics to Rebuild a Better Economy*   *161*

Appendix B New Economics Tools and Techniques   *173*

Index   *181*

Acknowledgements

Writing a book about the emergence of the new economics is often a business of collecting, from the range of new insights, ideas and inspirational projects that are emerging all over the world, those that put people and planet first. It is about shaping an argument around them.

That is difficult enough at the best of times, but we started this book at an unprecedented moment of crisis for the financial system – the emergence of what was then referred to as the 'sub-prime crisis'. We finished it at an even bigger moment: what will undoubtedly become known as the Crash of 2008. The continuation of the financial system in its present form is now in doubt. We have adapted the message to suit the times, as they changed, and can only apologize if that adaptation has not taken into account some new, unknown twist in the story just over the horizon.

This book is also a collection of the work of, and a tribute to, the founders, trustees, staff and supporters of the New Economics Foundation (**nef**), the E. F. Schumacher Society in the USA and our other allied think tanks around the world. It is intended as a statement of where the new economics now stands, and it would not be possible without their pioneering endeavour.

We particularly want to thank those at **nef** who have been involved most closely in advising on drafts, corrections and ideas, especially Saamah Abdallah, Pat Conaty, Corrina Cordon, Lindsay Mackie, Susanna Mitchell, Ruth Potts, James Robertson, Stephen Spratt, Jim Sumberg, Veronika Thiel, Perry Walker, Stewart Wallis, and Lorna Arblaster, David Adshead and the Network for Social Change, for their time, effort, advice and for making the project possible. We did not always take their advice, so the mistakes are all ours.

Many of the ideas and examples are drawn from **nef** reports since 2000, and we very much want to acknowledge their many authors, including Jody Aked, Jessica Brown, Molly Conisbee, Elizabeth Cox, Emma Dawnay, Deborah Doane, Aniol Esteban, Victoria Johnson, Petra Kjell, Eilis Lawlor, Alex MacGillivray, Sarah McGeehan, Nic Marks, Ed Mayo, Richard Murray, Eva Neitzert, Sargon Nissan, Julian Oram, Ann Pettifor, Rachel Prance, Polly Raymond, Josh Ryan-Collins, Paul

Sander-Jackson, Lisa Sanfilippo, Jessica Sellick, Lucie Stephens, Nicola Steuer, Sam Thompson, David Woodward and many others.

We also want to acknowledge the enormous patience of our families while we struggle away at the computer, now and always: Sarah, Robin and William (David's family) and Rachel and Scarlett (Andrew's family). Without them we couldn't manage it or be who we are today.

David Boyle
Andrew Simms

List of Acronyms and Abbreviations

CDCU	community development credit union
CDFI	community development finance institution
CDO	collateralized debt obligation
CEO	chief executive officer
CHP	combined heat and power
CND	Campaign for Nuclear Disarmament
Democs	deliberative meeting of citizens
DIY	do-it-yourself
DTQ	domestic tradable quota
EBCU	emissions-backed currency unit
Escos	energy service companies
GDP	gross domestic product
GM	genetically modified
GPI	Genuine Progress Indicator
HPI	Happy Planet Index
IMF	International Monetary Fund
IP	intellectual property
ISEW	Index of Sustainable Economic Welfare
km	kilometre
Lets	Local exchange and trading systems
LM3	Local Money 3
m	metre
MDGs	Millennium Development Goals
MDP	Measure of Domestic Progress
MDR-TB	multi-drug resistant tuberculosis
mph	miles per hour
nef	New Economics Foundation
NHS	National Health Service
RESOLVE	Research Group on Lifestyles Values and Environment
SDRs	special drawing rights

SERs	special emission rights
SIV	structured investment vehicle
SROI	social return on investment
T-bills	Treasury bills
TEQ	tradeable emissions quota
TOES	The Other Economic Summit
TRIPS	Trade-Related Aspects of Intellectual Property
WEEE	Waste Electrical and Electronic Equipment (Directive)

1
The Economic Problem

Man talks of a battle with nature, forgetting that if he won the battle, he would find himself on the losing side.

E. F. Schumacher, *Small is Beautiful*, 1973

Industrial humanity is behaving like King Midas. He turned his daughter into gold before he realised the limitations of his own conception of wealth.

Paul Ekins, *Wealth Beyond Measure*, 1992

What can Walt Disney teach you about financial crises? When the sub-prime mortgage crisis took hold in the spring of 2007, with the big financial players desperately beginning the search for exactly what lay in those structured debt investments they had believed were assets, the front line investigators were employed by a company in Connecticut, outside New York City, called Clayton Holdings. Clayton specialized in checking out risky mortgage loans for the big Wall Street firms, before or after they had been bundled up into the notorious structured investment vehicles (SIVs) that they were buying. It was at this point, checking one mortgage portfolio, that they found one that had been signed by the borrower simply as 'M. Mouse'.

This was a symbolic moment. If Mickey Mouse can take out a mortgage, then the system is revealed to be without any of the checks and balances that are supposed to safeguard us all. Especially in the UK, people still believe that the great institutions that underpin our lives, known as banks, are dedicated to careful scrutiny and prudent lending: in practice, these institutions – like so many others – have been hollowed out, removing those checks, as well as those bank managers who might once have scrutinized Mr Mouse's mortgage application and rejected it earlier.

It was a serious crisis, but it wasn't exactly unprecedented. The Wall Street crash followed the great radio stocks boom. The 1987 crash followed the junk bond boom.

The dot.com 'bust' followed the dot.com boom. Now the 2008 crash has followed the property and credit boom. Although it always comes as a surprise to the people the novelist Tom Wolfe dubbed the 'masters of the universe', financial panic follows financial over-excitement, as surely as night follows day.[1] A handful of sacrificial lambs are blamed and sometimes even gaoled; regulations are tightened and loosened again. But the fundamental problem that the financial markets are the epicentre of a massive system, the main purpose of which is to make its key players unimaginably rich, is never properly addressed. Nor are the other structural problems of the economic system, which forgives the powerful their mistakes, and which cushions them against the hard times, and provides them with enough money to achieve their dreams, but exhausts the rest of us and punishes and corrodes the lives of the poorer two thirds of the world. 'The economic problem', as John Maynard Keynes put it, has not been solved, and there sometimes seems to be little prospect of solving it – even when its institutions suffer the kind of catastrophic collapse they suffered in 2008.[2]

The crucial fact is that the collapse of the financial markets is only a small part of the problem. It is simply the visible part of an iceberg that represents those crises the world faces which are driven by economic assumptions that no longer work. This latest unravelling – and there have been more than 40 currency crises since the Second World War – is the beginning of the end of the flawed dream that a handful of us could consume our way to economic nirvana. The planet can't take it; the human psyche can't take it; but economics seems to insist that we do it anyway. That looks increasingly like an impossible contradiction. Is there a way out?

This book suggests that there is: a 'new economics' approach, or to be more accurate, a bundle of approaches, that values real, rather than illusory wealth, and puts people and planet first. The good news is that there have been symptoms now for decades of the seeds of this new economics, which sets out to organize the muscles of the world differently. It is there in the emergence of local and ethical food, the rise of people's demand for authenticity, in the rise of ethical business, ethical investment, fair trade and the massive growth in 'downshifting', in everyone from architects to economists learning from nature, of people deliberately earning less to have a better life. This new economics is based on a different framework: it recognizes a different yardstick of success. It is aware of the gap between money growth and real wealth. Its basic tenets are accepted in communities and in business alike, but have barely filtered into the ivory towers of government and their orthodox economic thinking.

The idea is not new. Books on the new economics have been written already, even if they did not use that term. But what was urgently needed was a book, written as much for non-economists as for the experts and specialists, which could set out the tradition, parameters, practicalities and claims of this new economics, and set these out in terms that policy makers can understand and use. We have tried to do that here by looking at the way the world works through the lens of the new economics, and finding there some bizarre questions that seem to fly in the face of orthodoxy. Why do we work longer hours than some medieval peasants? Why are the best mechanics in the world Cuban? Why do we export as many chocolate waffles out of the UK as we import? Each one of these serves as an introduction to a different aspect of the new economics, whether it is the critique of the idea of wealth that lies at the heart of new economics, or whether it is the implications of that critique for money, trade, work or resources.

Those bizarre questions overlap, but they broadly cover the basic issues of the new economics, with a chapter of the book devoted to each – measuring wealth, money, markets, work, resources, trade, community and debt.

* * *

The sheer diversity of the immediate crisis – in credit, climate and energy – is also, paradoxically, an opportunity. Its sheer seriousness compels some response. The crunch is a combination of a credit-fuelled financial crisis, accelerating climate change and volatile energy prices underpinned by the encroaching peak in oil production. These three overlapping events threaten to develop into a perfect storm, the like of which has not been seen since the dustbowls, bankruptcies and unemployment of the Great Depression and quite possibly never before.

These immediate crunches are underlain by three fundamental crises: ecological, human and spiritual. These are not usually understood as economic problems, but that is exactly what they are: a by-product of faulty measurement and misleading values pedalled by an ill-directed economic system. These central crises are as follows:

The ecological crisis
The rising temperature of the biosphere is being caused by human economic activity, burning fossil fuels to drive the growth economy. As a result, the year 2005 was the hottest year ever. Carbon dioxide is at its highest level in the atmosphere for the last 2 million years, predominantly driven by industrial and human use of fossil fuels: the destruction of our natural capital for economic reasons, leading to climatic upheaval, more extremes of weather including increasingly severe droughts and floods, species loss and a real threat to the viability of the human food chain. If all the ice in the world melted, the sea would rise by up to 70 metres (m). But even a single metre will displace tens of millions of people in a country like Bangladesh, slightly more will be catastrophic for many parts of the world, flooding major cities and large parts of certain countries. Estimates also suggest that in the foreseeable future we are going to lose a quarter of our mammalian species, 12 per cent of our bird species and something like a third of our amphibians. The future for polar bears is bleak.

Then there is the inappropriately named 'positive feedback', when these changes cause knock-on domino effects. As the ice melts, there are less reflective surfaces, so less heat is reflected back. As more carbon dissolves in the sea, its ability to absorb carbon goes down, besides becoming more acidic and destroying coral reefs. As the sea warms, other greenhouse gases trapped in the sea bed stand to be released. As the tundra melts, it gives off methane and carbon dioxide. As the Amazon rainforest is destroyed, there is more drought, more fires, more destruction, less carbon absorbed and more released. These and many effects are described in the last report of the Intergovernmental Panel on Climate Change.[3]

The human crisis

This is the crisis of distribution. Despite two centuries of economic expansion and unprecedented growth in recent decades, around 1 billion people are going to bed chronically malnourished every night and 30,000 children are dying every day of preventable diseases. Behind those statistics lie individual stories of human tragedy all over the world. Worse, the inequality between those people and the wealthy has actually been increasing. In the late 19th century, the ratio of the richest 20 per cent in the world to the poorest was somewhere between 3:1 and 10:1. By 1960, the ratio between the richest and the poorest had grown to 30:1. By 1997, that had grown to 75:1.[4] These are accelerating figures: now the richest 1 per cent of the world earn as much as the poorest 57 per cent of the world combined. At the same time, the poorest 5 per cent of the world actually *lost* a quarter of their real income.

The spiritual crisis

Yet even those who are among the winners under the current system are largely failing to benefit. Although gross domestic product (GDP) in the UK has doubled over the last 30 years, most measures of well-being have remained steady or dipped down. Similar studies are showing even some decline in well-being in most developed countries. The winners in the system are suffering from rising debt, rising stress, rising depression and mental ill health.

At the same time, the social glue that holds our lives together, and makes the economy possible, is also unravelling: families, neighbourhoods and relationships are fracturing under the pressure of high mortgages, benefit regulations and the kind of monoculture that drives out local enterprise, institutions and community life from many areas in the name of efficiency, centralization and corporate success.

When 12 million people in Europe are involved in some way in downshifting – earning less money for greater well-being – then you know the mainstream, which demands we should constantly accelerate our earning and spending, has a problem.[5] Downshifting is incoherent in conventional economic terms, where people are assumed to maximize their income at all times. It is also evidence that high growth economics does not necessarily produce greater well-being even for those who benefit financially.

* * *

Major change tends to emerge with the aid of economic catastrophe, though that is a depressing conclusion. Even so, it would have been hard to imagine, when the property boom was still at its height in the spring of 2007, that, within 18 months, governments would have been dusting off economic ideas that had been rejected for a generation or more, and would be desperate for new ones. The crash was predictable; the scale and speed of collapse was less so.

The immediate cause of the great unravelling was the so-called 'sub-prime' market, which was in itself nothing new. It was one aspect of the market that lent money to poorer people, at higher risk of default, in return for higher rates of interest. It had previously been a whole industry carved out between door-to-door loan sharks, shunned by the mainstream lenders. The big banks had been criticized on both sides of the Atlantic for failing the third of the population they considered unworthy for credit. But instead of expanding their own operations to cover them, they invested in 'sub-prime' companies to mop up the marginally bankable instead, and foremost among these was HSBC.

So it was hardly surprising that it was HSBC that revealed, in February 2007, that they were setting aside extra funds to cover bad debts in their American sub-prime lending portfolios. On the same day, one of the biggest sub-prime lenders in the USA, New Century in California, experienced a catastrophic loss of confidence after revealing a quarterly loss. Its senior executives were away in Ireland planning future projects: another metaphor for the faults of the system as a whole.

What had happened was that the investment banks believed they had discovered a way for mortgage lenders to lend money to poorer people at high rates of interest, but at negligible risk. What they did was to bundle the loans they had made together with a range of other loans from other markets, with varying degrees of risk, and sell them as safe investments. Then they could lend money from the sale to more investors and so on.

The disastrous model used by so many lenders meant bundling up their mortgages and selling them on, then using the proceeds to lend more. It meant that banks and other investors would buy the SIVs, getting the full value of the repayments over the years. The SIVs were then taken apart and reassembled into parcels called collateralized debt obligations (CDOs) and sold to hedge funds, which sold them on all over the world. Because these CDOs included debts from a range of different markets, they were believed to be insulated against risk: the mortgages might cause problems, but the other loans would offset the risk. That is how the credit ratings agencies Moodys and Standard & Poor saw it, giving them AAA ratings.

The trouble was that, once the truth about the sub-prime loans – M. Mouse and all the rest – became clear, this very safety aspect of the CDOs became their undoing. They could all rely on safe loans being in the package, but it also meant they could also rely on unsafe sub-prime loans being in there as well, and, as the default rate began to rise, that rendered them of doubtful and uncertain value.

By July 2007, Standard & Poor was threatening to cut its ratings on $12 billion of sub-prime debt. A month later, the European Central Bank was pumping €95 billion into the money markets, as the flow of interbank lending, which banks need to deal with day-to-day withdrawals while their deposits are out on loan, all but dried up. A month after that, reports that Northern Rock was looking for emergency financial support from the Bank of England led to the first run on a British bank for over a century, with the alien sight of savers queuing for hours in the rain outside branches.

Since then, as we know, the crisis accelerated until most of the investment banks on Wall Street had disappeared, and – spurred by the bankruptcy of Lehman Brothers – most of the banks in Europe and North America were forced to accept state bail outs and partial state control, or went cap in hand to the sovereign wealth funds in the Middle East, to avoid bankruptcy. The economic assumptions of the past generation lay in ruins, the advice provided by the best financial minds had been disastrous, and occasionally fraudulent, and the architecture that runs the world's economies was broken beyond repair.

The epicentre of the disaster on the ground was by then the city of Cleveland, Ohio, where one in ten homes was repossessed and vacant, nearly every street blighted by boarded up properties and street gangs.[6] With one in five US mortgages now sub-prime, many of them facing major hikes in the repayment rate after two or three years, more than 2 million foreclosure proceedings began in the USA in 2007 alone, many of them against people sold mortgages where the terms and interest rates were misrepresented to them, which is what happens when products are believed to be risk free by those selling them. Especially when those selling them are often paid on a commission basis, and are normally rewarded for the number of sales they achieve.

These sales were complicated by the bizarre packaging and repackaging of the actual mortgages into SIVs, and many families have been rescued by the fact that the final owner of their mortgage has, not surprisingly, mislaid the relevant paperwork, without which they are powerless to foreclose. The less fortunate mortgage payers found that huge unexplained fees had been added once they asked for help to delay payments, putting them even further in debt.

By October 2008 – financial crashes usually take place in October for some reason – the real question was whether not the financial system could survive. One estimate puts the total value of credit default swaps in the system, most of which include risky sub-prime loans, at as much as $45 trillion: twice the total value of the

US stock market and three times the GDP of the US.[7] The veteran investor Warren Buffett has already described derivatives, and other investment vehicles used by hedge funds and others, as 'financial weapons of mass destruction', and he may well be proved right.[8] Certainly the events of the autumn of 2008 implied that something more serious was happening, as a series of major names – HBOS, Lehman Brothers, Merrill Lynch and all the others – were wiped off the map, driven out of business as much by the hedge funds as by any other mistakes they might have made. Governments have run up huge deficits propping up a banking system that may or may not be able to deliver any kind of recovery, except for itself.

The collapse of the New York and London economic model in 2008 may turn out to be as significant as the collapse of the Soviet model in 1989. If the financial system survives the crisis – and it usually does survive, despite the upheaval – it may briefly focus the minds of policy makers worldwide on the problems that lie behind these activities. As we write, the minds of most policy makers are obsessed with how to return to what they might call 'business as usual', but the sheer intractability of that – and the inevitability of another bust not far off when they do – might allow them to consider how self-destructive the system is and to ask themselves what kind of alternatives there are.

When, in February 2009, the bankers who were at the helm of the big UK banks gave evidence to the House of Commons select committee, they were unanimous that 'nobody' at the time had pointed out the risks. This was nonsense, of course, and evidence of the ivory tower where the masters of the universe have their dwelling. But if they had peered out of the window of that tower, and if the politicians do now, they might be forced to ask themselves why the system requires huge indebtedness, from rich to poor, just to chug on. Nearly all the money in circulation was created in the form of bank loans: under the current system we need these loans in order to have the money to exchange goods and services. And since most of that money began as mortgages, we need them – in this sense at least – in order to survive.

There is also the peculiar irrelevance to real life of this bizarre dance in Wall Street and the City of London, justified by their occasional ability to raise loans for productive expansion, but actually leaching vast fees and bonuses from the income of savers, pensioners, insurance payers and taxpayers. And behind that, there is a more fundamental problem: this global financial system, underpinning all our lives yet increasingly disconnected from real life, accelerates $3 trillion through the system every day, nearly 90 per cent of which is speculation, mostly speculation in the foreign exchange markets.[9] We find ourselves colluding in that system through our savings, pensions and credit card debts, but it has nothing to do with the job that the financial system is supposed to do – to facilitate the exchange of goods and services, to make capital available for people so that they can create productive businesses in the future.

The money system is no longer designed for this basic work of economics. Perhaps it never was, but its power is now huge. And, those who manage the world continue to accept the enrichment of those who run the system, under the misapprehension that some of those rewards will filter down to the rest of us.

We are living through a period when the politics of money has shifted. Fewer of the electorate are prepared to accept that enrichment of others, especially when the banks have so mismanaged the world. Fewer of us are prepared to be taxed more to prop up a failing financial system. The political shock of the collapse has led more people to look increasingly closely at money and where it comes from. Many of them are surprised to find that what they had assumed was no longer true. No, money hasn't been based on gold since at least 1931. No, money is not produced at the Royal Mint (no more than 3 per cent anyway). We have comforted ourselves with these cosy myths for generations. In fact, of course, the pound is worth what it is because of millions of transactions by foreign exchange dealers around the world. Most of the money in circulation is created by the private banking system as interest-bearing debt, and has to be paid back, plus a bit. We owe more than there is money to pay it off, but we keep the dance going by pulling off the trick year after year of growing the economy a little bit more – at least until the music stops.

These revelations, and the fury at the cost of bailing out the system again, may be enough, in themselves, to justify a mainstream search for a new kind of economics. The new economics is certainly a reaction against the narrow form of globalization that has gripped the planet, a combination of global deregulation of capital, a moral vacuum at the heart of the economic system, and a process whereby the powers and resources of nation states are handed over to monopolistic global corporations. This has been described as the 'neoliberal' agenda, though there is nothing very new and certainly nothing liberal about it, and its failures are increasingly obvious. But it is not just a reaction against globalization. In practice, the 'new economics', which has been emerging over the past three decades, has been as much a reaction against the results of the previous consensus, which drew on aspects of Keynes – the inflation, centralization and narrow measurements of success – as it has been against modern corporate globalization. It has a more fundamental critique at its heart, about the distance between money and real wealth.

* * *

'It may work fine in practice,' goes a joke the French make at their own expense, 'the trouble is, it doesn't work in theory.' Anyone who has sat through debates in Brussels or conferences in Paris will know all about the French love of theory, in contrast to the nuts and bolts obsessions of Anglo-Saxons about whether things will actually work. So it is strange that Paris became the birthplace of an unusual revolt against the pre-eminence of theory over practice, of economic abstractions over reality and of statistics over real life. What is more, the rebellion by economics students had an impact that has echoed through the French establishment. A top-level inquiry recommended sweeping changes in the way economics was taught in French universities, backed by their education minister. It was one of the most successful coups by a branch of the new economics anywhere.

Calling themselves 'post-autistic economics'– 'autistic' is intended to imply an inward-looking, disengaged preoccupation with numbers – the movement spread quickly, but more quietly, to other universities in Britain and America. The movement's leaders at the Sorbonne – Gilles Raveaud, Olivier Vaury and Ioana Marinescu – may not have had much of an impact on thinking outside academia, beyond causing mild consternation among econometricians. But their efforts may mark something more important: a growing disenchantment with the whole cult of measurement, statistics, targets and indicators, which has become such a feature of modern life, not just in the UK government, but around the world; and with the drift of mainstream economics away from the human reality it attempts to describe. As long ago as 1985, an article in *Atlantic Monthly* by Robert Kuttner suggested that universities were churning out economics students who were 'brilliant at esoteric mathematics yet innocent of actual economic life'.[10] The post-autistic campaigners were determined to do something about it.

Their campaign began with a web petition in June 2000 (www.paecon.net), protesting against the dogmatic teaching of neoclassical economics, to the exclusion of other points of view, and the 'uncontrolled use' of mathematics as 'an end in itself'. Within two weeks, the petition had 150 signatures, many from France's most prestigious universities, and *Le Monde* had launched a public debate. The call was taken up by students across France and, by the autumn, education minister Jack Lang had announced that he took the criticisms seriously, appointing the respected economist Jean-Paul Fitoussi to head a commission of inquiry.

He reported in 2001, backing many of the 'post-autistic' points. By then, there had also been a vitriolic exchange of articles by French and American economists, a counter-petition launched by the Massachusetts Institute of Technology, and a peculiar post-autistic petition by Cambridge PhD students in the UK – unusual in that the Cambridge signatories were too scared for their future careers to put their real names to it. There is certainly growing concern about the narrowing of economics: Cambridge economics professor Ha-Joon Chang has complained that economic history has been dropped from the curriculum.

But while post-autistic economics sprung from the economics profession, 'new economics' emerged from outside it. Both represent a critique of conventional economics – the ideas that underpin the rules by which the world is run – that is primarily critical of the way that money measures the world. Both are sceptical of the claims that economics is a scientific and accurate representation of the real world. Together, and with other strands and critiques, they are reacting against economic assumptions that work so badly for most people and the planet, assumptions that may no longer be shared by most economists, certainly not all of them, but that have long since been adopted by those who advise policy makers. 'Practical men, who believe themselves to be quite exempt from any intellectual influences, are usually the slaves of some defunct economist,' said John Maynard Keynes.[11] Unfortunately for us, the current batch of practical men now rule the world. And the brand of economics they use is open to the following criticisms:

It ignores the planet

Conventional economics largely disregards environmental issues, and fails to take account of the damage done to the planet and to people. It ignores those side effects of economic success, the loss of rainforest, the pollution, the crime, dislocation and depression, all of which come under the heading of what economists call 'externalities'.

It measures the wrong thing

Money measures value badly, and – to be more specific – measures of economic growth measure success badly as a result. The GDP is the money value of all the goods and services produced and exchanged in the nation in a year: it is the cornerstone of conventional economic success. Yet it is actually a means and not an end. Forgetting this skews the economic system, encouraging bad things that increase GDP and discouraging good things that don't.

It misunderstands real life

Conventional economics assumes that markets work. It assumes that people have money or assets and can operate in the marketplace. It assumes we are isolated, rational individuals with all the information we need to make free choices, and that the uneven distribution of power is not a problem. It assumes that the price is an accurate reflection of such markets. In fact, of course, those perfect conditions never exist: many people have no power or assets to operate economically, and are anyway overwhelmed by the power of others.

It encourages vulnerability

Speak to poor cotton farmers in the majority of the world, and you realize that they are dependent, not so much on their own efforts, but on what happens to the world price of cotton, and on the $4 billion of subsidies being paid to other cotton farmers, mostly in Louisiana and Texas, which allows the United States to dump cotton at virtually no price onto the world market and devastate other producers.[12] What ought to be a level playing field – and is assumed to be in conventional economics – is often an unclimbable cliff, dominated by a handful of corporate monopolists, subsidised by tax paid by poor people in rich countries.

It colludes with short-termism

Most democratic systems are highly short term, based on a short electoral cycle, which encourages politicians to trade long-term change for short-term illusions of success. Financial bonuses in the private sector also fuel a short-term cycle, trapping their employees on the business equivalent of a hamster wheel, having to produce ever greater quarterly earnings.

It overvalues owners

Ownership by individuals of their home and enough land to make them independent is some guarantee of independence. But perpetual ownership by investors of companies excludes and devalues the work and imagination of other people involved in their success, and – since ownership extends way beyond most investment horizons – means an inefficient overpayment to investors.

It remains blind to values

The pursuit of pure markets by conventional economics blinds economists to those aspects that are beyond price – the ethics behind a product or the pursuit of well-being by earning less, rather than more. There is an increasing minority of people who want to reflect their values in the way they shop, invest and work.

It encourages consumption for its own sake

Because of the design of money, which has to be paid back plus interest, and the requirement for constant growth, the economic system has to move faster and faster just to keep still, generating new desires and unsatisfiable wants, leading to depression, disaffection and environmental degradation.

It encourages and relies on debt and indenture

Most of the money that circulates around the world was created in the form of debt that must eventually be paid off by somebody, plus interest. This represents a huge demand, not just on the indebted populations of the Earth, but on the planet's ability to produce enough to meet this constantly increasing demand.

Taken together, these criticisms reveal not just an economic system that is partially blind, but one that has no moral compass and is destructive of the environmental conditions on which civilization depends. It is an economics that assumes there is no morality but supply and demand. Economics may have begun as a branch of moral philosophy, but it ignores the moral aspects of humanity, and other human aspects, as inconvenient for its theories. The result is a narrow economic system, which fails to reflect the real world, and is hurtling towards human and environmental limits. By putting economics back into its proper psychological and biological context, the new economics tries to return to those moral roots.

None of these are criticisms of markets in themselves. On the contrary, markets with clear social and environmental parameters can be effective ways for human beings to interact and get what they need. Amartya Sen, the Nobel prize-winning economist, said that 'to be generically against markets is like being generically against conversation'.[13] Markets are part of life, but they are not the same everywhere. They can be vibrant and bustling at street level in towns and villages, binding communities together. And, on a larger scale, they can be faceless, bland and destructive, the economic equivalent of aerial bombing, in which the pilot never gets to see the damage they cause on the ground. Their problem is the imbalance of power between those taking part, the measuring system they use, and the ecological context in which they have to provide feedback.

Behind them is a more fundamental problem about the claims to pre-eminence of conventional economics. Despite its flawed representation of the world, economics claims pride of place in policy discussions. Even media debates about the benefits of supermarkets or new airports end with this conundrum: the economy makes everything else possible, so it comes first.

This has led to a perverse upending of nature. The economy is supposed to serve the needs of people and planet, but the reverse is increasingly true. The privileges given to the private and financial sectors are justified by the way their success is supposed to serve the interests of society. People's worth is increasingly judged by the value they create in the economy contributing to GDP growth, a process that seems to have been internalized so that people often see material possessions as the main source of self-worth. Yet beyond a relatively low level of satisfying needs, we are no happier.

Thanks to the deregulation of capital controls, the state itself is also increasingly subordinate to the needs of business and finance, and openly so. This is partly a logical consequence of the focus on income and profit growth: the business and financial sector are seen as the means through which this can be delivered, and so their needs are given priority. Also, the state's tax revenue is, directly or indirectly, connected to the activities of these sectors, making their views influential.

The combination of all this means that the purpose of social, health or education spending, for example, is not to make people healthy and well for their own sake, but to increase their productivity. In the same way, education is not seen as a good thing in itself, but is valuable because it equips people with the skills needed for business to compete in a globalizing world. In fact, everything becomes important and defined according to the ways in which it can increase this narrow profitability, primarily for corporations. Policy regards people simply as passive consumers of goods or services, which are 'delivered' to them by service providers. Energy consumption is profitable under this narrow interpretation of economics, but energy conservation is more problematic, so we consume. Health care consumption is profitable in the short term for providers, preventative health is not, so we become consumers of health 'solutions'.

The pre-eminent profit motive also makes companies grow to increase their profits and grow yet more. This is facilitated by financial institutions, which have themselves grown to an enormous scale, but which also profit from arranging mergers and acquisitions in the business world. In the public sector, cost considerations, and the desire to centralize control, fosters a culture where bigger is better, and narrow economic efficiency considerations preclude holistic approaches and local participation in the delivery of public services. Even voluntary sector organizations, charities and social enterprises find that narrow short-term efficiencies of scale allow them to undercut smaller competitors when tendering for contracts, enabling them to grow yet more and drive out smaller organizations.

The result is a centralized sclerosis where giant corporations, public and private, dominate the details of people's lives, alienated from the people they serve and – measured by narrow short-term profits – are increasingly 'efficient'. But in their failure to engage the imagination and efforts of the vast majority of people on the planet, and their failure to deal with the holistic needs and skills of those they serve, they are massively inefficient.

At the heart of all this is the problem of money, its design, what it does and how it is allowed to behave, and the fundamental and ruinous disconnection between the idea of money and wealth. Conventional economics measures money, and assumes that it is real and valuable in itself; worse, that everything can be reduced to it, and so misunderstands the way the world is. That critique is both ancient, as old as money itself, and newly urgent, because it goes some way to explain why the economic system is working so badly for most of us.

But there is a more important implication than that. Conventional economics justified itself on the grounds that it was necessary to drag people out of poverty. 'We have to pretend for a while that foul is useful and fair is not,' wrote Keynes, warning that economics still needed to use people's competitive instincts more than their collaborative ones.[14] But it is increasingly clear that the reverse is true: like a casino the economic system that dominates our lives does not improve people's lives, except for the tiny minority that it makes massively wealthy. It creates poverty every day, encouraged by faulty measurement and rigged institutions that favour the very rich. We can leave that economic system in place and battle to ameliorate its effects, or we can build a new economics that does what the economic system claims to do. How to do so is the question that the new economics struggles with.

* * *

You can see the real economic effects of casinos if you climb 250m up into the Rocky Mountains in Colorado, where the air begins to thin, to the former Gold Rush town of Black Hawk. 'Population: 350', it used to say at the foot of the hill, but the legalization of gambling in Colorado in 1991 changed that overnight, and changed everything else too. Go there now and you find yourself directed by men in dark glasses at the tiny crossroads in the town centre, and almost every building from the Silver Hawk Saloon to the end of the town is now devoted to gambling – Doc Holliday's Casino, Bonanza Casino, Crook's Palace, Bronco Billy's.

You can go there virtually as well, at www.blackhawkcolorado.com, to see what gambling does to a local economy. 'We might point out that if you visit Black Hawk, leave your children at home,' says the website. 'Black Hawk is not a friendly place to people under the age of 21.' Almost every economic activity apart from gambling has been driven out. Thanks to the legalization of gambling, nothing else is viable in Black Hawk. Which is why the manager of Central City, which has all but merged with Black Hawk, now says anyone thinking of opening their community to gambling 'needs to have their head examined'.

So when other governments around the world, notably the British, began to consider super-casinos as a source of steady income for local government, this was based on a fallacy, itself based on a fundamental misunderstanding about money. Because all money is emphatically not the same. There is money that comes into the town, shakes a couple of hands, and disappears again outside the area into the pockets of investors and multinationals. There is also money that stays put, and re-circulates among productive local enterprises, building local wealth.

But there is another kind of money as well: the kind that drives out everything else because it is so profitable and so corrosive. Gambling is one of those activities that replaces productive business and people by shady figures in dark glasses. For some reason, policy makers and old-fashioned economists find it bizarrely difficult to distinguish between these – perhaps because highly centralized nations listen only to their Treasuries, and they get the money either way. But this is another example of the short-term thinking that led those same Treasuries into the economic disaster of 2008 and its consequences, and that may lead to some broader thinking as a result.

What Black Hawk reveals is a more fundamental problem with the way money behaves through what Keynes called the 'activities of a casino'. Those activities are so immensely profitable to those who run the casinos that other businesses become uneconomic. Speculating with money has so many rewards, which is why so many previously productive corporations have hived off their production and remain empty shells run by their financial service departments, shifting what assets they still possess between shady tax havens to avoid national taxes. Porsche, the car maker, for example, made far more from speculative financial deals than from selling cars. So is it really a car maker that dabbles in finance, or a hedge fund that happens to sell a few cars?

The problem is that money used to measure value – real, human value – does it very badly: that is the starting point of the new economics. Money measures some aspects very well, such as short-term financial risk and returns, but it is also partially blind to the assets represented by people and planet. An economic system based on the idea that money measures value effectively is likely to devalue those assets, to forget them and ultimately to preside over their destruction – and therefore ultimately its own destruction.

The outlines of the new economics, and how it emerged, are the subject of the next chapter. But, fundamentally it is a new definition of wealth. It is everything that follows from the central discovery that money and wealth are not the same, that money is a means to an end – and not the only means required either. By unshackling itself from this ancient mistake, the new economics subsumes the old idea of an economic science into broader ideas of the way the world works. It resumes its proper place as a subset of biology or psychology in the way it explains the planet and the way people behave. It becomes the study of how human beings, and the places they live, can reach their full potential – using the far broader assets that they have at their disposal, which are not always reducible to money. The new economics is the rejection of money as the totemic centre of a pseudoscience. The next chapter describes how it came about.

Other books to read

Ha-Joon Chang and Illene Grabel (2004) *Reclaiming Development: An Alternative Economic Manual*, Zed Books, London
Herman Daly and John Cobb (1994) *For the Common Good*, Beacon Press, New York
Herman Daly and Joshua Farley (2004) *Ecological Economics: Principles and Applications*, Island Press, Washington, DC
Jeff Gates (2001) *Democracy at Risk*, Perseus, New York
Oliver James (2008) *The Selfish Capitalist: Origins of Affluenza*, Vermilion Books, London
David Korten (1995) *When Corporations Rule the World*, Earthscan, London
Bernard Lietaer (2001) *The Future of Money*, Century, London
Erik Reinart (2007) *How Rich Countries got Rich and Why Poor Countries Stay Poor*, Constable, New York
Vandana Shiva (1999) *Stolen Harvest*, South End Press, New York
Joseph Stiglitz (2002) *Globalisation and its Discontents*, Penguin, London

Notes

1   Tom Wolfe (1988) *Bonfire of the Vanities*, Cape, London.
2   Arts Council (1946), *First Annual Report*, London.
3   Intergovernmental Panel on Climate Change (2008) *Climate Change 2007*, Geneva.
4   United Nations Development Programme (1998) *Consumption for Human Development*, Oxford University Press, New York.
5   *Daily Telegraph* (2003) 16 April.
6   *Daily Mail* (2008) 21 March.
7   Richard R. Zabel (2008) 'Credit Default Swaps', *Pratt's Journal of Bankruptcy Law*, Sept. The original $45 trillion figure came from the Bank for International Settlements.
8   *Fortune* (2003) 3 March.
9   International Financial Services (2006) *Foreign Exchange*, London, October.
10 Robert Kuttner (1985) 'The Poverty of Economics', *Atlantic Monthly*, 1 September.
11 John Maynard Keynes (1936) *A General Theory of Employment, Interest and Money*, Macmillan, London.
12 Oxfam (2002) *Cultivating Poverty: The Impact of US Cotton Subsidies on Africa*, Oxford.
13 Amartya Sen (1999), *Development as Freedom*, New York, Knopf.
14 John Maynard Keynes (1931) *Essays in Persuasion*, Hart-Davis, London.

2
No Wealth but Life: A Brief History of the New Economics

We destroy the beauty of the countryside because the unappropriated splendours of nature have not economic value. We are capable of shutting off the sun and the stars because they do not pay a dividend.
John Maynard Keynes, *National Self-Sufficiency* (1933)

Today's army of accountants, bankers, tax-people, insurance brokers, stock jobbers, foreign exchange dealers and countless other specialists in money, is the modern counterpart of the medieval army of priests, friars, monks, nuns, abbots and abbesses, pardoners, summoners and other specialists in religious procedures and practices. The theologians of the late Middle Ages have their counterparts in the economists of the late industrial age.
James Robertson, *Future Wealth* (1989)

The legendary Gold Rush in California in the 1850s was a bitterly disappointing and brutalizing experience for many of those taking part. But for a few, it meant a fortune. One of those, carrying his gold home with him on a ship that foundered in the Pacific, became the subject of a cautionary tale by the great Victorian critic John Ruskin a few years later.[1]

He described how the passenger, who was carrying 200 pounds of gold with him, was loathe to abandon his hard-won wealth when the ship disappeared beneath the waves. He therefore strapped as much as he could to himself, and jumped over the side. Once in the sea, the gold dragged him down to the bottom.

'Now, as he was sinking,' asked Ruskin rhetorically, 'had he [got] the gold, or had the gold [got] him?'

This neat story, written in the style of a morality tale told by preachers, could have been no more than a short homily about laying up treasure in heaven. But for Ruskin, it was an economic parable as much as a spiritual one. Quite deliberately, he put it at the heart of his controversial 1860 essay series on economics in the *Pall Mall Gazette*, commissioned by the editor, novelist William Makepeace Thackeray. Ruskin launched this polemic with an attack on the people who were supposed to be experts – and in this case, the economists who believed that scarcity was the basic existence of humanity. 'No,' says Ruskin to Malthus and Ricardo. 'The real science of political economy, which has yet to be distinguished from the bastard science, as medicine from witchcraft, and astronomy from astrology,' he wrote, 'is that which teaches nations to desire and labour for the things that lead to life: and which teaches them to scorn and destroy the things that lead to destruction.'

The essays caused such controversy that Ruskin was never invited to write about economics again. But when they were published as *Unto This Last*, it had the most enormous influence on the next two generations. Gandhi read it from cover to cover on his journey from London to South Africa and it inspired his political struggle. E. F. Schumacher was inspired by its principles to develop his concept of Buddhist economics. That tradition – economics as if people mattered; economics that recognizes that money can also be a hindrance, and that the economic system is creating a deeper poverty – is the basis of the emerging understanding we know as the new economics.

The phrase 'new economics' is, of course, not that new. It was used to describe Keynesian economics in its early post-war days of success. There is a deliberate implication that, like Keynes's ideas, a 'new economics' can conjure the wealth we need to satisfy the growing population of the planet. Even so, the *new* new economics does claim this ability for itself. In fact, it argues that it is uniquely able to do so, but it also reaches back into the past.

This is an approach to economics that has E. F. Schumacher as its father, and John Ruskin as its grandfather, and probably aspects of it go back to some of Jonathan Swift, the Country Party, the Diggers and medieval agrarian reformers, even perhaps the Peasants Revolt. It claims a broader remit than conventional economics, and draws inspiration from aspects of the spirituality of William Blake, the radical self-sufficiency of William Cobbett, the localism of G. K. Chesterton. It draws from the Toryism of Ruskin (or so he put it), the socialism of Morris, the liberalism of Jefferson, and the visions of peaceful co-existence of Gandhi and Kropotkin.

What all these thinkers have in common is an approach to economics that is sceptical about money: which understands that human happiness and well-being are not measured very well in terms of money wealth, and that just as money is subservient to morality, spirituality and humanity, so economics is part of a wider ecosystem that explains it, limits it and makes it real. It is an economics that broadens our definitions of wealth, rather than narrows them down to an abstraction that may or may not relate to human fulfilment.

This is an economic tradition that has a long history, but lies consistently outside what has been the mainstream so far, though even mainstream economists have embraced many of the same ideas. When John Maynard Keynes made his famous distinction between art and ideas, which should be international, and goods, which should be primarily local, he was setting out a truth that new economists have been developing ever since.[2] When Sir William Beveridge urged that voluntary action was a vital ingredient of the new welfare state that he had outlined, he was providing a glimpse of the ideas about social capital that would also be so central to the new economics.[3]

But the new economics does not derive primarily from economists like Keynes or Beveridge, but from people whose vision reached beyond economics and beyond those renegade economists who were seeking to turn the whole edifice upside down. It reaches back to the origins of economics in moral philosophy, putting economics back in what they regard as its proper place – embedded in ethics, or in biology, psychology and the sciences of the Earth. For the new economics, there is no great gulf between economics and the environment: the economic cycle that takes raw material and turns it into products and then waste is just a tiny part of a much bigger cycle. It is the cycle of life that turns seeds into trees and takes millions of years to create those raw materials. Nor is there a gulf in the new economics between economics and morality. There is no excuse, for example, for the cult of the chief executive officer *übermensch*, to whom ordinary morality does not apply. The new economics embraces art and spirituality; it learns from ancient traditions of wisdom, convinced that there are higher truths than those of the narrowly economic world before us.

That distinguishes the set of ideas that we now know as new economics from some of the other radical critiques that emerged in the early years of the 20th century. Social credit, for example, was a critique of the way money was created, not necessarily of its accuracy of measurement. Fabianism, for all its good intent, was quite the reverse: a worship of money as the only source of wealth. The one 20th-century movement that embedded elements of what is now new economics was Distributism, inspired by Hilaire Belloc's 1912 book *The Servile State*, an influential diatribe against big business and Fabian collectivist policies.[4] Distributism knitted together the old Catholic social doctrine of Pope Leo XIII that was so close to Belloc's heart, inspired originally by Ruskin via Cardinal Manning. It mixed a generous dollop of land reforming Liberalism with unworldly Gandhian simplicity, borrowing the old slogan of Joseph Chamberlain and Jesse Collings from the 1880s, 'three acres and a cow'. At its heart was the redistribution of land and property so that everyone had some – on the grounds that small enterprises, smallholdings and small units were the only basis for dignity, independence and liberty.

Belloc and his friend G. K. Chesterton and the Distributists were equally hostile to socialism and capitalism, and set out to prove they were the same thing, and that both tended towards slavery. They were anti-industrial, anti-finance, anti-corporation, anti-bureaucrat, and most of all anti-giantism, either big bureaucracy or big business – the 'Big Rot' according to Belloc. What it was actually for was a little hazier, but it included Jeffersonian solutions of workers' cooperatives, smallholdings and land redistribution, and savings boosted by the state. Capitalism is unable to satisfy human needs for stability, sufficiency and security, said Belloc, and is therefore only a phase.

One of their earliest campaigns was in support of the small London bus companies that were being driven out by the monopolistic London General Omnibus Company. In response, they bought a series of Distributist buses, painted them red, green and blue and called them names like 'William Morris' – and briefly took on the big company buses.[5] But while Belloc provided the ideological underpinning, Chesterton provided the rhetorical firepower. His passionate denunciation of corporate power, of large-scale corporate shopping – not shops at all, he said, but 'branches of the accountancy profession' – was based on a sense that neither corporate power nor consumerism could provide for people's material or spiritual needs, and that both implied a mechanical tyranny that was increasingly wielded over people as the monopolies took hold.

He claimed he had only twice been censored by newspaper editors and once it had been for criticizing big shops – one of those things you were no longer allowed to say. 'I think the big shop is a bad shop,' he wrote in *An Outline of Sanity*. 'I think it bad not only in a moral but a mercantile sense; that is, I think shopping there is not only a bad action but a bad bargain. I think the monster emporium is not only vulgar and insolent, but incompetent and uncomfortable; and I deny that its large organisation is efficient.'[6]

Chesterton and Belloc thundered from their respective platforms, or in the pages of Chesterton's newspaper *G. K's Weekly*, or debated with Fabians like George Bernard Shaw and H. G. Wells. But the real vulnerability about Distributism was that it lacked practical policy solutions. 'I think we can explain how to make a small shop or a small farm a common feature of our society better than Matthew Arnold explained how to make the State the organ of Our Best Self,' wrote Chesterton, but he in fact couldn't. The whole prospect seemed impossible, and the very tone of both men was melancholic, as if the tidal wave of giantism would inevitably sweep them away: 'Do anything, however small,' urged Chesterton in 1926. 'Save one out of a hundred shops. Save one croft out of a hundred crofts. Keep one door open out of a hundred doors; for so long as one door is open, we are not in prison.'[7]

Distributism fizzled out after the Second World War. Its land schemes of the 1940s failed and the Distributist League was wound up in the 1950s. There have been

Distributist gestures from governments (Mrs Thatcher's sale of council houses with often tragic, or Lincoln's Homestead Act in the USA), but little more. Its proponents were disappointed that those who had taken it to heart most were not the urban poor, but craftsmen like Eric Gill or journalists like Beachcomber. Once Chesterton had joined Belloc in the Roman Catholic church, then Distributists were increasingly regarded as the political wing of Catholicism. Today they are all but forgotten, and those who worry about such things are liable to remind anyone mentioning them that Belloc was an admirer of Franco's and that Chesterton's vitriol for the financial services industry looked worryingly like anti-semitism.

Where the Distributists developed practical and progressive new economics was in their recognition that the muddle between money and well-being is not just an awkward error but a threat to human life.

***

A leading economist then who reorganized the foundations of the new economics in the second half of the 20th century. Fritz Schumacher had been an associate of Keynes himself before he was appointed as economic advisor to the National Coal Board, during its innovative years under Lord Robens where it attracted an array of talented economic pioneers. 'If my mantle is to fall on anyone,' Keynes told a friend in the Treasury just before he died, 'it could only be Otto Clarke or Fritz Schumacher. Otto Clarke can do anything with figures, but Schumacher can make them sing.'[8]

It was to be nearly four decades before Schumacher's ability to make words and numbers sing captured the public imagination in the UK, and very quickly beyond. The publication of his ground-breaking essays *Small is Beautiful* in 1973, at the height of the oil crisis, was the most important articulation of new economics so far.[9] The title was actually coined by his publisher Anthony Blond, and went some way towards its initial success, but Schumacher was quickly lionized as an expert on the future, and provided with special protection after death threats in the USA on a visit to the White House to see Jimmy Carter.

Schumacher had also managed to capture people's attention with his insistence that there was a new kind of economics emerging. He already had an impressive body of work behind him as a social entrepreneur, as we now call it, founding the Soil Association and Practical Action – which used to be known as the Intermediate Technology Development Group – but *Small is Beautiful* made him a household name, and catapulted his neat phrases about 'Buddhist economics' and Gandhian economics into national debate.

What Schumacher managed was to inject spiritual questions at the heart of practical economic ones. What was a good life about? What was the ultimate purpose of the economic system? Bringing ethical and moral questions into a discipline that, at the time, considered itself immune to such considerations provided the shock value of Schumacher's writing, especially when it came to writing about what he called 'Buddhist economics':

> *The Buddhist economist would insist that a population basing its economic life on non-renewable fuels is living parasitically, on capital instead of income. Such a way of life could have no permanence and could therefore be justified only as a purely temporary expedient. As the world's resource of non-renewable fuels – coal, oil and natural gas – are exceedingly unevenly distributed over the globe and undoubtedly limited in quantity, it is clear that their exploitation at an ever-increasing rate is an act of violence against nature which must inevitably lead to violence between men.*[10]

He died only four years later, in 1977, but his lead was followed by other pioneering books like James Robertson's *The Sane Alternative*, George McRobie's *Small is Possible*, Paul Ekins' *The Living Economy* and Herman Daly and John Cobb's *For the Common Good*. All in their own way drew both from a sense of disillusionment with mainstream economics – Robertson had been director of Interbank Research – but also from older sceptical traditions, reinterpreted and reapplied by Schumacher.

Similar prophets were emerging all over the world, though mainstream economics was shifting very quickly from a corporate Keynesianism – blamed for the combination of stagnation and inflation that followed the ruinous Vietnam War – to a vigorous agenda of free market deregulation under the auspices of Margaret Thatcher and Ronald Reagan. The new economics' critique came together in London in 1984 at the same time as the G7 summit in the same city that summer, challenging the right of the leaders of seven countries to dictate the economic future of the planet.

There was something about the year 1984 that gave it a peculiar resonance for the post-war generation. Those who grew up with George Orwell's novel with that year as its title looked ahead to 1984 as a symbol of everything that could go wrong with society – and with the hope that the world might be different from that experienced by Big Brother and Winston Smith.

In the event, there were certainly convulsions enough – the British Miners' Strike, the emergence of Mikhail Gorbachev and the arrival in the UK of cruise missiles. There was the Greenham Common Women's Peace Camp, and the start of the countdown towards the Big Bang deregulation in the City of London, and the wild worldwide speculation that we have become used to since. There was no one Big Brother, but there was – in a sense – a series of them. They were the six Big Brothers and one Big Sister of the G7, the leaders of the seven richest industrial countries of the world, whose increasingly influential summit meetings every summer presumed to decide the economic future of the planet.

It was a different world in those days. Later on, under the influence of the counter-summits and the green and development movements, the G7 final communiqués would eventually pay lip service to the great issues – poverty and the environment. But back then, there was no hint that there might be any other way than economic growth, environmental destruction, and the hopeless dependence of rich and poor alike on an economic system that only delivered for a privileged elite. 'There is no alternative,' said Margaret Thatcher only a few years before. And the economic assumptions of the G7 were challenged by a discredited intellectual Left, but little else.

The idea of a counter-summit to change that came from the Ecology Party activist Sally Willington. She presented the idea to the party council as the WEDGE project in July 1983 – a bid to get to grips with the economics of *more* – after an article by the *Guardian* columnist Harford Thomas, urging the members of the G7 summit, that year in Williamsburg, to tackle the issue of the unemployment on their own doorsteps. She and colleagues planned to fly to Williamsburg to confront them, but were warned that the American authorities would refuse them entry. But still, wasn't the summit going to come to London next?

Sally persuaded Jonathon Porritt, about to be appointed director of Friends of the Earth and then Ecology Party chair, to take a lead. Porritt believed a counter-summit required a new organization to manage it. He contacted James Robertson and his partner Alison Pritchard, coordinator of the Turning Point network, and together they hammered together a committee which met in Jonathon's flat, around the corner from King's Cross Station in London.

The steering committee included many names that were going to become familiar as the sustainability debate took hold – especially after Mrs Thatcher's surprise declaration three years later, under the influence of Prince Charles, that she was a 'friend of the earth': David Cadman, John Elkington, Liz Hosken, Gerard Morgan-Grenville, Duncan Smith, Jakob von Uexkull and Paul Ekins.

The result was The Other Economic Summit (TOES), which brought together a diverse mixture of environmentalists, radical economists, futurists, mystics and community activists.[11] The three-day event attracted more than 140 people, and launched with a rally at Friends House on the Euston Road, chaired – rather unexpectedly – by the former British Ambassador to Washington and future BBC economics correspondent Peter Jay. Among those on the platform was the World Bank economist Herman Daly, shortly to make his name as one of the godfathers of green economics.

TOES, taking place around the corner at the RAC Club in Pall Mall, was certainly not the only challenge to the G7 leaders over at Lancaster House. There were protest vigils outside by Quakers, protest drumming by Buddhists and a major Campaign for Nuclear Disarmament (CND) rally in Trafalgar Square. But TOES ignited something. When economics seemed constantly to be the end of the argument for sustainability, when economists seemed lined up hopelessly for the narrow status quo, it was an attempt to pull together a new kind of economics that would work for people and planet. Or, more accurately, it was an attempt to bundle together work by a wide variety of people in a range of fields as a single school of thought – a new economics with popular appeal that could be understood by non-economists too. It was ad hoc and makeshift, but it was enormously hopeful.

TOES met again in a much bigger event the following year, and the papers of the two conferences were edited together by Ekins as *The Living Economy*.[12] By then, he had also been appointed as the first director of the New Economics Foundation (**nef**). The trouble with the idea of a 'new economics' is that it remained hard to pin down, except in list form. 'I do not believe that such an economics yet exists,' said the Chilean radical economist Manfred Max-Neef at the original TOES conference in 1984. There were copious lists of attributes, and a shorter list of questions, summarized then by George McRobie as:

- What work will people do?
- How will it be paid for?
- How will the Earth sustain it?

The answers were more difficult, he said:

> *The answers to emerge will entail new ways of organising work and meeting human needs, and of guaranteeing incomes; a new emphasis on economic self-reliance, including local economic regeneration and enrichment of poor countries through self-reliant development strategies rather than increasing third world dependence; new awareness of ecological constraints, of human needs for survival, social justice and self-fulfilment, and new economic concepts to take these into account; new growth areas for economic activity in energy-efficient and resource-conserving industries and in care and maintenance of the built and natural environment. It is a formidable agenda for a massive advance in human welfare and wealth, in the widest sense of the word, worldwide. With apologies to my old friend, Fritz Schumacher, it is not a small agenda, but it is beautiful. It is also becoming increasingly obvious that it is possible.[13]*

The Living Economy put more flesh on this new economics skeleton. It was the first text book of the new-style economics and it was an immediate success. In a speech to the Society for International Development in New Delhi in March 1988, he set out a more measured list that described this emerging paradigm:

1 A commitment to the satisfaction of the basic needs of all people, through personal responsibility, mutual aid and governmental action.
2 An expanded concept of human welfare, expressed through an accounting system that gives value to social and ecological factors as well as to output and employment.
3 A concomitant awareness of the social, ecological and ethical implications of economic activity, resulting in a determination that the benefits of such activity be justly distributed and its costs be borne by the activity concerned.
4 An emphasis placed on the process of production and exchange, as well as on the ownership of their means and on the product itself: as in concepts like good work, cooperation and appropriate technology.
5 Increased local economic self-reliance, recognizing different levels of locality, both through increased use of local resources to satisfy local needs and through a reorientation of trade.
6 An understanding that much human activity essential to human well-being, such as reproduction, home making and child rearing, is carried out, and is better carried out, in a non-monetary economy. Those engaged in such activity should not be excluded from the recognition, status and rewards accorded by society to productive work.
7 An insistence on intergenerational equity, so that future generations have at least as good economic prospects as the present one.

'Many of these features already exist to some extent in contemporary economics, although often only in embryonic form,' he said, 'and they are nearly everywhere dominated by opposite economic characteristics.'[14]

That was the problem. The new economics was an attempt to knit the very beginnings of trends together into a narrative, while the old assumptions were shared powerfully in every elite business and governmental body in the world: trying to push forward the monetary economy, maximizing economic growth and ignoring the damage to the operating systems of society and planet, putting huge rewards for the few before the basic needs of the many. The old assumptions had power and money behind them.

But there was already a sign that some people in mainstream politics and economics were slowly awakening to the intractable problems before them. Within a couple of years of TOES, the speakers were beginning to find their way into government circles. Professor David Pearce became advisor to Environment Secretary Chris Patten; Jose Lutzenberger became Brazilian environment minister, and a whole string of ideas shifted into the mainstream as well, almost without anyone noticing.

The *Green Consumer Guide* was beginning to shift shopping habits.[15] Some ethical or greener products – like free range eggs, organic milk and lead-free petrol were becoming market leaders (lead-free petrol drove the old lead-based petrol out altogether). The ethical investment market was expanding, and by the end of the century, there were up to 9000 local currencies around the world, many of them – as in debt-ridden Argentina – actually keeping people alive.

David Pearce was strictly speaking an environmental economist: his expertise was the business of pricing the environment into the mainstream economy so that it was treated with respect. New economics was, in many ways, clarifying itself as the reverse of this: a scepticism about price and a determination to hold to what is important despite prevailing economic values. This is the difficulty when new economics encounters the mainstream. It is taken up, where it is taken up, by policy makers to solve specific problems, often without the ideological baggage that guaranteed its humanistic roots.

Alternative economic indicators and social auditing, both developed at **nef**, became completely mainstream, but at some cost – government targets suffocated local initiative and social auditing pigeon holed corporate social responsibility in the public relations and accountancy departments. Energy taxation has been muddled by many of the governments that have enacted it – including the EU – but it is at least in place. Credit unions and community banks have sometimes bucked this trend, and remain a small but potent force. Other thinking, to underpin thriving local economies – local money flows, complementary currencies or the critique of the doctrine of comparative advantage – have barely filtered into mainstream assumptions at all, except among those creative and forward-thinking early adopters that exist in any government, however backward.

The developing new economics was also informed by a range of successful initiatives to put those ideas into practice, like the pioneering Grameen Bank micro-credit operation, or the massive Seikatsu consumer co-op in Japan.[16] Grameen allowed people, mainly women, to borrow very small amounts to underpin small businesses. Seikatsu allowed people to band together and buy healthier, local food wholesale, and in the end produce their own. It also soon became clear that there was a sizeable and growing minority of people who are involved in the emerging new economics paradigm in their everyday lives, and a sector is emerging to support them, providing green energy, ethical investment, community-supported agriculture and organic food. There was some evidence that this was the growing portion of the UK population known to marketers as 'inner-directed', or 'cultural creatives' in the USA, who sympathized with this even if they were not involved in buying organic themselves. They seem to make up around 40 per cent of the UK population and maybe a quarter of Americans.[17]

But as the new economics developed, the background was also shifting. The Keynesian consensus that had motivated a reaction from people like Schumacher and others had given way to a new narrow emphasis on growth and profit, and a renewed belief that money earned by the richest would trickle down to the poorest.

* * *

James Carville is one of the most successful political consultants in the world, the man behind Bill Clinton's unexpected election as president against the first George Bush in 1992, made even more famous by his marriage to his rival in the Bush camp, Mary Matalin.[18] It was he who struggled to find some antidote to Bush's poll ratings after the first Gulf War, which had been in the region of 90 per cent, and who hung a notice on the Clinton campaign headquarters in Little Rock that set out the three messages of the campaign:

1   Change vs more of the same.
2   The economy, stupid.
3   Don't forget health care.

The sign was intended for other campaign workers, but the phrase 'it's the economy, stupid' became something of a slogan for the Clinton campaign. It was the same campaign, and the same Carville, who came up with the phrase 'trickle down doesn't work'. By itself, this seems like a simple statement of fact, but it was important that a successful presidential candidate should spell this out so clearly. Since Margaret Thatcher and Ronald Reagan, and in many ways before them as well, 'trickle down' was the conventional economic assumption that replaced Keynesian economics. If you helped some people get rich, then they would spend more and it would trickle down through the economy to the poorest. It survives to this day in most of the assumptions of mainstream regeneration and economic development, though it is even more obvious now than it was to Carville that wealth doesn't trickle down, it floods up.

In fact, of course, the great days of trickle down economics were still to come. Every government conditioned by the so-called Washington Consensus, as well as the all-powerful International Monetary Fund (IMF) and World Bank, believed that cutting taxes would in the end stimulate the economy, and – to start with – it did. But in the constant failure of regeneration, redistribution and community revitalization, it was increasingly obvious to most people outside that consensus that trickle down simply did not work.

This was an era dominated by the set of policies that became known as 'neo-liberal', though they bore no relation to any liberalism worthy of the name. The heart of this consensus was a redoubled reliance on money as the only measurement tool, and a major commitment to trickle down economics via private corporations. It was more accurately an application of Darwin's evolutionary theories to economics: a kind of survival of the economically fittest. But their interpretation of the 'fit' – the marketable, the profitable, the global – was not only a misreading of Darwin, but deeply inadequate. The financially 'fit' survived; those that *did not* fit into the shape of the new world, people, communities and nations, were bled dry.

The Washington Consensus built a devastating machine that could bear no variation, and it assumed a kind of adolescent approach to morality by business, as if it were somehow exempt in the sacred duty of creating wealth. The corporate pioneer John D. Rockefeller once boasted that he was quite willing to pay someone a salary of a million dollars if he were brutal enough. 'He must be able to glide over every moral restraint with almost childlike disregard,' he wrote, 'and has, besides other positive qualities, no scruples whatsoever and be ready to kill off thousands of victims – without a murmur.'[19] If you pretend that business is beyond morality, that is unfortunately the kind of business you get.

But the globalization era, when governments handed over their powers to corporations in the belief that their profits and spending would 'trickle down' through society, was already making way for something else, more related to the worship of sheer economic power that Rockefeller's business morality implied, and ushered in by the presidency of George Bush Jr. This was a strange amalgam of Keynesian economics with deregulated globalization: a massive handover of assets to the wealthiest, racking up vast budget deficits, reorganizing welfare away from those in need and towards the wealthiest businesses, with little awareness of the economic risks to the world. This marks the last stages of what you might call 'old economics', a perverse caricature of the worst propensities of the old paradigm, and hideous amalgam of state and unrestrained corporate power without competition, imagination or enterprise, that mirrors a similar combination emerging from China.

Of course, using a phrase like 'old economics' makes it an easy target, more of a caricature than a genuine school of economics. In many ways, economics itself has moved on from this kind of fake Darwinian vision of money, where people and planet are sacrificed apparently – according to the ideology – for their own greater good, because the benefits trickle down to the poorest. Most economists know perfectly well that they don't, but the old assumptions are kept alive, not so much by economists, as by policy makers and those who cluster around governments. Those advisors who, as we write, are struggling to force the world financial system back to some disastrous business as usual.

Even so, the development of the new economics has reacted against that background of narrow globalization. It has been underpinned by a range of new disciplines and ideas that were emerging from economics itself, realizing that the classical economics of William Stanley Jevons, Leon Walras and Vilfredo Pareto were based on the assumptions of Victorian physics, borrowing from Newtonian physics long after it had been superseded by Einstein, using economic variables in their equations as if they were equations in physics. They simply replaced energy with economic concepts, when there was little evidence that energy and money or the economic concept of 'utility' behaved in the same way at all, as if people's economic behaviour bore any relation to the behaviour of atoms. Behavioural economics, heterodox economics, ecological economics, neuroeconomics (scanning people's brains while they decide), and a whole range of new mini-disciplines have emerged from inside the mainstream, trying to take account of the divorce between the old assumptions of economics and the real world.

What the new economics recognized was that there was just a possibility that conventional economics could be turned on its head – that there were hidden resources among ordinary people and in impoverished communities that could be brought to bear to provide solutions. It recognized that the narrow measure of value pedalled by economic practitioners was often transforming the poor into dependent supplicants to big corporations or centralized government. It also recognized that, even as it was being reformed, the economic system was accelerating its ability to create poverty around the world, sucking the resources and work out of those subservient populations. Looking more closely at economic institutions, and exactly how they reinforced the existing power relationships, might provide a way out.

These are both new ideas and practical solutions – the new economics is, above all practical – and in some ways these are the very solutions that eluded the Distributists and their allies. But the new economics combines these solutions with ideas that emerged from a much older tradition, that built on the distinction that Ruskin originally made between wealth and what he called 'illth', the ruined, dehumanized lives that narrow economic measures have reduced us to all over the world.

'There is no wealth but life,' he wrote at the end of *Unto This Last*, the central idea of new economics.[20] 'Life, including all its powers of love, of joy, and of admiration. That country is the richest which nourishes the greatest number of noble and happy human beings; that man is richest who, having perfected the functions of his own life to the utmost, has also the widest helpful influence.'

Other books to read

David Boyle (ed) (2003) *News from Somewhere,* New Economics Foundation, London
Guy Dauncey (1988) *After the Crash*, Green Books, Totnes, UK
Paul Ekins (ed) (1986) *The Living Economy*, Routledge, London
Paul Ekins, Mayer Hillman and Robert Hutchison (1992) *Wealth Beyond Measure*, Gaia Books, London
Edward Fullbrook (2009) *Pluralist Economics*, Zed Books, London

Paul Hawken (1993) *The Ecology of Commerce*, Harper Business, New York

Bill McKibben (2007) *Deep Economy: The Wealth of Communities and the Durable Future*, Times Books, New York

George McRobie (1982) *Small is Possible*, Jonathan Cape, London

James Robertson (1978) *The Sane Alternative*, James Robertson, Cholsey, UK

Vandana Shiva (1998) *Monocultures of the Mind: Biodiversity, Biotechnology and Scientific Agriculture*, Zed Books, London

Vandana Shiva (2005) *Earth Democracy: Justice, Sustainability and Peace*, Zed Books, London

Notes

1   John Ruskin (1862) *Unto This Last*, Blackfriars, London.
2   John Maynard Keynes (1933) 'National self-sufficiency', *The Yale Review*, Vol 22, No 4, June.
3   William Beveridge (1948) *Voluntary Action: A Report on the Methods of Social Advance*, Allen & Unwin, London.
4   Hilaire Belloc (1912) *The Servile State*, Foulis London.
5   A. N. Wilson (1984) *Hilaire Belloc*, Hamilton, London.
6   G. K. Chesterton (1926) *Outline of Sanity*, Methuen, London.
7   G. K. Chesterton (1926) *Outline of Sanity*, Methuen, London.
8   Quoted in David Boyle (2001) *The Tyranny of Numbers*, HarperCollins, London.
9   E. F. Schumacher (1973) *Small is Beautiful: Economics as if People Mattered*, Anthony Blond, London.
10 E. F. Schumacher (1973) *Small is Beautiful: Economics as if People Mattered*, Anthony Blond, London.
11 David Boyle and Andrew Simms (ed) (2003) *News from Somewhere: 20 Years of the New Economics Foundation*, New Economics Foundation, London.
12 Paul Ekins (1986) *The Living Economy*, Routledge, London.
13 David Boyle and Andrew Simms (ed) (2003) *News from Somewhere: 20 Years of the New Economics Foundation*, New Economics Foundation, London.
14 Paul Ekins (1986) *The Living Economy*, Routledge, London.
15 John Elkington and Julia Hailes (1988) *The Green Consumer Guide*, Gollancz, London.
16 For Grameen Bank see www.grameen-info.org
17 David Boyle (2003) *Authenticity: Brands, Fakes, Spin and the Lust for Real Life*, HarperCollins, London.
18 James Carville and Mary Matalin (1994) *All's Fair: Love, War and Running for President*, Simon & Schuster, New York.
19 Quoted in Robert C. Solomon (1997) *It's Good Business*, Lanham, Oxford.
20 John Ruskin (1862) *Unto This Last*, Blackfriars, London.

3
Measurement: Why Did an Apparently Poor Pacific Island Hit the Top of the Happy Planet Index?

We are happy to proclaim that we are the people of Vanuatu.
                                                    Vanuatu national anthem

*The sentence 'let's get out of this airy stuff and look at the bottom line'
ends with one small phrase, and yet a whole civilisation can disappear
through that small hole.*

                                                                Robert Bly

Vanuatu is an archipelago in the western Pacific, made up of over 80 islands, 65 of which are inhabited by a population approaching a quarter of a million. The chorus of their national anthem goes: '*Yumi, Yumi, Yumi* – "We, we, we … We are happy to proclaim that we are the people of Vanuatu".'

Vanuatu has over 2500 kilometres (km) of exposed coastline, and no regular military. Despite its tiny ecological footprint per person – no higher than developing countries like Mali and Swaziland – it has a life expectancy matching Turkey and an estimated life satisfaction as high as nearby New Zealand.

Not only is the life expectancy high, but the islands have an extremely rich natural history, with unspoilt coastlines and unique rainforests. They are also effective democracies. Vanuatu has only been independent since 1980, but has been consistently democratic and peaceful, despite its immense cultural diversity. There are over 100 local languages. The economy is based largely on small-scale agriculture, which provides livelihoods for 65 per cent of the population. The local market is also served by an indigenous light industry. It has few commodity exports and is remote from international markets. Government revenue comes largely from duties imposed on imports so the taxes are low. The climate is warm and fertile.

'Don't tell too many people, please,' Mark Lowen of Vanuatu Online, the country's online newspaper, told the *Guardian* newspaper.[1] 'People are generally happy here because they are very satisfied with very little. This is not a consumer-driven society. Life here is about community and family and goodwill to other people. It's a place where you don't worry too much.'

Life in Vanuatu is not entirely worry free. Like many other Pacific islands, it is vulnerable to tropical cyclones and typhoons, and those are likely to get worse because of global warming. But the positive attributes combined to put it top of nef's first Happy Planet Index, which ranked the nations of the world according to the efficiency with which their economies transform the Earth's natural resources into long and happy lives.[2] The index put Vanuatu first and Zimbabwe bottom and had a rather unexpected impact on the world's media. Within 48 hours of its publication, the report about it had been downloaded 37,000 times around the world. Within six months, that figure had risen to nearly a million. You could argue about the exact position of countries in the league table, but the idea that there is a wealth beyond the usual definitions of money growth and gross domestic product (GDP) seemed to attract people's attention and interest because it began to explain better the meaning of the real world around us.

There have been many attempts to measure 'real' wealth. Happy Planet was the first to combine environmental impact with well-being to measure the environmental efficiency with which countries provide long and happy lives. The results were surprising, even shocking, because the ranking unmasked a very different world order to that promoted by our leaders. In the rankings, very rich countries did badly because of over-consumption and very poor countries did so too, often due to low life expectancies. It put the UK at a disappointing 108th and the USA still lower at 150th on the index.

The index stripped the view of the economy back to its absolute basics: what goes in (resources), and what comes out (human lives of different length and happiness). No nation got everything right, but – taken as a whole – the index revealed patterns that showed how we might better achieve long and happy lives for everybody, without ruining the planet. Vanuatu's climate gives it a great advantage, but its citizens have so little apart from that, and if they can manage all this with so few resources, then why not the rest of us?

The success of Central America

One of the peculiarities of measuring the efficient production of human well-being like this was that Central America managed to achieve the highest average score in the index. The region combines relatively good life expectancy (an average of 70 years) and high life satisfaction with an ecological footprint below its globally equitable share. Central America has had a notorious history of conflict and political instability, but the last 15 years have been relatively peaceful, and Central America has strong traditions of community engagement, which may explain its success.

Colombia may not be strictly in Central America, but South America scored well too and the fact that it managed to come second in the first Happy Planet Index was shocking to many. It has high life expectancy (the same as Hungary) and high life satisfaction (the same as Germany), all for a quarter of western Europe's per capita consumption of natural resources. The British writer Matt Rendell spends half the year in Colombia (he is married to a Colombian) and he explained the result by digging a little beneath the movie caricature of a country whose public image is dominated by the drugs trade:

> *In some respects Colombia is similar to Italy – a country with particularly high levels of reported social capital. It has very strong regional identities, each with its own cuisine, use of language or dialect, its own music and dance. It has almost every climate in the world and, as a result, one of the widest ranges of fresh fruit and vegetables on earth. It is also one of the most modern and economically stable countries in Latin America and has been so for a hundred years. Colombia has never had the type of hyper-inflation common to other countries in the region and its brief experience of military dictatorship was not of the malignant kind found elsewhere.*[3]

One reason why people may be surprised about Colombia's position is because the Western media focuses on the country's problems, but not on its vibrant civil society. Colombians love music, sport and beauty. They also have very high educational and health care standards. There is certainly high corruption and cocaine, and pressure from the insatiable appetite for drugs in Western economies makes it virtually impossible for Colombians to shed a trade that most people there regard with shame. But the vast majority of the 40 million Colombians have never seen cocaine, and live generous, law-abiding, colourful and valuable lives. 'Colombians are surrounded by natural splendours and haven't grown immured to the beauty of their own country,' said Matt Rendel. 'In my experience they tend to be amazed on a daily basis by the beauty of their landscapes. In this sense, it is a country of elevated spirits who look towards the sky.'[4]

The success of small islands

One of the other fascinating insights provided by the index was how happy people are when they live in small, island nations. They tend to have higher life satisfaction, higher life expectancy and marginally lower footprints. Even within regions, islands typically do well. Malta tops the Western world with Cyprus in seventh place (out of 24). The top five nations in Africa are *all* islands, as well as two of the top four in Asia. Even Bahrain, the island that scores lowest due to its high footprint, ranks above the other Gulf states.

But why islands? In many cases, isolation and relative vulnerability have encouraged adaptive and supportive forms of economic and social organization. Traditional Pacific agriculture, for example, has shown remarkable resilience to disasters, especially weather-related incidents like cyclones. During the 1990s, Samoa was hit by two '100-year' cyclones and lost its main crop, taro, to disease. Instead of famine, Samoa recovered because of its traditional food production system, which uses a wide diversity of crops selected for their hardiness over generations and grown together in a robust mixed-crop pattern.

Island economies based on sharing and gift-giving, such as that of Nanumaea – one of Tuvalu's islands – give rise to highly cooperative and mutually supportive communities. According to anthropologists Keith and Ann Chambers: 'In a sharing system, maintaining supportive social relationships is so intrinsic to the exchange process that short-term tallies of material benefit are meaningless. As a result, sharing equalizes access to resources across a community and serves as a socio-economic levelling mechanism.'[5] By comparison, profit-seeking enterprises promoted by aid projects 'support the weakening of sharing obligations' that are central to coping when disaster strikes.

Geographical isolation may insulate populations from mainland political turbulence and conflict, the presence of which is known to seriously undermine well-being, though Fiji and Haiti certainly provide counter-examples. If you live on islands – especially small islands – it is also impossible to be removed from nature, as happens to people in large urban areas. This may lead societies to develop more culturally ingrained notions of environmental stewardship. Perhaps the high cost of importing goods to geographically remote islands has a restraining effect on personal consumption. These questions need further investigation, but as we all become increasingly aware of our vulnerability and isolation on island Earth, it is logical to learn the lessons – both good and bad – from those who survive and often thrive on small islands.

The basic problem: Money doesn't measure real wealth

Indices like Happy Planet are compilations of statistics. One of the reasons they seem to be so compelling is that they can allow people to take familiar truths unawares – to look at them in whole new ways. What this index managed was to encourage people to unpack the accepted definitions of wealth.

One of the tragedies of classical economics has been its determination to be a science. To be scientific, economics needed to reduce itself to hard measures, to reduce itself in turn to econometrics, to formulae and graphs. The difficulty was that, actually, this undermined its ability to describe the world, and the behaviour of human beings, very accurately. It assumed that people always maximize their broad wealth in any given situation – which is, almost by definition, true (though there is some room for argument about deferred gratification). But economics then defined wealth so narrowly, as little more than money, when everyone knows – at least outside the economics lecture room – that this is nonsense. Human beings constantly accept something that is both less and more than money, from quiet or calmness or good relationships, to any other aspect of life that brings them fulfilment and excitement. Any economics that fails to recognize this blinds itself to the way the world is, so that it finds it hard to understand decisions to downshift or to pay more for an ethical choice, and is – only now – struggling to come to terms with the obvious.

Yet while economics may now be moving on, the policy makers are often trailing behind them: as Keynes said, they are 'often the slaves of some defunct economist'.[6] They find it hard to recognize that some of the side-effects of more money, the so-called externalities – the ill health, depression, alienation, crime, murder, divorce, environmental destruction and pollution that sometimes happen as a result of wealth as well as poverty – are part of the same picture and need to be tackled together.

The first rule of the new economics is to see the world clearly, not through the distorting lens of economic theorems, which by their very nature are bound to be inaccurate when it comes to individuals or specific places. That means having a view of what human beings really regard as wealth. Once we realize that, suddenly the problem of what Ruskin called 'illth' – the opposite of wealth – becomes clear. Loneliness, isolation, stress, depression, chronic ill health, all stand in the way of genuine success. There are less of these in Vanuatu: that's why it is more successful, in this respect, than the UK.

When you move on from nations and start measuring UK institutions in this way, the spread of illth becomes more obvious. **nef** carried out a study of young people in Nottingham, on behalf of the city council, which came up with some disturbing results. It showed that 32 per cent of young people were, at the very least, unhappy and could be at risk of mental health problems, and that there tended to be a collapse in the way young people felt about themselves as they moved from primary to secondary level.[7]

The data show that not only did both their satisfaction with life and their curiosity in life – a measure of personal development – fall as they got older, but also that their satisfaction with their school plummeted between primary and secondary school, and never climbed back again. Their levels of interest in school and the belief that they were learning something also dropped a great deal. Those findings have been echoed by the recent United Nations study that found that UK young people were the most miserable in the world out of 21 nations they looked at. These are not conventional economic problems, but misery undermines wealth in its broadest sense. The problem is that conventional policy, based on the maxims of classical economics, has generally failed to realize that this is an economic problem and to broaden economics to cover it.

Add into this mix the fact that up to a fifth of the population will suffer from some kind of mental illness at some time in their lives, and that 10 per cent are suffering from depression, the full scale of the problem becomes clearer. Much of this may also be attributed to the collapse of social networks and family life, both of them corroded by economic change, high house prices and high levels of debt – forcing both partners out to work – all of which happens, paradoxically, in the name of money and economic growth. None of these are conventional economic problems, yet they are by-products of faulty economic policy.

The real question is: how can economics have got it so wrong?

The measurement problem

Part of the basic mistake is counting the wrong thing. In his novel *Hard Times*, Charles Dickens imagined the character of Sissy Jupe, the circus girl sent to school for the first time, who was asked a tough question about national wealth. '"Here we are in this nation with fifty million pounds," says the teacher: "…Girl Number twenty, isn't this a prosperous nation, and a'n't you in a thriving state?"'[8]

Sissy was confused: "I thought I couldn't know whether it was a prosperous nation or not, and whether I was in a thriving state or not, unless I knew who had got the money, and whether any of it was mine. But that had nothing to do with it. It was not in the figures at all," said Sissy, wiping her eyes.

"That was a great mistake of yours," observed Louisa.'

Nearly a century after the publication of *Hard Times*, British politicians developed the idea of GDP, simply the sum total of the nation's money earned in a year. They believed they could see a new era of prosperity stretching before them, all because they could 'count' a nation's wealth in one figure and see how much it was growing. The idea was introduced during the 1954 Conservative Party conference as an antidote to wartime rationing and post-war austerity. If Britain could 'grow' by 3 per cent a year, then living standards could double by 1980, said the Chancellor of the Exchequer R. A. Butler. That was his repeated message at the general election the following year.

'It's not pie in the sky but a sober picture,' he said.[9] 'Moreover we don't have to wait until 1980. Progress will come year by year if we concentrate on production and investment. The government will help with great new schemes. We will build roads and railways, develop atomic power and help with the re-equipment and modernization of the whole of industry.'

In fact, the idea of GDP dated back further than 1954, to the battle to rescue the world from the Great Depression, and then from Hitler. It was developed by some of the young economists around Keynes and Simon Kuznets in the USA as a way of working out the total productive power of the economy, a by-product of those techniques of investment that allowed Britain to out-produce Nazi Germany. Once the war was over, this seemed to provide the perfect scorecard for an impoverished nation: measure national success by the total amount of money that changed hands, and nothing else.

As a result, the 'growth' has been gigantic, the technological innovations astonishing, and the living standards – if you measure them in terms of money – have shot up. But real life has often become less healthy, more stressful, more polluted or all three. Nor has there been an accompanying growth in well-being: quite the reverse in fact. Most measures show the trend of well-being mostly unchanged or falling in the developed world. After a certain level of income, which might be as low as £22,000 year in the UK, there is very little extra impact on improved well-being of any additional income. And if that extra income adds to the stresses and environmental destruction, then new economics says the trade-off is neither fair nor efficient.

The blindness of growth
The Fats Waller song 'My very good friend the milkman' suggests that this loving couple ought to move in together to save money. That is how GDP falls when people get married: they spend less. On the other hand, every divorce that leads to one parent paying another to look after their children raises GDP and gives us the impression that the nation is growing wealthier. Growth goes down when people love each other and up when they fall out. Nor does GDP take any account of non-financial aspects of well-being, such as working time. If production were increased by 10 per cent as a result of everyone working 10 per cent longer, people would not be 10 per cent better off, because of the extra time they were working, unless of course they preferred going to work.

National accounts also include what is known as 'defensive consumption', without taking account of the social problems that give rise to it. This includes the extra spending required to clean up pollution, treating it as if it were a bonus, to maintain security in the face of increasing crime or social unrest, or for national defence in response to increasing international tension. Nor do they take any account of the distribution of income. National accounts treat £1 of income identically, whoever receives it. This is clearly unrealistic and counter-intuitive: the effect of an additional £100 on the well-being of a household with an income of £100 is clearly far greater than for a household with an income of £1 million.

The impact of the new economics is such that most European politicians now recognize that GDP is not an effective way of measuring progress. It is not a genuine bottom line. Yet, as they have done since the 1950s, governments still fall over themselves to compete for growth, sacrificing their wildlife, nature or people's sanity – and sometimes even their populations – to make way for great dams or motorway projects. Anyone who questioned whether it was a good idea to flatten a wetland for a road or a neighbourhood for a tower block was told, fatuously, that you 'can't stand in the way of progress'. Back in the 1950s and 1960s, this was an irritating inversion of the meaning of the word. But the same blindness continues.

As a result, in the half century since Butler unveiled his 'growth' concept, there are many signs of increasing wealth and luxury for many people, but there is also more ill health and less creativity, fewer people in sports teams, less amateur dramatics, less learning of musical instruments or painting. There are more people with asthma, depression and cancer. There is more crime, more people in prisons and more divorce. But the key measure of success used by politicians and economists recognized none of these things as important. By narrowing the definition of what constituted 'wealth', we ended up narrowing all our lives. Worse, if the whole of public policy was devoted to improving this one bottom line figure, it was a kind of self-fulfilling prophecy. Things that money could never buy were driven out. 'A country that cut down all its trees, sold them as wood chips and gambled the money away playing tiddly-winks, would appear from its national accounts to have got richer in terms of GNP per person,' wrote one economist in 1988.[10]

What makes this most distressing, and most urgent to reverse, is that we all know – at least ordinary people who are not tainted by the blindness of conventional economics know – that money and wealth are not the same thing. We act on that knowledge every day of our lives, though our ability to do so is increasingly curtailed. 'To my big brother – the richest man in town!' says George Bailey's brother in *It's a Wonderful Life*, even though we know George has very little money. We understand that meaning of the word 'rich', but public policy has forgotten it.

The missing aspects of life
When the New Zealand politician Marilyn Waring, author of *If Women Counted*, was chair of the New Zealand public accounts committee, it opened her eyes to the problem of how the work of women was being excluded from the measures.[11] She noticed that a range of aspects of life that mattered most were completely ignored by the government, because officials only counted money. One of these aspects of life was the work done around the world by women, often in the home, which had previously been regarded by economists as an infinite resource. She wrote a paper for the Women and Food conference in Sydney in 1982, and submitted it for comment to Australia's deputy chief statistician. 'His memo of reply to me – a classic of sexist economic assumptions – was one of the major incentives to write this book,' she wrote in the introduction.

She also discovered the lists of students who worked under the economist Simon Kuznets (who originally warned against over-reliance on growth as a measure) in the 1930s to develop national accounting in the first place, before it had become the theory of economic growth. The names were all men, but at the bottom was an important note: 'Five clerks, all women with substantial experience and know-how, assisted importantly in this work.' These women – all with substantial experience apparently – had become non-persons. Their invisibility then spread to the system they created that still ignores women's work. In the UN accounting system, farmer's wives and children are excluded from the statistics of agricultural labourers because there is no money changing hands.

The issue of measurement reached a much wider audience in a long article in the magazine *Atlantic Monthly* in 1995 called 'If the GDP is up, why is America down?'[12] It was intended to mark the foundation of a new think tank in San Francisco called Redefining Progress. It was written by Clifford Cobb, with the journalists Jonathan Rowe and Ted Halstead, and it had an enormous response. This was the period in the UK when politicians were searching for the elusive 'feel-good factor' that explained why people were so stressed, unhappy and angry with the government even though the numbers said they were wealthy. It was the same in the USA: 'There seemingly inexplicably remains an extraordinarily deep-rooted foreboding about the economic outlook,' said Alan Greenspan of the Federal Reserve. People had money in their pockets, but they weren't content. It appeared to be a mystery.

The *Wall Street Journal* had just worked out that the O. J. Simpson trial had cost the equivalent of the total GDP of Grenada. Was that progress, asked the authors? Then there were the liposuction operations – 110,000 of which take place every year in the USA, each of them pumping $2000 into the growth figures. GDP seems to win both ways – there is growth, making people overeat the least healthy foods, then there is growth operating on them to make them look thin again. There is growth making pesticides that cause cancer and growth selling drugs to cure it. Not only did GDP ignore the collapse of environmental and social underpinnings to the world, but it pretended this was a gain.

The impossibility of growth
But there is another problem about measuring success in terms of money, which is the assumption, lying behind it: that this growth will trickle down from the beneficiaries to the poorest. Economic growth is the official method by which we will reach the Millennium Development Goals (MDGs), the first of which – to halve the proportion of the population of developing countries living below the '$1-a-day' poverty line – is supposed to be met by 2015.

The trouble is that economic growth is an extremely inefficient way of achieving poverty reduction, and is becoming even less effective. Between 1990 and 2001, for every $100 worth of growth in the world's income per person, just 60 cents found its target and contributed to reducing poverty below the $1-a-day line.[13] To achieve every single dollar of poverty reduction therefore required $166 of additional global production and consumption, with all its associated environmental impacts. Here is the paradox whereby ever decreasing amounts of poverty reduction can only be won by ever increasing amounts of over-consumption by the already rich. Using this model of flawed belief in the possibility of infinite growth, coupled with trickle down, just getting everyone in the world onto a modest income of $3 per day would require the natural resources of around 15 planets like Earth.

The scale of growth this model demands would generate unsupportable environmental costs; and the costs would fall disproportionately, and counterproductively, on the poorest – the very people the growth is meant to benefit – through climate change and pollution. The basic assumption that growth in the amount of money spent would bring widespread success by itself has now broken down. 'Growth' is the wrong question: some kinds of economic growth are going to be worthwhile, if they improve well-being and reduce aspects of consumption; some are not. But in conventional economics, the meaning of 'growth' is unbreakably attached to the rise of GDP.

New measures of success

The resistance to economic growth began less than 15 years after Butler unveiled it as a political weapon. The maverick economist E. J. Mishan wrote a book called *The Costs of Economic Growth*, filling the prefaces of successive editions with long rants about schoolgirl pregnancies, junk mail, gay hotlines and one-parent families. 'The suburbs were quiet and pleasant,' he wrote nostalgically in 1993 about the days before economic growth.[14] 'Nobody's ears were assailed by low flying aircraft or the neighbours stereophonics, nor indeed by screaming chainsaws and long-wailing lawnmowers. In English seaside resorts it was still possible to smell the salt sea air. The Mediterranean coastline had not yet been wrecked by "development" and the waters were clear and fit to bathe in.'

His critics accused him, with some justification, of extreme conservatism. What about the costs of not growing, said his critics? What about the poor people who need economic growth? What about the fact that raw materials haven't actually run out yet? 'A man who falls from a hundred-storey building will survive the first ninety-nine storeys unscathed,' he replied. 'Were he as sanguine as our technocrats, his confidence would grow with the number of storeys he passed on his downward flight and would be at a maximum just before his free-fall abruptly halted.'

But what was the alternative? Recent decades have seen a range of efforts by new economists to find alternatives to GDP that can reflect the world more accurately. But what was to be done about this? The first step was to come up with an alternative to GDP. One of the earliest and best known was the Index of Sustainable Economic

Welfare (ISEW), which measured money but also subtracted the 'bads' from the total – the pollution, disease or depletion of natural resources. It was drawn up by the green economist Clifford Cobb, whose father, theologian John Cobb, teamed up with the World Bank economist Herman Daly to publish the idea in their book *For the Common Good*.[15] Their ISEW demonstrated alarmingly, in both the USA and UK, that – despite all the rise in money wealth over the past generation – well-being was actually going down.

The invention of the ISEW has been mirrored at local level by the search for better local indicators of success, based on John Kenneth Galbraith's famous maxim that 'if it isn't counted, it tends not to be noticed'. The city of Seattle was one of the first to embark down this path, looking for sources of measures of wealth that might be obscured if they only measured money. They wanted to know how cultured, how educated and how clean the city was, to measure their success by the number of books sold or lent out by libraries, by attendance at arts events, by participation in sport. They set out to measure the number of latchkey kids, the amount of blood donated, or the number of hours people volunteered. They also wanted a series of ratios. They wanted to judge the city's success by the number of vegetarian restaurants as a proportion of the number of McDonald's. Or the amount of bird seed sold at local garden centres as a proportion of the pesticide.

This was important knowledge, but it has had unexpected side effects, especially on a formidably utilitarian British government. The Blair administration used the idea of targets to increase their control over local administration, and what had been distinctive local indicators of success were soon a battery of centrally imposed targets – covering everything from hospital waiting lists to the tooth decay of sailors in the Royal Navy. Just three years into the new Blair government, there were 10,000 targets, and they have continued to grow ever since.[16] Worse, GDP remains enthroned as the target beyond targets, the very apotheosis of success.

What was needed instead was a simple concept of wealth, even if it was difficult to measure. The economist Richard Layard was among those who have put forward happiness as the ultimate wealth, and to sketch out a series of policies that might target happiness instead of money. But even happiness somehow misses the point: people defer happiness, sometimes deny themselves happiness for other goals, and it may be anyway that happiness is not possible if you strive for it directly – like friendship pursued for its own sake. That focus also led to an overly utilitarian emphasis on quick fixes with near universal application. Hence, while often useful, cognitive behavioural therapy is not right for everyone and every problem.

Well-being has emerged instead as the substitute 'wealth' in new economics. Some academics argue that well-being is best understood in terms of our overall happiness or satisfaction with life. But evidence shows that there is much more to life than satisfaction: people also want to be leading fulfilling lives – developing their capabilities, fulfilling their potential and leading socially useful lives. The new economics model of well-being has a number of different dimensions:

- People's satisfaction with their life, which is generally measured by an indicator called life satisfaction: this captures satisfaction, pleasure and enjoyment.
- People's personal development, including being engaged in life, curiosity, 'flow' (a state of absorption where hours pass like minutes), personal development and growth, autonomy, fulfilling potential, having a purpose in life, and the feeling that life has meaning.
- People's social well-being – a sense of belonging to our communities, a positive attitude towards others, feeling that we are contributing to society and engaging in pro-social behaviour, and believing that society is capable of developing positively.

New economics means replacing money at the heart of human endeavour with well-being, because this will cause fewer side effects, fewer corrosive externalities, and will enable us to have a little of the best aspects of life in Vanuatu without losing some of the other benefits of life here. That does not, of course, mean getting rid of money completely – even if such a radical shift were actually possible. But it does mean relegating it to its proper place.

The riddle of Vanuatu, and why life is 'better' there, is primarily an issue about the blindness at the heart of economics. Measuring success entirely in terms of money blinds us to those aspects of wealth that are not measurable in that way. Worse, by blinding us to their existence then, in the end, they tend to disappear. Using the tinted spectacles of GDP, we see no forest in the way of the airport so that, by the end – as if by magic – the forest isn't there. The danger of measuring success in this one-dimensional way is that we become blind to the causes and effects in society, just as we become blind to the real wealth.

The impoverishment of language is supposed to cause the impoverishment of thought. The impoverishment of economics – and measurement systems that go with it – has this same effect. When we can no longer see the causes and effects of social breakdown, all we can do is posture, and gaol people. When we get blind to society around us, we get more desperate and authoritarian. We can see that there is more mental illness or youth crime, but not those aspects of life that money has driven away that used to keep them in check.

So many of the levers of our political system – if they work any more – are geared towards GDP and money growth. Only through the critique of new economics, and other critiques of money-based economics, can we begin to question whether they provide the only way forward.

A new economics way forward

Having looked critically at our measurement systems, and chosen well-being as a better measure of success, then we need some kind of political response: what would a political agenda look like if it were based on well-being and not growth? How should we stitch together a new politics to go with a new economics that is based on human well-being? What would politics look like if promoting people's well-being were one of government's main aims?

The first thing to ask is where well-being comes from. Research suggests that there are three main influences: our parents, through our genes and our upbringing (about 50 per cent), through our circumstances, which include our income, as well as other external factors such as the climate and where we live (about 10 per cent), and our outlook and activities like friendships, being involved in our community, sport and hobbies as well as our attitude to life (about 40 per cent).[17] This last category is where we have the most opportunity to make a difference to well-being.

Policies can't make us happy or more engaged with life, but they can shape the culture and society in which we live. If enhancing people's income by growing the economy only has a small effect on well-being, and may be achieved at the expense of our time with others, the environment in which we live, or the vibrancy of local communities, then what can governments do? The key item in the new economics manifesto is to *measure success differently*. That means, at least in the UK, we need to consign the GDP figures to some dusty corner of the Treasury, released on a quiet day in Parliament, and put centre stage in the annual budget statements a detailed set of national well-being accounts that would allow us to understand well-being better and track changes over time. A number of possible measures are already available, including the Index of Sustainable Economic Welfare and the Happy Planet Index: Bhutan already measures Gross National Happiness.

Like so much else that is vital to our futures, this is something the government will find it hard to achieve by itself. The well-being figures will have to be treated as important by opposition politicians and media alike: they must fight their political battles over them as evidence of progress. That means dethroning GDP not just because it fails as a measure of national progress, but because the new economics wants to undermine the idea that only money 'growth' can provide what we need for national spending. If we can find money from elsewhere, from land tax or from other local resources, or from interest-free credit issued by the Bank of England, then GDP figures are that much less critical to national debate, though they may provide information about safe levels of credit. GDP will still have a role, but it will be one which suits it – not to pretend that it is somehow a measure of everything good, the pursuit of which requires ever more sacrifice of environmental and social capital. Herman Daly argues, with only mild irony, that GDP is best used as a measure of the depletion of scarce natural resources.

In the long run, well-being accounts will be part of the infrastructure for a *steady-state economy* or *dynamic equilibrium* with the natural world, that does not have to grow, at least in its use of resources. The nation may grow in wisdom, happiness, knowledge and activity, but – if you can de-link growth from public spending – there is no reason why it should have to grow just to stand still, the besetting sin of classical economics.

An economy that does not grow in the conventional sense raises a number of other difficult issues that are not wholly solved (though, of course, an economy designed for infinite growth raises many more survival-threatening problems for which no solutions exist). Some answers to the challenge of a dynamic equilibrium economy are in this book – about how we can provide for pensions and social services and the other business of welfare, or how we deal with a rising population. There are resources for these, human and in other forms of money, but we need more experiment to find out precisely how these can be turned to human benefit.

A change in how we see ourselves, from passive consumers to active producers, is at the heart of a progressive transformation. If we work shorter weeks, for example, it will have the double benefit of freeing up time to enhance our well-being and create more employment opportunities for those without any paid work – tackling the culture of overwork and the harsh reality of total unemployment simultaneously. Of course, working less will reduce our money income, making material over-consumption harder – an awkward but necessary transition. But, with more time on our hands, there is more opportunity for ourselves to do, swap or make many of the things that we would once have had to pay for. With other people doing the same, a vast pool of skills, tools, knowledge and goods becomes available to share. What's the point of a street of 50 houses all going to work to earn money to each buy a separate lawnmower, if you could work shorter hours, earn less money, then buy one lawnmower for the whole street and take turns to share it? Different forms of sharing and reciprocity can gradually displace the treadmill of money – commodity – accumulation. And different forms of cultural activity, that we engage in ourselves, can replace ultimately dissatisfying, passive consumerism.

In the meantime, UK local governments now have a general power to enhance well-being, though they do not yet have much idea of where the deficits are and where the levers are to do anything about them. Being able to tracks changes will help them do so. The difficulty is that many organizations, even voluntary ones, find themselves stuck with bottom line financial measures of success, with little idea of the real impact they have on people's lives – even the output measures demanded by funders are often irrelevant and easily manipulated. We need better ways of measuring progress, and finding ways to make the invisible value of things – essential to our well being – visible and more measurable. The problem is that what gets counted, counts – but what is most important is the hardest to measure. We need to focus instead on engaging people and building capacity. Whether we are measuring trust or local money flows, we know that involving local people and working with their strengths, not their deficits, is vital to making sure that measuring leads to action and improving people's well being.

Other ways forward mean we must:

Create a well-being economy
High-quality work can profoundly affect our well-being by providing us with purpose, challenge and opportunities for social relationships. That means a major shift in the way we work, making workplaces less stressful, more flexible and more productive, and finding new ways of reconnecting people to meaningful work, aware that this might not be paid or marketable. Breaking the link between earnings and work is also part of it. A 'citizen's income' is one long-discussed approach, paid to every citizen as of right, leaving them free to earn more or to work more creatively without pay, or do something completely different, as they choose. This could be modernized and combined with tradable personal carbon entitlements, designed to tackle both climate change and fuel poverty.

Reclaim our time
We systematically overestimate the amount of happiness extra income will bring us and work too many hours to get it. We fail to account for the fact that our expectations also rise with our incomes. On the other hand, spending more time with our children, families, friends and communities could bring us more well-being. It may be that we need to take our productivity gains in the form of time, introducing a shorter working week – perhaps only three days. A shorter working week could redistribute work – simultaneously tackling unemployment and over work, whilst freeing up more time to do things that generate real well-being.

Massively cut house prices
One of the main factors that add to our workload is the need, often for both partners, to work long hours to pay massive mortgages, limiting their choices and undermining their relationships with their families. Reducing house prices by taxing capital gains or capping mortgages at three times people's salary, or providing access to home ownership via community land trusts (see Appendix A), would mean we would have to provide alternative ways of saving for retirement. This is not a simple matter, but tackling the cost of homes would have an effect on the insane prices that we only endure because they provide us with the possibility of retirement nest eggs. It would be politically difficult for exactly that reason, but it would transform people's lives.

Create a holistic education system that promotes creativity

The purpose of the education system should be to create capable and emotionally well-rounded people who are happy and motivated, and not to provide subsidised workforce training for global corporations. At its heart, education policy must acknowledge that the best way of enabling people to realize their potential is to value them for who they are rather than their performance against targets, or their ability to slot neatly into jobs. The curriculum needs to be broadened to include more opportunities around sports, arts, creativity, well-being and other engaging activities.

Refocus the health system to promote health

So much health spending is geared to curing disease, when it needs to be shifted towards preventing it, and towards tackling the growth of chronic ill-health that takes up about 80 per cent of its resources and against which it is fighting a losing battle. A well-being agenda would also mean a shift of resources towards promoting mental health, making the massive burden of mental ill-health a much higher priority, and providing more accessible talking cures for psychological need. That will probably mean a health system which recognizes that we will have to support each other better in recovery and maintaining health, and to rebuild the human, voluntary aspects of health care (see Chapter 9). It will probably also mean a different kind of health system that is able to reach out into the community and tackle the causes of ill-health.

Discourage materialism and clamp down on damaging advertising

We don't, of course, become sexier and more attractive by switching brands of shampoo or buying a new car. So the media generally, and advertisments specifically, should stop using imagery that suggests we do, because they seriously undermine people's well-being and promote discontent. Young children particularly lack the critical capacity to distinguish between facts and selling messages, and so do many of the rest of us. Advertising to children probably needs to be banned altogether, certainly for sweets, sugary drinks and toys. The point is that materialism is not only bad for the environment: it upsets our lives and drives us to do and buy things that will undermine our mental health. We should try to make the well-being choice the easy choice, to wean us off our national pastimes of shopping and TV watching.

Measure social effects

In 2008, unprecedented investment in banking stability was justified on the grounds that doing nothing would be much more expensive. Social auditing was developed largely at **nef** in the 1990s, and became a method whereby organizations and companies could reach out to stakeholders and report on their social and ethical performance. Organizations that take on social auditors make themselves accountable to stakeholders and commit themselves to following the audit recommendations. The same logic can be applied to public services, when failing to deliver effective services is more expensive than paying for them. For example, for every pound spent on alternatives to prison that reduce reoffending, **nef** research found that an extra £14 worth of social value is generated. This comes from a technique developed at **nef** called social return on investment (SROI), which involves putting a money value on externalities as a way of demonstrating the way that conventional bottom lines fail to tell the whole story. SROI is an impact measurement tool that helps any organization define the relationship between its inputs, outputs and outcomes in terms of the value to each stakeholder group, and then provides a way to put a money value on them.[18] It allows investors to look at the real effect of their investment beyond the simple bottom line.

Other books to read

Richard Douthwaite (1992) *The Growth Illusion*, Green Books, Totnes
John Elkington (1999) *Cannibals with Forks*, Capstone, London
Clive Hamilton (2003) *The Growth Fetish*, Allen & Unwin, London
Oliver James (2007) *Affluenza*, Vermilion, London
Richard Layard (2005) *Happiness: Lessons from a New Science*, Penguin, London
Alex Macgillivray, Candy Weston and Catherine Unsworth (1998) *Communities Count!*, New Economics Foundation, London
Lisa Sanfilippo (ed) (2007) *Proving and Improving*, New Economics Foundation, London
Julian Tudor Hart (2006) *The Political Economy of Health Care*, Policy Press, London
David Woodward and Andrew Simms (2006) *Growth Isn't Working*, New Economics Foundation, London

Notes

1   Quoted in Nic Marks, Andrew Simms, Sam Thompson and Saamah Abdallah (2006) *The Happy Planet Index,* New Economics Foundation, London.
2   Nic Marks, Andrew Simms, Sam Thompson and Saamah Abdallah (2006) *The Happy Planet Index,* New Economics Foundation, London.
3   Quoted in Nic Marks, Andrew Simms, Sam Thompson and Saamah Abdallah (2006) *The Happy Planet Index,* New Economics Foundation, London.
4   Quoted in Nic Marks, Andrew Simms, Sam Thompson and Saamah Abdallah (2006) *The Happy Planet Index,* New Economics Foundation, London.
5   Keith and Ann Chambers (2001) *Unity of Heart,* Waveland Press, Long Island.
6   John Maynard Keynes (1936) *A General Theory of Employment, Interest and Money,* Macmillan, London.
7   Nic Marks (2004) *The Power and Potential of Well-being Indicators*, New Economics Foundation, London.
8   Charles Dickens (1854) *Hard Times,* London.
9   Quoted in Richard Douthwaite (1992) *The Growth Illusion,* Green Books, Totnes.

10 Marilyn Waring (1988) *If Women Counted*, Macmillan, London.
11 Marilyn Waring (1988) *If Women Counted*, Macmillan, London.
12 Clifford Cobb, Ted Halstead and Jonathan Rowe (1995) 'If the GDP is up, why is America down?' *Atlantic Monthly*, October.
13 David Woodward and Andrew Simms (2006) *Growth isn't Working*, New Economics Foundation, London.
14 E. J. Mishan (1967) *The Costs of Economic Growth*, Staples Press, London.
15 Herman Daly and John Cobb (1989) *For the Common Good*, Beacon Press, Boston.
16 David Boyle (2001) *The Tyranny of Numbers*, HarperCollins, London.
17 Sam Thompson and Nic Marks (2008) *Measuring Well-being in Policy*, London, New Economics Foundation.
18 David Aeron-Thomas, Jeremy Nicholls, Sarah Forster and Andrea Westall (2004) *Social Return on Investment: Valuing What Matters*, New Economics Foundation, London.

4
Money: Why did China Pay for the Iraq War?

When enterprise becomes a mere bubble on a whirlpool of speculation, the job of capitalism is likely to be ill-done.

John Maynard Keynes

The notion of multiple target currencies opens up a new way of thinking in economics... Multiple parallel systems, with permeable membranes between them, give very stable systems – as in the human body. This is a whole field which needs, and will get, attention.

Edward de Bono on parallel currencies

When the USA marched into Iraq in 2003, with the fury of what Defence Secretary Donald Rumsfeld called 'shock and awe', one of the aspects of the operation that inspired the most awe was the economics of it all. The direct cost of the invasion by the end of 2008 was around $3 trillion. But the USA was, like many countries, technically bankrupt.[1] Its income is consistently below its spending and has been for decades. Its national debt increases at the rate of $1.4 billion every day. It now stands at over $10 trillion.

Why don't the bailiffs call round? Partly because of the impact on the global economy, but largely because the government of the United States can and does borrow enough to get by – day by day – and the world believes in its ability to pay its debts. The by-product of the situation is that the daily operations of the Federal Reserve to borrow enough to keep the American government operating has become one of those shadowy engines of global events that nobody really talks about. The office of the Federal Reserve in New York, in its vast renaissance-style palace around the corner from Wall Street, sells Treasury bonds and Treasury bills (the so-called

T-bills) every day. These bonds mature at set intervals and pay a set interest rate. They are bought by investors the world over looking for a reliable but unexciting investment, and they are also sometimes bought by the Federal Reserve itself, creating the money to buy them with a simple entry in the books.

It remains a controversial business, especially in the USA, although most countries conduct similar operations. Every sale adds to the dollars in circulation, because the T-bills have been conjured out of nothing. When the Fed buys them itself, then it has also created the dollars with which to do so. Every new dollar dilutes the total amount in circulation, which would normally mean inflation.

The fact that prices do not rise is largely because there are enough foreign investors willing to buy these official bonds, keeping the value high. This is where the peculiar ironies creep in, because much of that demand globally has come from the prudent investors of what came to be called 'old Europe' – countries like France and Germany – which were implacable opponents of the Iraq war, but were financing it by buying US dollars. But old Europe made hardly any contribution compared to the savers in the Far East, in Singapore, Japan and China. China alone, officially a communist country and in uneasy tension with the USA over issues like Taiwan and North Korea, now holds over $1 trillion in dollar-denominated assets, of which about a third are Treasury bonds and bills.

The situation is getting more extreme. Before the recession, the US trade deficit was running at around $2 billion a day, as American consumers binged on luxury foreign goods.[2] A similar amount of money flows out of the USA every day, just because people take money abroad or offshore – in fact a third of all dollars now circulate outside the country. There are massive inflows of dollars to offset this loss, but it isn't enough. The US trade deficit now stands at $27 billion.

The basic problem: The money system no longer serves its purpose

The peculiar way that China has been financing the Bush administration is just one of the quirks of how money has begun to flow internationally. The world's financial system creates new billionaires every day, but presides over grinding poverty and debt. It is also increasingly unstable, managed by testosterone-pumped youths in red braces in London and New York who make more money the more it fluctuates. It is a spectacularly unstable combination.

The financial establishment believes that the sloshing of vast sums of money across the wires of the money system – $3000 billion a day, most of it speculation – makes the global economic system more efficient. The traders react quickly to compliant governments by buying their currency – the majority of world 'trading' is actually foreign exchange speculation – and just as quickly to punish uncompliant ones. This is what the writer Thomas Friedman calls the 'electronic herd'.[3] George Soros'

Quantum Fund became the most famous hedge fund in the world during the 1990s, until he withdrew from active management after mistiming his reaction to the dot.com boom. It was Soros who was one of the first insiders to warn the world of the perils of the system's built-in instability, when traders earn more if the market veers wildly than they do when it is stable. 'The collapse of the global marketplace would be a traumatic event with unimaginable consequences,' he wrote. 'Yet I find it easier to imagine than the continuation of the present regime.'[4]

He did not just blame the dangerous interconnections in the global marketplace, or the computers that are programmed to sell automatically when the market drops a certain amount. He blamed the whole theory. The global markets do not, in fact, tend towards equilibrium at all: they tend to overshoot and veer dangerously off in the wrong direction. This becomes potentially catastrophic when combined with financiers' casual and almost complete disregard for the impact of their behaviour on the financial infrastructure of the economy as a whole, something that the economist J. K. Galbraith noted was a key characteristic of the 1929 Wall Street crash. In the 1998 crisis, where currency after currency across the Far East collapsed in the markets – with devastating consequences for the people who lived there, patients thrown out of hospitals at gunpoint in some places – people began to ask whether there were alternatives, or at least some speed bumps to slow down the flow of capital.

Slowing down the speed of money

The most practical solutions involved slowing down the furious and often ruinous flow of capital. Malaysian Prime Minister Mohamed Mahathir re-established exchange controls, preventing people taking large sums of money out of the country, the situation all over the world until 1979. He credited this solution with being the reason the Malaysian economy recovered faster than its neighbours after the East Asian crisis of 1997–1998. Colombia now allows foreigners to invest in local businesses but not to buy debt or shares, which means they can't simply sell up over night. The Chilean government insists that foreigners investing in the country have to keep their money there for at least a year, which deters speculators.

A more radical solution was a brainwave by the Nobel prize-winning economist James Tobin, who suggested a small levy on foreign exchange transactions of 0.05 per cent, to 'throw sand in the wheels of our excessively efficient international money markets'.[5] This would have a calming effect on the speculation, although a debate continues on the level at which it should be set, and would also raise money to put UN poverty reduction and sustainable development programmes into effect. The Tobin Levy, as he preferred to call it, is still resisted – partly because Tobin himself changed his mind about it – but has been backed at various times by the Canadian and the French governments. It would be difficult to implement if one of the main financial centres remained aloof: they would all have to agree. But even if the sums raised were not as large as its supporters claim, they could still contribute significantly to the meagre current redistribution of wealth, and the levy would have the effect of calming the markets by making very marginal speculation far less profitable.

The growing gap between rich and poor

So for the time being, the financial markets rule. The old economics claims that this new 'wealth' spreads down through society though, actually, one of the peculiarities of the speculative success of recent years is how little it has trickled down. The economist Paul Krugman, in his book *Peddling Prosperity*, estimates that as much as 70 per cent of the extraordinary economic growth of the 1980s in the USA was delivered to the richest 1 per cent of the population.[6] There were 13 billionaires in the US in 1982, and by 1999 there were 268 – and that was before the dot.com boom.[7]

We have already seen how Bill Clinton won the 1992 presidential election with the help of the slogan 'Trickle down doesn't work'. Despite this definitive statement, most economic policy is based on this flawed old economic dictum that helping the wealth-creators will automatically help everybody else. If that wealth is not productive, or if the bargain driven with the producers is manifestly unfair, then the wealth will not trickle. Even so, the complete failure of so-called 'trickle down economics' seems to require some other explanations. Why, despite the apparent success of recent decades, has that not benefited the poorest?

Some possible explanations are covered in the previous chapter, but a glimpse at some of the workshops that manufacture clothes for the big brand names is enough to see that there is a problem. Often the basic work is carried out by offshore packagers, who transform a pair of jeans made for big brand names for 20 US cents each (including wages) and sold in New York or London for $30, sewed by women and girls in Nicaragua working sometimes 20-hour shifts, sleeping in cramped breeze-block rooms.[8]

Then there are the taxes that benefit big over small, rich over poor. Poor people pay taxes when rich corporations increasingly don't: among the big corporations that pay almost no tax worldwide is Rupert Murdoch's News Corporation. Instead, the offshore financial centres, tiny pin-pricks on the atlas, like Jersey or the Bahamas, the British Virgin Islands or Labuan in Malaysia – though Luxembourg, Switzerland and even offshore aspects of London, New York and Dublin ought to be included as well – now host a staggering amount of the world's wealth.

Of course, because of the secrecy that surrounds them – the Jersey authorities prefer the term 'confidentiality' – we can't know how much. A recent estimate is around $11,500 billion, or around one third of all global wealth.[9] Half of all global trade is now routed via offshore accounts to avoid tax. More money simply passes through the offshore centres on its way somewhere else. One American study estimates that up to half of all global transactions are conducted electronically via the offshore financial centres.

Inward investment into the UK or any EU member state has no need to route itself via tax havens, other than where it is trying to obtain an unfair tax or regulatory advantage, or where it wants to avoid disclosure of its provenance. Too much of the capital flowing through the offshore circuits is engaged in speculative activity rather than being committed to long-term investment. The impact of such vast sums moving rapidly in and out of equity markets and currencies, without effective multilateral regulation, has created a global economy that is probably beyond the control of nation states.

The cuckoo in the nest effect

But look more closely at Jersey, and another problem with international money flows becomes clear. When very small islands like Jersey become tax havens, other sectors of the economy are driven out. Anyone who has looked for affordable accommodation in London knows what it means when financial services start driving everything else out: in Jersey, banking has made agriculture unviable, and tourism is difficult as well. The capture of Jersey by the awesome power of world capital is frighteningly reminiscent of the UK, where economic policy has been tailored to suit the financial services industry, while manufacturing struggles away unsupported.

The truth is that financial services tend to price out of existence the business of actually producing anything. Of all the commodities you might put your money into, none can compete with money itself, which offers far bigger returns – by people who have access to almost infinite credit – than the small returns offered by any productive process, still less any natural process. The money markets offer, and we therefore demand, returns that no natural system could ever provide – and we are threatened with economic disaster when this inexorable growth starts to slide. When it slackens off to less than 2 per cent a year, policy-makers wander around white faced with fear. That is, in itself, a kind of financial slavery.

The truth is that the money system is no longer designed for the use of ordinary people. Only around 5 per cent of those titanic daily money flows has anything to do with the facilitation of goods or services. Money is designed for the money markets, and it therefore carries within it the familiar faulty measurement of value.

Faulty measurement: The struggling local economy

We rely, for example, on economic forces to protect the small local bakeries or local cafes that we enjoy around the corner. We know other people enjoy them too. They represent aspects of local wealth, yet they close: the debt or rent burden is too high to take on the limitless resources of the multinationals. When they close, the balance sheets of their international competitors will rise but, locally, we lose something too.

Why don't these aspects of wealth show up in the figures? If money is supposed to reflect people's preferences, why doesn't it reflect the preferences of the locals? One reason is that the yardstick the global players use – an international currency like the pound or the dollar – is unable to measure the fine mesh of local wealth like that. The problem for the rest of us is that these international currencies are all we have got.

In a modern economy – even in a modern city – there is really more than one economy at work, and these big currencies do not suit them all very accurately. Take the sheer diversity of London, where all of us have to get by, using the one currency, the value of which is decided by tens of thousands of youthful traders in the financial service centres. They are doing so with one eye on their own short-term needs and another on the needs of the international economy. But there is another economy in London, and in any city, which just about survives off the pickings from the rich table above it, but is not directly part of it: it runs the services used by the traders but otherwise it remains outside the world of bonuses. These are the bar, club and restaurant staff, the office cleaners and the hotel workers. This economy governs those aspects of life that have nothing to do with financial services.

The international economy brings in executives from all over the world, whose employers will pay their hefty expenses, forcing up the value of London homes beyond anywhere else in the country, and pricing London services beyond the other economy. Because of this, London struggles to employ nurses or teachers or bus drivers because their salaries are not valued in the same way by the international currencies, so the basic services suffer and – if they have to live in London – their accommodation has to be subsidized. Worse, London's rich economy threatens very slowly to drive out the poor economy completely.

Faulty measurement: The struggling social economy

There is a third economy in London that is also threatened because the international currencies fail to value it at all. It makes up the crucial human transactions that build families and neighbourhoods, look after old people, and without which nothing we can do can be successful. Economists call this 'social capital'. The co-production and time banking pioneer Edgar Cahn refers instead to the 'core economy' of family and community (see Chapter 9). This is what underpins the money economy.[10] Market forces do not apply here and, without it, police, teachers and doctors cannot do their jobs.

As we saw in Chapter 3, the deep operating system of the social economy is not measured in GDP. Politicians assume it is inexhaustible, so they largely ignore it. That is a mistake. It is like being more concerned with your wallpaper than your walls. One reason it happens is that big, international currencies fail to measure the needs and assets in these other economies very accurately. What they miss out gets ignored, then forgotten. Currencies are not just measuring systems; they are eyeglasses. They are the way we see the world. If our currencies are unable to value things, then society often fails to see them at all.

We have already seen how using measures of success like GDP means that the environment, human dignity, community and family are all in danger of being driven out. Monoculture money systems drive out other cultures, other species, other languages, other opinions and other forms of wealth. This phenomenon is happening so slowly that we barely recognize it. Money is pushing out life, and we need new kinds of money, new measuring systems, that don't drive out life. Otherwise we face a dwindling, impoverished economy for the vast majority of us, sidelined by the electronic herd, what Keynes referred to as 'a peregrination in the catacombs, with a guttering candle'.[11]

Faulty measurement: The loss of feedback

In many ways, the world now has one, massive, interconnected currency. The problem is that, the broader these electronic links are between currencies, the less ability national governments have to take economic action, at local as well as national levels. Both sovereignty, and by implication democracy, get undermined. The merest hint of disapproval from the global markets and the value of their currency can collapse overnight. There is also evidence that large currency zones, where the same currency – and therefore the same interest rates – is shared across nations, tend to increase the economic divisions within and between nations and that they can cause continuing unemployment.[12]

The key problem for large currencies is unemployment. This has been a continuing problem across western Europe, before and after the euro. Clearly large currencies are unlikely to be the only *cause* of joblessness: the connection is more complicated than that. Western Europe built up this jobs backlog under many currencies, while the USA reduced its unemployment to an unprecedented low in the 1990s with a single currency. The issue is whether large currencies can make the situation worse so that it becomes more difficult to do anything about it. The larger the geographical area covered by a currency, the more likely it is for regions within it to be at different stages of the same economic cycle and hence respond better to different interest rates.

Even within the UK, the effect of having one currency – and one interest rate – probably increases divisions: certainly the Governor of the Bank of England said he believed this to be the case. 'Any national policy that makes enough national spending available to enable Liverpool to generate healthy levels of economic activity there, is bound to create inflationary conditions in other parts of the country,' wrote the economist and former civil servant James Robertson.[13] That situation is probably even more pronounced under the euro.

The problem with big currencies is that they undermine the kind of information small currencies can provide to cities and regions. This was the argument that the radical economist Jane Jacobs put forward in 1986:

> *Imagine a group of people who are all properly equipped with diaphragms and lungs, but share only one single brainstem breathing centre. In this goofy arrangement, through breathing they would receive consolidated feedback on the carbon dioxide level of the whole group, without discriminating among the individuals producing it... But suppose some of these people were sleeping, while others were playing tennis... Worse yet, suppose some were swimming and diving, and for some reason, such as the breaking of the surf, had no control over the timing of these submersions... In such an arrangement, feedback control would be working perfectly on its own terms, but the results would be devastating.*[14]

Hong Kong and Singapore are cities with their own currencies, said Jacobs; Detroit is not. In practice, once again, this loss of feedback undermines the ability of nations and regions to respond to international events. If a recession in Latin America meant a decline in Spanish exports, for example, then the Spanish peseta used to weaken and interest rates fall. That automatically reduced the impact on unemployment by stimulating other exports. But now that the peseta has been replaced by the euro, Spain can no longer use this method of easing their unemployment. Nor can the Spanish government be allowed to cut taxes or raise spending to offset a fall in demand. The precise effect of the euro during a recession remains to be seen.

New ways of organizing money

Money and its creation can be a topic fraught with difficulty in the new economics, which is heir to complementary – possibly contradictory – traditions to deal with this basic problem at the heart of money. It is contradictory because the problems of money are contradictory, depending on the prevailing economic climate.

If there is too much money in circulation, most of it created as interest-bearing debt by the banking system, and we are heading for one of our regular bursting bubbles, then the problem is one of rooting money to reality. It is an issue about the way money has cast itself adrift into an imaginary world where anything is possible, but unrelated to the real wealth of people and resources. A series of new currencies have been proposed to tackle this problem, notably Bernard Lietaer's terra, the value of which would be rooted in a basket of commodities, and which hold national currencies to this basic reality.[15] Another is Richard Douthwaite's suggestion of an energy backed currency unit. This would be a way of connecting the economics of trade in fossil fuels both to their limited resource, and their environmental impact. As the amount we are able to burn goes down, so the currency in circulation reduces.[16]

Commodities also corrode or 'rust', as the original money – corn or tobacco – did and there is, in this tradition, a range of corroding currencies, known as *demurrage*, which have a negative interest rate to encourage spending. These were used to great effect in towns on both sides of the Atlantic during the Great Depression until they were declared illegal.[17]

But if there is too little money in circulation, then there are ways that these negative interest currencies can help as well. There were thousands of local scrip systems in the USA in the 1930s, designed to reconnect people with needs and people with resources. Recent years have given us a series of similar currencies like local exchange and trading systems (lets), which do just that. These currencies suit a prevailing climate when there is too little money in the right places, where there are people available to do the work, people who want work doing, but no cash to bring the two sides together. They are currencies based on the information function of money. People create it themselves by their own efforts.

The last 15 years have seen a range of other kinds of printed local currencies, starting in cash-strapped Argentina, where the Global Barter Clubs were at one stage keeping up to 2 million people alive. The beautiful notes of Ithaca hours in upstate New York, issued into circulation partly as no-interest loans, partly as grants to local charities, have inspired a whole generation of similar projects, most of which have struggled to survive – though Ithaca is still going strong. The berkshares system in Great Barrington, Massachusetts (see Chapter 11) has replaced dollar notes with local notes that are intended to circulate faster locally, and keep spending power circulating locally.

Local currencies are now being used in most continents, but especially in Latin America – coping with the consequences of linking their own currencies to the dollar – as a method of involving people on the fringes of society in economic activity. The idea has attracted government at every level, from local to European, and has begun to involve business too. They can be used as a tool to regenerate local economies and as a protective shield for people against the worst excesses of the market.

Ever since the state took for itself a monopoly of the coinage, there have been radical dreams of inventing new kinds of money that would be able to provide for local needs. The pioneer social reformer Robert Owen printed labour notes in his 1832 National Equitable Labour Exchange, but they failed because they could not buy food. The most recent phase of development emerged out of Michael Linton's lets in the Comox Valley in Canada.

A decade on, the argument has progressed and so have the possibilities. Every community has assets in its people and their skills, even if the market economy doesn't recognize them. But these assets can be used as the basis for new kinds of currency that can invigorate those sections of the economy that the big currencies ignore. Inventing new currencies is a way of refusing to accept the narrowing of life by measuring everything by what it is worth in pounds or euros.

The idea of multiple currencies, possibly competing ones, would have been nightmarish until a decade ago, with complicated wallets, expensive exchanges and a juggling of different notes and cards. But the advent of ubiquitous information technology now makes this relatively simple, and currencies can now be downloaded onto cards by phone, can be spent by phone, can be collected, exchanged and managed by software. Meanwhile, there have been exciting developments in the printed hours currency in Ithaca in New York state; Michael Linton's Community Way model, which also raises 'real' money for local charities; the *talent* system and regional currencies in Germany; the system run by South African New Economics (Sane); and – most recently – the Dutch *qoin* system has learned some of the lessons of the commercial barter currencies. The Argentine models ran into difficulties with counterfeiting, and there remains the issue of how to pay for the back office systems that any currency requires, but these are still working models with great potential.

The power of information technology and mobile phones make a range of new innovations possible. Those who are concerned about the corrosion of the social economy have adopted Edgar Cahn's time banks ideas, of which more in Chapter 9.

Creating new money via the state

But those whose concern is that the basic problem of money is that it is created by banks, along with considerable private profit, rather than by governments, with the benefits going to the public purse – that the original sin at the heart of money is the interest that goes along with it – have a different solution (see Chapter 5). Reformers like the social credit pioneer Clifford Hugh Douglas, or the Nobel chemist Frederick Soddy, urged that banks should be banned from creating money, and that it should be created instead by elected governments and used (in the case of social credit) to pay a citizen's income to everybody as of right.[18] Trickle up rather than trickle down.

There is clearly a case to be made that the laborious business of government borrowing, via T-bills and their various equivalents, is massively profitable for financial institutions and increasingly unviable for the rest of us. Thomas Edison and Henry Ford teamed up to urge that government borrowing for capital projects should be done differently: the government should create the money themselves, lend it to the project without interest – or as the Islamic banks do, at a fee – and withdraw it from circulation to avoid inflation as the project began to pay.[19] At present, the profits that come from creating money – known as *seigniorage* – nearly all go to the banks, when it is argued that they properly belong to us as citizens. It is certainly true that the power to create unlimited sums, which has been taken up by the banking system as a whole, is a privilege that ought to be taxed at the very least and certainly better regulated.

But the idea that governments alone should create money, while it is clearly part of the alternative economics tradition, is not strictly 'new economics' in the sense that it does not share the new economics scepticism about money and its measuring power. Social credit, important though its ideas are, believes that money is the key and believes that, by making it 'real' in a different sense, then the basic economic problems of society are solved. The new economics urges a greater scepticism about money as a real measure of anything.

The other objection to a wholesale state takeover of money creation is that it remains an elite – a democratically elected though centralized one – which decides on the amount of money in circulation. It also leaves the problem intact of money's faulty measurement of value, which is where the complementary currencies come in.

Multiple currencies

If, as seems likely, the world is about to plunge into a combination of financial, environmental and energy crises, then a new generation of complementary currencies – using smartcard and mobile phone technology – will probably come more firmly into our lives. They will provide money to connect up needs and wants when success has moved elsewhere, will provide a boost for local production and local skills – a new way of keeping local spending power circulating locally – and provide the kind of diversity of measuring systems that underpins diversity itself. Different people need different kinds of money, which behave in different ways and are based on the value of very different assets. We also all need different kinds of money for different aspects of our lives. Without them, some parts of our cities will be rich and some poor, and some parts of our lives will be rich and some poor.

Ironically, the original 'single currency' – the euro – is now slowly becoming a second currency in Britain. You can use it in the phone booths in London, for example, and a range of shops. But that is just the beginning. If we need a range of yardsticks, we need a range of currencies. Time banks to underpin the social economy, local currencies to keep money and resources circulating locally. Regional currencies to provide low-cost finance to small business. Each of them can give value to assets and resources that the big currencies are unable to recognize, like recycled computers or old bicycles, just as barter currency exchanges can let us exchange unsold plane seats or hotel rooms or toothpaste in last year's colour, when the market fails to recognize them as valuable.

Big monocultural currencies are unable to do that because the messages they carry are too distant and too complex, but complementary ones can. The new economics provides an escape from the old idea that money is indivisible and objective.

Complementary currencies can reveal to us that, even in the poorest places, there are vast living assets – ideas, skills, time, love even (in the case of time banking) – that can turn our ideas of scarcity on their heads.

A new economics way forward

So how was it that the USA funded its invasion of Iraq with money from China and the Far East? The answer is that the demands that the American government places on its own money system are too much for it to bear (and also because invasions are, quite appropriately, ruinously expensive). China, made rich by its massive trade surplus and Walmart's fondness for cheap imports to the USA, was only too happy to convert its currency reserves into the holding of secure US Treasury bonds and bills – in the process, lending the US government billions. In fact, the global money system no longer meets the needs of the vast majority of people on the planet, partly because it is out of control, partly because it is focused on speculation rather than production, and partly because it is pricing production out of existence.

This chapter has proposed a number of ways forward. The key task in the new economics manifesto is to find ways of taming the destructive money flows. That will mean persuading *local authorities to take development decisions on the basis of their impact on local money flows*, measuring the effects of potential developments on whether they keep money flowing locally or whether they encourage money to seep out. The short- to medium-term solution is to use a measuring tool like LM3 (Local Money 3) to measure how much money stays circulating in the local economy, to maximize the life it can generate. It can also help them refuse developments that would simply hoover up the money and send it elsewhere.

But, in the long term, we need a *multi-currency world*, a multiplicity of local, regional, volunteer, social and reward currencies to underpin different aspects of our lives. Local and regional currencies are an excellent tool investing in low or no interest loans in productive local business, which uses local people and assets. There are a range of models already at work, and the new ones – often linked to smartcards, and building on the parallel success of business barter – will be coming online soon. We need hard currencies, online currencies and global currencies underpinned by commodities and which are created in a range of different ways, because – in the long run – single currencies are single yardsticks, and when it is all created by debt in the same way, we risk a further descent into monoculture.

The manifesto might also include measures to:

Calm the international money hurricane

That means putting in speed bumps to the flow of capital that prioritize productive loans against speculations. This can be done by allowing investment only on the basis that it stays for a certain amount of time, or even then – after the investment horizon where it barely matters any more (say 20 years) – the ownership should revert to the stakeholders.

Tax currency speculation

The best option here is the Tobin levy on currency speculation, part of which goes to the collecting nation – a perk to encourage the financial centres to take part – and part of which goes to the United Nations to fund its poverty reduction and sustainable development goals. Proposed levels at which to set the levy range enormously, from 0.1 per cent, considered by many to be high, through to a very modest suggestion from the group Stamp Out Poverty for a 0.005 per cent levy on sterling exchanges anywhere in the world, which would be difficult to avoid and would be collected in London wherever they took place.[20] It would yield an estimated £2 billion a year and could be done without international agreement.

Clamp down on offshore financial centres

This is a way to insist that multinationals pay their fair share of the tax burden, as their smaller competitors have to. In fact, the UK is in an excellent position to make this happen, because many – if not most – of the more respectable tax havens in the world are also British crown dependencies. Since 2001, it has been far more difficult to hide money offshore, and the time has come to prevent corporations avoiding paying their fair share of tax.

Link to a global reference currency

Keynes imagined one called the bancor, just as Bernard Lietaer's terra currency is designed as a way to underpin the value of other currencies. His terra would be based on the value of a range of real commodities, which would have the effect also of providing the nations with stocks of these – mainly developing countries – with more status and financial clout. Joseph Stiglitz has also proposed a global currency he calls the global greenback to replace the estimated $3 trillion in dollar reserves around the world, and which can also be used by developing countries to meet their development goals.[21] A simple way of providing a global reference currency would be to price dollars in terms of oil, rather than the other way around.

Set up new local savings schemes to make capital available locally

Local government in the UK urgently needs to be able to raise its own finance, as cities can in the USA by issuing their own bonds. They could and should also be able to issue their own currencies, and provide low-interest loans in them. The biggest shift in the UK would be to set up a range of local pension products invested in safe and reliable projects like low-cost housing. This would have the twin benefits of setting people's pension pots partly free from the vagaries of the stock market, and providing the capital we need locally to house ourselves.

Back a new generation of complementary currencies
These will almost certainly emerge without government backing, especially business-to-business currencies like the Wir model in Switzerland, which underpins the building and restaurant trades by providing very low interest loans in a parallel currency to the Swiss franc. But government at every level can underpin these currencies by accepting them for a proportion of local and national taxes.

Experiment with the creation of public money
We need new kinds of no-interest loan finance by governments, to replace government borrowing and as a way to make public investment in vital infrastructure affordable again. If they are withdrawn from circulation in the same way as more conventional loans, there are no reasons why this need be inflationary. In fact, it is hard to see how the major investment needed by the UK – let alone anywhere else – to educate students, and build railways and renewable energy infrastructure, can be afforded any other way.

Other books to read

David Boyle (ed) (2004) *The Money Changers,* Earthscan, London
J. K. Galbraith (1976) *Money: Whence it Came, Where it Went,* Penguin Books, London
Tom Greco (2001) *Money,* Chelsea Green, White River Junction
Keith Hart (2000) *The Memory Bank*, Profile, London
Doreen Massey (2007) *World City,* Polity Press, London
Peter North (2007) *Money and Liberation*, University of Minnesota Press, Minneapolis
Ann Pettifor (ed) (2003) *Real World Economic Outlook*, Palgrave Macmillan, London
James Robertson and Joseph Huber (2000) *Creating New Money*, New Economics Foundation, London
Joseph Stiglitz (2007) *Making Globalisation Work*, Penguin Books, London

Notes

1   Joseph Stiglitz and Linda Bilmes (2008) *The Three Trillion Dollar War*, Norton, New York.
2   Ann Pettifor (2006) *The Coming First World Debt Crisis*, Palgrave Macmillan, London.
3   Thomas L. Friedman (1999) *The Lexus and the Olive Tree*, HarperCollins, London.
4   George Soros, Byron Wien and Krisztina Koenen (1995) *Soros on Soros*, Wiley, New York.
5   James Tobin (1978) 'A proposal for international monetary reform', *Eastern Economic Journal*, Vol 4, July–October.
6   Paul Krugman (1995) *Peddling Prosperity*, Norton, New York.
7   Jeff Gates (2000) *Democracy at Risk: Rescuing Main Street from Wall Street*, Perseus, New York.
8   Anita Roddick (2001) *Take it Personally*, Thorsons, London.

9 Tax Justice Network (2005) *The Price of Offshore*, London.
10 Edgar Cahn (2000) *No More Throwaway People: The Co-production Imperative*, Essential Books, Washington DC.
11 Robert Skidelsky (1992) *John Maynard Keynes Vol 2: The Economist as Saviour*, Picador, London.
12 David Boyle (2003) *Beyond Yes and No: A Multi-currency Alternative to EMU*, New Economics Foundation, London.
13 James Robertson (2002) 'The euro will prompt further monetary reform', *European Business Review*, Vol 14, No 1.
14 Jane Jacobs (1986) *Cities and the Wealth of Nations*, Random House, New York.
15 Bernard Lietaer (2000) *The Future of Money*, Random Century, London.
16 Richard Douthwaite (1999) *The Ecology of Money, Schumacher Briefings Number 4*, Green Books, Totnes.
17 Tom Greco (1985) *New Money for Healthy Communities*, Greco, Tucson.
18 See, for example, David Boyle (ed) (2002) *The Money Changers: Currency Reform from Aristotle to e-cash*, Earthscan, London.
19 *New York Times* (1921) 4 December.
20 Stamp Out Poverty (2005) *Submission to the Intergovernmental Working Group*, London.
21 Joseph Stiglitz (2002) *Globalisation and its Discontents*, Norton, New York.

5
Markets: Why has London Traffic Always Travelled at 12mph?

If you build it, they will come.

Catchphrase in the film *Field of Dreams*

Commercialisation of blood and donor relationships represses the expression of altruism.

Richard Titmuss, *The Gift Relationship* (1970)

London in 1900, the centre of empire. The Central Line underground railway is being constructed with picks and shovels. The vast majority of London's traffic is horse drawn, but it clutters the streets nonetheless, leaving a layer of manure that – so some believe – will eventually lie feet deep and overwhelm the capital. Getting across Piccadilly Circus or Parliament Square can be a laborious and dangerous business. What research has been done shows that the average journey time, door to door, across central London is just 12 miles per hour (mph).[1] It wouldn't be quicker to walk, but it feels frustratingly slow.

Just over a century later, research across all the European capitals into traffic speed put London at the bottom of the league. The average traffic speed, door to door, was 11.8mph.[2] The extraordinary aspect of this loss of 0.2mph in a century is that it comes, not just after billions spent on traffic management and urban motor ways – on the North and South Circular roads and the M25 – but after the congestion charge introduced by Mayor Ken Livingstone in 2003.

Traffic speeds in cities are one of the jokes of the modern age. There is hardly a city in the world where traffic has not choked people's road space and lungs. But the amazing consistency of London traffic speed implies that, despite all that spending, some other factor is at work here – some other hidden hand. The man who helped uncover what it was and helped to popularize the answer was one of the most unusual transport planners of the century. Martin Mogridge was originally a physicist who wore long hair and leather trousers, with a cultivated air of exoticism. His interests included science fiction and Victorian eroticism, and just before his untimely death in 1999 at the age of only 59, he began studying Hebrew.

Over the previous three decades, while the major cities of the world enthusiastically demolished their slums and built massive urban highways, transport experts had been puzzling over the phenomenon of how new roads – even widened roads – seemed to increase traffic. Economists had noticed that, if there is more road space, people find it worthwhile to pay to use their cars, if they have one. Then public transport attracts fewer paying passengers and the fares go up or services reduce, and even more people go by car. Even in the 1930s, they had noticed that new roads released what they called 'suppressed demand'. Worse, then the traffic goes faster and the buses find it more difficult to negotiate traffic streams or cross big highways. It all combined together to create what was called the Downs-Thomson Paradox, described like this:

> *If the decision to use public or private transport is left to the free choice of the individual commuter, an equilibrium will be reached in which the overall attractiveness of the two systems is about equal, because if one is faster, cheaper and more agreeable than the other there will be a shift of passengers to it, rendering it more crowded while the other becomes less so, until a position is reached where no-one on either system thinks there is any advantage in changing to the other... Hence we derive one of the golden rules of urban transport: the quality of peak-hour travel by car tends to equal that of public transport.*[3]

That was a vital clue: the speed of road transport and public transport are linked, and the journey times door to door for both are often very similar. Mogridge realized that, in London, everything depended on the speed of the underground system. If you build more roads, people go back to their cars because it is then quicker than going by underground – until the point when the speed is so slow that underground travel is faster. Then they leave their cars behind and go by tube.

The solution to speeding up the traffic is therefore to speed up the main public transport infrastructure. What's more, said Mogridge, this works even if you take space away from cars to make room for public transport.[4] It was the thinking that led to plans like Crossrail – the new high speed underground line across London – as well as Zurich's successful strategy to reduce car use based on better pedestrian access and investment in trams. By the end of his life, Mogridge reckoned that traffic speed could be doubled just by reducing space for cars, though it remains difficult for public officials – at least in the UK – to act on this new law of traffic management.

It is also difficult for the kind of assumptions that policy makers have about economics, often based on the ideas of those defunct economists. Even classical economics understands that price can be one of a number of factors that make people decide things, though it also assumes that most people will decide according to price. Its concept of 'utility' has never just been about money, though it usually is. But the old-fashioned version of classical economics used by those who rule us understands the way people make these decisions entirely in terms of money, and in terms of the ratio between costs of petrol, tickets or parking and speed. Classical economics has to explain the simple business of deciding which method of transport is quickest in terms of what it costs to go faster, believing that people want their time spent more efficiently so they can earn more elsewhere. It does not see that there is another kind of market going on here, which goes beyond money. It really is a kind of market in time.

The basic problem: A blindness about human motivation

Price undoubtedly matters when we decide what journey to take, and time is a component of price, but it is the question of how much time each journey takes that is paramount. There is some kind of market going on here, but it is not really about price. People are involved in it even if getting there faster earns them no extra money at all. The kind of economics that reduces everything to money finds it hard to understand what is going on.

New economics accepts that markets exist – that much is obvious – but denies that these markets are simply a matter of price. There is nothing special about money, and concentrating only on the role that money plays fails to describe our decisions very clearly. In fact, any of the human needs described in the 'hierarchy of needs' set out by the radical psychologist Abraham Maslow are likely to be involved in the highly complex decisions we make.

One reason why the version of classical economics our rulers use gets it wrong so consistently is that it fails to understand why people behave the way they do, and the changes in our behaviour when those motivations change. Economics simply has to describe the world accurately. But more than that, it also has to understand human interactions, and to do that economics needs to see itself partly as a branch of psychology. The failure of traditional economics to understand the complexity of human psychology is part of its tragic mismanagement of the world.

Standard economic theory stops short of trying to explain where people's preferences come from, so it takes no account of the direct influence of other people's behaviour and social norms on our behaviour. The narrow economic ideas of politicians and policy makers, based on the economics of the past, assumes that we independently know what we want and that our preferences are fixed. This standard theory can be very good at explaining short-term decision making (I want green vegetables but choose beans as they are on special offer) but it fails to explain longer-term changes in preferences (I now only choose organic food).

Policy makers assume that, taken together, people's decisions are based on a rational understanding of all their available options. Actually, this is not what we have at all. We often just copy other people. It would need far too much effort to look up all the rules when we drive in an unfamiliar country, to find out all the fines and punishments for failing to meet the rules, to work out the probability of being caught and the possible costs, before deciding how to drive there. Instead, we just copy what the locals do and change our behaviour according to the feedback we receive (if someone hoots when I pull out of a junction, next time I might give way).

Social norms are important in psychology, but incoherent under the old defunct assumptions. As a result, policy-makers who focus only on neoclassical economic analysis may often devise a system that has an immediate effect, but then they are surprised that it doesn't last. Knowing that there is a fine for speeding and believing there is a high likelihood of getting caught, I will probably drive more slowly – but I will drive just as fast once I think nobody is looking or if I see several others doing so.

On the other hand, if policy-makers can change the social norm – perhaps in this case by encouraging us to frown on others who drive dangerously fast with campaigns against dangerous driving – then less enforcement will be needed after the change. In other words, policy-makers might want to take preferences as fixed in the short term, but they need to understand shifting preferences in the medium term. Malcolm Gladwell's ground-breaking book *The Tipping Point* is not a book about conventional economics, but the behaviour of consumers is often not explicable without it.[5]

The demand for well-being

The demand for well-being is key to the new economics, as we saw in the previous chapter. But the new economics goes further and says there is a sizeable minority (maybe 25–40 per cent, see Chapter 2, page 26) that is motivated by their well-being in the economic and social choices they make, even if it means earning less money. Perhaps that isn't so surprising given that 3.3 million British people work more than 50 hours a week, and nearly a quarter of those take no paid holiday at all, or when a quarter of British men and a third of British women are depressed or anxious at any one time. In the USA, nearly half those employed as executives say their lives are empty and meaningless.

These are people who barely see their families, whose choice of work is governed by the overwhelming demand to pay the mortgage, who commute up to four hours a day, half of whose marriages unravel, and who finally die miserable, meaningless deaths attached to tubes in hospital – and find that their predicament is on no political or economic agenda and, if they ask for help, are offered pills.

When Tom and Barbara Good, the popular characters in the BBC sitcom *The Good Life*, first emerged on British TV screens in the 1970s, the word 'downshifting' wasn't in common use. It was actually coined in 1994 by Gerald Celente, the director of the Trends Research Institute in Rheinbeck, New York.[6] But the idea of living a bit more simply, or going back to the land – as people put it then – was very much in people's minds. By the 1990s, downshifting had emerged as an option for being less busy, taking more time, and trying to get off the treadmill to live a bit more authentically – which by then often meant making relationships more central in our lives. The simplest definition of downshifting – deliberately earning a bit less – would mean that anything between a quarter and half of the British and American population are downshifters in one sense or another, because they have taken the decision to earn less in order to live better.

That figure may be even higher. In some way, though, downshifting was always an American phenomenon. Henry David Thoreau was downshifting when he went to live on Walden Pond, though he clearly wasn't making relationships more central to his life. Duane Elgin, the American author of the influential book *Voluntary Simplicity*, defined it as 'the deliberate choice to live with less in the belief that more of life will be returned to us in the process'.[7]

Downshifting is incoherent under the old assumptions. The assumption of the narrow version of classical economics that policy-makers tend to use is that people tend to maximize their 'utility'. The idea of them deliberately earning less in order to live more simply – and maximize their well-being – is outside its basic assumptions. Nonetheless, that is what increasing numbers of people are doing. They choose the option that allows them to lead better, more fulfilling lives.

The demand for ethics

Ethics can appear like any other luxury that raises the price. But that is to assume that ethical options are all about buying things, when often they are about buying nothing. They are about taking no option at all. In any case, the very idea of people spending more for something that is grown or produced ethically still flies in the face of the same defunct economic assumptions that assume only one dimension in the decision. That is why the growth of ethical consumerism has been such a harbinger of a new way of looking at economics.

Since the publication of the *Green Consumer Guide* in 1988, the whole phenomenon has been dismissed by economists and business commentators as a blip many times. In fact, it seems to be accelerating. The Co-operative Bank's annual Ethical Consumerism Report showed that sales of ethical clothing alone – including organic cotton, fair trade clothes and garments made from recycled material – shot up by 30 per cent from £33 to £43 million just between 2003 and 2004.[8] Ethical spending seems to be rising in most areas by about 15 per cent a year, with ethical investment breaking through the £10 billion barrier in 2003. In a number of areas, like lead-free petrol, the green or ethical option so dominated the market that it drove out everything else. Free range eggs and organic baby food seem likely to do the same. Whether that acceleration will continue during the recession remains to be seen, but the idea that markets were just about money and prices is no longer tenable: it probably never was, in fact, but the boiled-down version of defunct economics that is used to run the world still believes it.

The demand for blood

In practice, there is a struggle between these different markets. The difficulty comes in interpreting complex interactions properly, because, when economists get it wrong, it can have serious repercussions. Take, for example, the muddle about blood banks. In the 1960s, the demand for blood in hospitals was growing very fast. To work out how to meet the demand better, the free market Institute of Economics Affairs commissioned an investigation resulting in a report entitled *The Price of Blood*.[9] The authors assumed that paying donors for blood was bound to increase the supply. That would be the assumption under classical economics, but in his classic 1970 work *The Gift Relationship*, the pioneering social researcher Richard Titmuss set out some strong evidence against it.[10]

At that time, blood donors where not paid in England and Wales, but they were paid in various different ways in the USA. Titmuss was a former insurance clerk who had left school at 14 and taught himself to become one of the pre-eminent researchers in Britain. He looked carefully at the statistics and found that not only did more people give blood when it was unpaid than they did when there were financial incentives, but also that the voluntarily donated blood was better.

The problem was partly that people who gave blood for financial reasons had a strong incentive not to be honest about diseases that they may have that would mean their blood would be rejected. The truth was, he said, that the 'commercialisation of blood and donor relationships represses the expression of altruism'. In terms of price per unit of blood, the commercialized American system resulted in administration costs 5 to 15 times higher than the voluntary British system, and commercial markets were more likely to distribute contaminated blood. After the book was published, the World Health Organization adopted a resolution urging member states to 'promote the development of national blood services based on voluntary non-remunerated donation of blood'. For some, the way that conventional economics misunderstands human motivation has had life-wrecking consequences. In 2009, a decades long campaign came to court seeking compensation for British patients who were infected with conditions ranging from hepatitis to HIV/AIDS from contaminated blood bought by the National Health Service (NHS) from donor supplies in the USA.

Classical economics assumes that humans are rational and behave in a way to maximize their individual self-interest. While this 'rational man' assumption yields a powerful tool for analysis, it has many shortfalls that can lead to unrealistic economic analysis and bad policy making. The **nef** researcher Emma Dawnay published a briefing for policy makers in 2006 that set out some of the psychological ideas that economics needed to grasp.[11] These were:

- **Other people's behaviour matters:** people do many things by observing others and copying, and are encouraged to continue to do so when they feel other people approve of their behaviour.
- **Habits are important:** people do many things without consciously thinking about them. These habits are hard to change – even though people might want to change.
- **People are motivated to 'do the right thing':** there are cases where money is actually demotivating because it undermines what drives people in the first place (you might stop looking after neighbours' children if they insisted on paying you).
- **People's self-expectations influence how they behave:** they want their actions to be in line with their values and their commitments.
- **People are loss-averse** and hang on to what they consider 'theirs'.
- **People are bad at computation** when making decisions: they put too much weight on recent events and too little on far-off ones. They are bad at working out probabilities and worry too much about unlikely events, and they are strongly influenced by how the problem or information is presented to them.
- **People need to feel involved and effective to make a change:** just giving people the incentives and information is not necessarily enough.

The fact that these human truths are missing from the faulty version of economics that is used to run the world is not a minor problem. It goes some way towards explaining why economic decision making has provided the basis for many disastrous decisions for people and planet, because classical economics can only deal with one dimension, and it has given birth to a whole range of assumptions and economic formulae that bear only slight relevance to the world as it is.

New ways of framing economics

The most effective revolt against the version of economics that fails to understand human motivation was organized by economics students in Paris, who staged a revolt against the pre-eminence of economics theory over practice, of economic abstraction over reality, and statistics over real life (see Chapter 1). The original post-autistic economics petition said that its signatories 'wished to escape from imaginary worlds':

Most of us have chosen to study economics so as to acquire a deep understanding of the economic phenomena with which the citizens of today are confronted. But the teaching that is offered, that is to say for the most part neoclassical theory or approaches derived from it, does not generally answer this expectation. Indeed, even when the theory legitimately detaches itself from contingencies in the first instance, it rarely carries out the necessary return to the facts. The empirical side (historical facts, functioning of institutions, study of the behaviours and strategies of the agents...) is almost nonexistent. Furthermore, this gap in the teaching, this disregard for concrete realities, poses an enormous problem for those who would like to render themselves useful to economic and social actors.[12]

Post-autistic economics, with its demand for interdisciplinary dialogue, is clearly a key part of the new economics that is emerging. It is the long-awaited revolution from inside economics, which parallels the emergence of a new economics movement from outside. The struggle for the soul of economics is gathering pace.

A new economics way forward

All this has enormous implications for those at the sharp end of economics, especially those in business. The new economics is not a puritanical refusal to accept that there are markets out there. It accepts that human markets, like human conversation, are often good ways to distribute goods and services. But it is not blind to the markets we create all around us that have little to do with price, especially if we enjoy more than a basic income.

It has been apparent to anyone involved in retailing, at least since the *Green Consumer Guide*, that price competition is only part of the story. For a growing minority – but only just a minority in the UK – people are motivated less by where the next meal is coming from or by status, but by their own health, independence, self-actualization and well-being, and extended sense of responsibility towards people they will never meet, but whose labour provides them with everything from food to clothes. They are bending the economy in such a way that it is almost impossible for the policy makers who rely on the old assumptions of classical economics to understand. It will often be an appeal to altruism or health that motivates these people – at least as they see it – more than an appeal to financial betterment. Consequently, policy makers need new tools by which they can achieve what they want.

What is emerging instead is an economics that is as much a branch of psychology as it is a discipline in its own right, or – as ethics grows in importance, and people increasingly feel the need for some kind of ethical coherence – almost a branch of moral philosophy. There is a long tradition of psychology in economics, stretching back to the Victorians, but it is excised from most economics curricula. Once more, policy makers find themselves stuck in a defunct economic paradigm, while some businesses – already way ahead – seek out new ways to communicate the advantages of their products, not just in terms of price, or in terms of fashion and status, but using ethics, honesty, sustainability, simplicity, authenticity and local rootedness. Of course, the attractiveness of these factors means, unfortunately, that there are also numerous examples of ethical and green 'wash' – false or misleading claims by conventional businesses seeking to cash in on the desire for change.

The point is not that conventional markets are some kind of fiction, but that they are only part of the story. The new economics suggests that policy needs to reflect human aspirations as they really are, and not assume that they always have a price.

What this means in practice is that politicians and policy makers need to broaden out the economic assumptions they use so that they reflect the breadth of human motivations, in order to better understand the world as it really is. In the short term, this is something that individuals may have to achieve for themselves, by following in the steps of the growing number of people in the West who are deliberately earning less to have better, more fulfilled and more loving lives. That means helping people escape from the kind of markets that trap people in lives dominated by the frenetic pursuit of money, as if markets in narrow 'utility' were the only kind that exist.

That is why this chapter on markets ends with items for the manifesto that are about making a broader kind of life possible for people. Downshifting means getting off the treadmill and rearranging priorities, and it can hardly be described as easy, especially when our mortgages keep us chained to jobs we loathe – men and women alike – and our children in full-time nurseries. This is not to say that anyone's place has to be in the home, just that it ought to be possible to live more fulfilling lives and to live and work closer to our families if we want to. So any new economics manifesto should include measures to *help people downshift* while ensuring basic material security, which means making affordable homes available, facilitating the growth of community land trusts, making land available for more self-sufficient living in the countryside and in cities, and finding better and more reliable ways of saving for retirement and meeting the needs of the elderly more generally than endlessly (and self-defeatingly) inflating house prices. It would include People's Pensions, invested in low cost housing and other local bricks and mortar that can provide reliable income for investors (see p61).

In the long term, we need to set people free to lead the life that most fulfils them with a *citizen's income*, a basic living wage paid to every individual regardless of their situation. We probably also have to recognize that this may be too large a commitment ever to be paid out of direct taxation, and must come from some other source, whether it is interest-free money issued by the Bank of England and withdrawn through higher taxation or some other route. Some form of citizen's income will do more than anything else to turn the economy a better way up. It will mean that vital jobs like care and nursing will have to be far better paid to attract people more properly rewarding the real social value of the tasks involved. Other ways forward are going to include measures that:

End predict and provide

Martin Mogridge's findings about traffic have strong implications for transport infrastructure, and not just cars. The way to keep traffic moving is to speed up public transport infrastructure, not building roads. Reducing air travel will not involve building more airports just because people want to use them, it is about providing alternatives – ships, high speed trains and IT interconnectivity. It also means recognizing the way that airports, which are apparently about fulfilling demand, are actually subsidized retail outlets to cater for a captive population, which provide the money to keep the airport in business. This is also critical to reducing the energy we use. Simply predicting and providing airport or road capacity doesn't just mean subsidizing unsustainable transport methods, it also undermines the sustainable ones.

Maximize human contact in business

'Simple systems-based advice will be comparatively cheap; person-to-person advice will be comparatively expensive,' writes says Robert Bruce, accountancy editor of *The Times*. But human contact is effective, not just between staff and customers, and professionals and clients, but between managers and employees, and between employees themselves. Human contact is the driving force of self-help. The more you reduce things to internet connections or automated systems, the further you get away from the human relationships that actually make change happen. The new economics recognizes the important added value of human interaction, realizing that much of this is impossible to put on an old-fashioned balance sheet. Evidence is also emerging that suggests that public services that retain human contact at their heart tend to be more effective.

Provide moral coherence

A generation ago, people managed to keep different aspects of their lives in separate sealed containers. If they were campaigning against smoking but their pension was invested in tobacco, it barely bothered them. Now the advent of huge markets for ethical investment on both sides of the Atlantic is evidence that people crave more of a kind of congruence: contradictions, especially moral ones, worry them. The conventional market is providing them with apparent and sometimes token ways out of the dilemma, but there is a long way to go if they are not to be trapped in old economic compromises. The old debate between decisions for personal good (economics) and decisions for the common good (morality) is no longer so clear cut. It makes no sense in people's lives for either to be isolated from the other.

Be authentic
This doesn't just mean that companies and organizations have to be true to themselves in their dealings with those around them. That is hard enough. The company has to be itself, and that means being wise enough to track down the lies its leaders tell each other about the company, facing up to them, being honest about where they are failing. If there are contradictions between what looks authentic and the truth behind it: if it is actually based on an identikit formula from one side of the world to another, or if it is actually based on slave or sweatshop labour. The same goes for towns and cities. People are exhausted and depressed at the way they increasingly look exactly the same – the same formulaic shopping centres, the same glass towers and concrete spaces. There is a demand, which is completely incoherent in the defunct economic assumptions, for places to look distinctive and real. This implies a critique of the doctrine of comparative advantage (see Chapter 8).

Recognize that people have a spiritual side
Many people can't bear to devote their lives to companies whose only purpose is to make a profit. They need a sense of higher purpose, and sometimes to work cooperatively with people. Even then, they have creative and spiritual needs that most companies never dream of. Meeting these employees' needs is risky. Finding ways that employees can become the people they want to be is a risky business. They may leave, after all. But if they stay, their ability to come up with solutions, work loyally and with enthusiasm will be out of all proportion to what it was before. Nobody wants to work for a machine. In the same way, governments need to recognize that people – probably the majority of people – are themselves engaged in some kind of search for meaning, which they must understand and accommodate.

Recognize that people need to feel useful and involved
One of the insights of psychology is that people hate feeling helpless and out of control. Yet when they do feel in control they can be highly motivated to change things for the better. This implies that too much information or too much choice can actually get in the way of change, while a participatory approach to problem solving is probably much more effective as a way of making anything happen. New economists Roger Levett, Ian Christie, Michael Jacobs and Riki Therivel argued in a paper called *A Better Choice of Choice* that some consumer choices – having an out of town superstore, for example – can limit the choices of others to shop at small, local shops a walking distance away.[13] Equally, providing choices of which hospital to get treatment at may require technocratic systems that undermine old-fashioned choices like

having a long-term relationship with a GP, not to mention placing a stressful onus of decision making on patients who feel insufficiently informed and skilled to make the right choice. Some so-called 'choices' actually reinforce a corporate bias that turns out to be a kind of supermarket choice: a great deal of barely different options, but whole areas of real choice eliminated.

Other books to read

David Boyle (2003) *Authenticity: Brands, Fakes, Spin and the Lust for Real Life*, Harper Collins, London
Neil Crofts (2003) *Authentic*, Capstone, London
Emma Dawnay (2006) *Behavioural Economics*, New Economics Foundation, London
Joe Dominguez and Vicki Rubin (1994) *Your Money or Your Life*, Penguin, New York
Polly Ghazi and Judy Jones (1997) *Downshifting*, Coronet, London
Jonathon Porritt (2005) *Capitalism as if the World Matters*, Earthscan, London
Dorothy Rowe (1997) *The Real Meaning of Money*, HarperCollins, London

Notes

1   *The Times* (1988) 5 December.
2   *Daily Mail* (2008) 17 January.
3   M. J. H. Mogridge (1988) 'Jams and superjams: A systems approach to congested traffic networks', *Civil Engineering and Environmental Systems*, Vol 5, No 4, December.
4   Martin Mogridge (1987) *A Panacea for Road Congestion?* University College, London.
5   Malcolm Gladwell (2002) *The Tipping Point*, Abacus, London.
6   Judy Jones and Polly Ghazi (1997) *Getting a Life*, Hodder & Stoughton, London.
7   Duane Elgin (1993) *Voluntary Simplicity*, William Morrow, New York.
8   Co-operative Partnership (2004) *Ethical Consumerism Report 2004*, London.
9   M. Cooper and A. Culyer (1968) *The Price of Blood*, Institute of Economic Affairs, London.
10 Richard Titmuss (1970) *The Gift Relationship: From Human Blood to Social Policy*, New Press, London.
11 Emma Dawnay (2006) *Behavioural Economics*, New Economics Foundation, London.
12 Deborah Campbell (2004) 'Post-autistic economics', *Adbusters*, September/October.
13 Roger Levett, Ian Christie, Michael Jacobs, R. Therival (2003) *A Better Choice of Choice*, Fabian Society, London.

6
Life: Why do Modern Britons Work Harder than Medieval Peasants?

The plain fact is that a man and his wife, and with four children that are unable to work, cannot now, out of his labour, possibly provide them and himself with the means for living... And will anyone say that this state of things is such as England ought to witness?

William Cobbett

It is amazing that this monster interest has not devoured the whole of humanity. It would have done so long ago had not bankruptcy and revolution acted as counter-poisons.

Napoleon Bonaparte

New economics is partly a 21st century manifestation of a very old tradition of economic scepticism, but it is also something much more specific – a body of ideas that could only have grown up in the couple of generations following the great Keynesian hope after the Second World War. It was forged in reaction to a storm of technological development known as 'progress', visible in the 'green revolution' in developing countries, the emergence of technocratic food distribution systems, the demolition of swathes of western cities for urban motorways and tower blocks. Like the corresponding green consciousness in response to the planetary crisis, the new economics was driven by scepticism about a specific ideological interpretation of that idea of progress.

The world knows better now. To a small degree at least. We can see that this kind of 'progress' meant little more than change: and many of those changes were actually major steps backward for those affected. We have labour-saving devices that have revolutionized women's work, but we have also limited the choice for women and men by forcing them into mortgages that can only be paid for when they and their partners work full-time at highly paid jobs, whether they want that kind of lifestyle or not. We have a range of new communication technologies, but we have become convinced that they have led to fundamental changes in the human condition, when – compared to the shift to industrialization in the 19th century – they often mean very little. If anything, instead of setting us free we have become suffocated by information, permanently wired, slaves to the rhythm of non-stop wireless connection. We have health technologies that have kept us alive longer, but have not made the same strides in social innovation that can improve the lives of people in chronic ill health or older people living alone.

Those are among the many paradoxes of 20th century progress. But it came packaged as some kind of inevitable shift that insisted that we had to accept them all, good and bad. In recent decades, most academic disciplines have dispensed with this narrow view of inevitable progress. Second-hand bookshops are littered with titles of forgotten historians peddling the idea. One area where the idea clings on is in economics. The deeply flawed conception of economic growth (see Chapter 3) carries within it this discredited idea: that all economic growth – all change, in fact – must be positive progress, and that more money in circulation must inevitably mean more wealth.

This is a chapter about the new economics attitude to progress. If rising GDP is not, in itself, an indicator of progress – although rising income however achieved will be important for poorer communities whose basic needs are not met – then how do we judge it? And more important, why does it remain so elusive? Why has conventional economics delivered such an exhausting world for those of us who are favoured by the economic system, and such an impoverished world for those who are not? The new economics is not sceptical about the possibility of progress, just about conventional interpretations of it. Progress is possible; the question then is why has this been achieved, so patchily, so far.

We know from the Index of Sustainable Economic Welfare (see Chapter 3) that, even in developed countries, overall well-being has been dropping for the past three decades – or at least refusing to rise along with rising average incomes and health.[1] We know there are growing gaps between rich and poor, within cities, nations and the world as a whole. But at the heart of this chapter, there is also a mysterious question for economics. If you believe that economic growth over two centuries has represented uncomplicated progress worthy of the name, why are we working so hard now? Why did the average English medieval peasant have more days off a year than we do now in the UK?

Subscribers to the Whig view of history, and the heroic style of economics that went with it, have cast European medieval civilization as hopelessly dark and bestial. The new economics tradition, stretching back to Morris and Ruskin, has encouraged people to take a second look at English medieval life to see what we can learn from medieval work, creativity and sense of spiritual certainty. We need not swallow the idea that everything about the Middle Ages was better, any more than everything about it was worse. Medieval dentistry alone might put us off swapping our lives with theirs. There were barbarisms, diseases, intolerances and hunger that would be intolerable to us. But there is something about the economic arrangements in western Europe in the 12th century particularly that deserve a glance.

When archaeologists unearth skeletons in London from the 12th century, for example, they are as tall, and therefore as well fed, as skeletons in any other period of history, anywhere, except our own.[2] In the case of women, they are even slightly taller. They lived in a society that built some of the greatest works of art in history in three centuries, the limestone quarries of northern Europe produced more stone for gothic cathedrals than was used in all ancient Egypt to build the pyramids.[3] There was famine, even poverty, in northern Europe at the time, though it was largely brought about by war. In peacetime, there seems to have been little poverty, unlike in our own times. For the most part, the hundreds of thousands of small farmers produced debt-free economic security, with varying degrees of feudal control, and with more days off for the average farm worker than anything people now enjoy.

There was enough prosperity for the ruling classes and those that depended on them directly to pay for an unprecedented artistic and intellectual renaissance, for a new kind of tolerance, including widespread set-piece theological debates in the new universities between Christians, Muslims and Jews, jury trials (at least in England), and (at least in southern Europe) local offices and estates held by women.[4] It was a brief period of enlightenment, it is true, before the abuses of the church and the deliberate intolerance unleashed across Europe, not to mention the plague and the role it played in making labour more scarce and therefore more 'valuable'.

We have little information about actual incomes in the 12th century, but Victorian economists calculated that the average English peasant in 1495 needed to work annually for 15 weeks to earn the money he needed to survive for the year, supported as people were by access to the common land. In 1564, it was 40 weeks.[5] Now, when GDP tells us we are incomparably richer, it is extremely difficult to buy a house in southern England and live a reasonable life without both partners working flat out all year. Sometimes even then, it simply isn't possible. Whatever changes the collapse in the property market may bring, that has been the definition of a successful economy according to policy makers and politicians.

It was an economy that was far less monetized than our own, but that provided some security in itself. We may not want to catapult ourselves back there, but it is still worth wondering why – despite two centuries of economic growth – we have to work and earn so exhaustingly now. This is not to argue, either, that poverty caused by war is unimportant. The point is that the 12th century economy seems to have avoided causing poverty as a by-product of success, as our own seems to do. While we might not want to be medieval ourselves, many of those trying to develop new approaches to economics have looked back to medieval economic institutions – guilds, set prices and rules against usury – to see if we can learn from them, either because there was some aspect of their way of managing that we have lost, or because they organized economics in a way that is wholly different from us.

The basic problem: The system impoverishes

Take the small Hampshire village of Nether Wallop. It is hardly a disadvantaged area, with more than its fair share of thatched roofs and retired major generals, though it has council housing and playing fields too. Half a century ago, it boasted two village shops, a post office, two pubs, a butcher, a village policeman and police house, a doctor and district nurse, a railway station a short bus ride away, and a multiplicity of postal deliveries. That was in the austerity years of the late 1940s. Now, when we are incomparably 'richer', all that's left is one pub, some groceries available in the wine merchants and a very occasional bus.

Why has this local life disappeared over the past two generations? The obvious culprit is the shift in shopping patterns away from small shops to large supermarkets, often out of town, driven by higher car ownership. It may also be the deliberate concentration of public resources in cities – where, ironically, the services are also struggling – but that is barely enough to explain the extent of the decline. After all, those who live in villages are the loudest in demanding more local services, and a recent survey for Spar found that 80 per cent feel that a shop 10 minutes' walk away is more important than a police station, church or pub.[6] The advent of supermarkets is also not enough to explain the contraction of local services: police, health and postal.

It would be inaccurate to suggest that the mystery of why the 12th century should have some aspects of its economies right is the same as why Nether Wallop should have been so active economically a generation or more ago, but these are parallel mysteries. They both challenge the prevailing view of policy makers, which is that the economy, as conventionally measured, has raised the level for everyone in generations of continual improvement. The answers may be elusive in both cases, but the question remains.

What was it about medieval economics in western Europe that made it spread prosperity better than 21st century economics? The guild system may have operated a closed shop, but it also provided training and support for professions and set prices that protected resources like river quality and fish stocks. The opposition to usury from the church included all moneylending at interest, which meant that, apart from the aristocratic classes, people were largely debt free, though – of course – feudal duties were owed instead. The resources used for building the gothic cathedrals remain shadowy, but the latest research suggests these were not paid for by ruinous taxation but by the cathedral authorities issuing their own currencies in the 12th century, known to history as 'black money'.[7]

These cheap coins were called in and re-minted every few years – with a fee attached – encouraging local spending. But that explanation still remains fringe and obscure. Was it perhaps the medieval regulations against usury and debt that avoided the kind of mortgage-based work demands we now face? Was it the overwhelmingly local and independent structure of the economy, supplemented by some international trade only in luxury and a few specialist items – throughout the medieval period? Was it, perhaps, the spiritual basis on which the culture was based, as people like Ruskin and Chesterton believed?

The truth is that we really have no idea. We have a slightly better idea why the life represented by a thriving local economy in a large village like Nether Wallop should have decline more recently. The new economics does suggest places to look for answers, and in two areas: how conventional economics actually manufactures poverty and, for the better off, how it often drains local economies of their human life and bustle.

Money poverty

The new economics critique of the prevailing economic system in our own time suggests that, far from being a source of general 'progress' for the world, the system is a generator of poverty – not just in developing countries, where this is more obvious, but in our own. It impoverishes not just in incomes but in quality of life, well-being and the distinctiveness, charm and liveability of the places we live. Somewhere in the interaction between money, institutions and values, the system manufactures poverty: either because of speculation, debt, unfair trade rules, loopholes in the tax system or the slow, sclerotic narrowing of local life and work.

Recent research at the World Bank, released at the end of 2007, suggests that income inequality and absolute poverty in the world are very much worse than anybody thought.[8] The problem with World Bank estimates of absolute poverty (living on less than $1 a day) is that they relied on calculations of what the equivalent of a US dollar was in some of the most impoverished economies in the world, a formula known as 'purchasing power parity'. The latest World Bank research suggests that this was extremely inaccurate and that the 1.2 billion people living on $1 a day may be very much higher. Poverty, though, is not escaped by earning just over $1 or $2 a day, as we will see below.

The World Bank estimates that the number of people in absolute poverty will have halved by 2015. But even this improvement, if it comes about, will have taken place during a period of unprecedented economic growth in the wealthier countries – not to mention India and China – and may well not be sustained during a period of rising food and energy prices. It would have been surprising if none of that new money had filtered down at all. Yet at the same time, absolute poverty in places like sub-Saharan Africa is rising very fast – up 41 per cent over the last two decades (both Nigeria and Zambia have around two thirds living on less than $1 a day).

Even in the wealthy USA, the number of people in serious poverty is now pushing 40 million and rising. Nearly a quarter of single pensioners in the UK are in poverty; so are over half of all children in families of more than two being brought up by single parents. The goal posts, too, are poorly positioned. For example, the level of income at which there ceases to be a very strong correlation between earnings and life expectancy, meaning that if you earn a little more, your can expect to live longer, is not the commonly quoted $1 or $2 per day – and nearly half of humanity takes home $2 per day or less – but the relatively higher figure of $3–4.

But arguments about the precise fluctuations in the level of global poverty over the past two decades are, in a way, beside the point. We have had two centuries since the Industrial Revolution in the UK. If the conventional assumptions of economics were correct, this growth would long since have swept poverty from the globe in a cascade of wealth. In fact, for most of that period, it has exacerbated the divisions between rich and poor. As the size of the global economy has grown, so has the gap between rich and poor in a pattern of expansion and divergence. This is largely due to a combination of gunboat trade diplomacy and speculation.

The institutions and rules of global economics are weighted in favour of the rich. Even today, the USA and its wealthy allies control most of the decisions in the secretive meetings of institutions like the World Bank, the Bank for International Settlements and the IMF.[9] The intellectual property laws recycle indigenous knowledge as profit-making assets for big corporations. Massive development projects like roads and dams have dislodged millions of the poorest people on Earth, continuing and accelerating a process that divides the poor from the commons, or from productive land, which used to sustain them, and earned millions for the civil engineering firms of rich countries. The growth of speculation (see Chapter 4), either in money or food and raw materials, has prevented poorer people from planning productive futures, and has often ended with surplus food or goods dumped in their own markets by subsidized corporations in the wealthy countries.

Life poverty

The new economics also suggests that, by undermining diversity – locally and globally – conventional economic measures also drive out bustle and complexity and those other prerequisites for wealth in its broadest terms. What seems to happen is that high streets, small towns and villages reach a 'tipping point'. There is no slow, smooth curve downwards, but a sudden collapse, in the same way that fish stocks suddenly collapsed in the Grand Banks off Newfoundland. Each closure is bad enough on its own: a quarter of all bank branches and fishmongers' shops disappeared in the 1990s, and the 222,000 grocery shops that existed in 1950 have come down to 35,000 today.[10] But when the number of local retailers falls below a critical mass, the quantity of money circulating within the local economy seems to suddenly plummet, as people find there is no point trying to do a full shop in town.[11] Nor is it just retail outlets: it is playing fields, community centres, banks and pubs as well.

But a similar process is happening, in a sense, to individuals who are finding their own lives narrowed and rationalized. The Harvard economist Juliet Schor has made particular studies of this phenomenon in the USA.[12] In 1987, she found that the average North American worker worked 163 hours a year longer than they had 20 years before. It is true that the average time people spend in each job is coming down, thanks to the enormous rise in part-time working, but many people – especially women – are forced to take more than one job. Even a generation ago, it seemed perfectly possible for one partner (usually the woman) to stay at home while the other went out to work. Until the collapse in house prices in the UK, home buyers found it increasingly difficult to have even one of the partners staying at home.

Even pointing out these twin impoverishments – in money and in broader wealth – does not really explain why old-fashioned economics has been having this effect. The new economics always suggests that we look at the way success is measured so narrowly (see Chapter 3), but also looks at three other parallel processes that seem to be part of the engine of this poverty-manufacturing machine: rising debt, rising monopoly power and the narrowing definition of work.

More debt

Rising personal and national debts are clearly part of the problem, and part of the reason why the massive rise in incomes has not been reflected in a corresponding rise in well-being. UK consumer debt has passed the £1 trillion barrier (see Chapter 10), and is known to be a contributing factor in the rise of stress, depression, mental health problems, relationship breakdown and even suicide.[13] We may not be deliberately signing our lives away when we take on the mortgages for our home, but at the very least our choices for the next quarter of a century will be more circumscribed. We may not be able to live where we want, work how we want at the kind of job we want, or spend as much time with our children as we want. Our grandparents were also circumscribed, but for different reasons. Most of them lived in rented accommodation, and those with mortgages paid them for about 15 years, and they normally took about 10 per cent of their salary; now it is 25 years and anything up to a third of our salaries, sometimes more.[14]

As individuals, our propensity to borrow is the subject of serious marketing pressure. In the USA, credit card companies market themselves by sending cheques for $5,000 through the post. The average American has been offered 32 credit cards regardless of credit history. All you have to do to open an account and spend the money is fill in your name – 'like feeding lettuce to hungry rabbits', according to one commentator. A quarter of all homeless people in South Korea were sent credit cards during one year alone (2001).[15]

Rising debt was one of the key causes of the economic collapse of 2008–09, because unsustainable borrowing had fuelled the speculative boom that unravelled so spectacularly with the rescue and bail out of so many of the biggest banks in the world. It is also a major reason why we have not managed the kind of economic progress that was claimed for us a generation ago. The debt is also underpinning nearly every institution, public and private, that we deal with every day. At least a third of the price of the goods we pay for, or the rooms we rent, goes on interest payments to cover the money borrowed. An average of 28 per cent of the income of UK businesses goes to service their debt.[16]

The rise of indebtedness is not just among individuals but among companies that are forced to take on debt to avoid their clean balance sheets being used against them by corporate raiders (see Chapter 10), who will load prudent companies up with debt in order to pay for their own takeover. More debt means that money increasingly has to be directed at the most profitable aspects of the economy, often financial services or the pillaging of natural resources, so that it can be paid off; just as we have to accept the best paid jobs, rather than the jobs which suit us, in order to pay our mortgages.

Behind this is the debt that underpins most of the money in circulation. Most money is created and pumped into the economy largely as loans created by the banking system, and which eventually have to be paid back, plus interest. Only 3 per cent of the money in circulation is made up of notes and coins that carry no interest. A generation ago, more than 20 per cent of the money in circulation was still issued interest free by the government, in the form of notes and coins.[17] This weight of debt, which lies behind so much of the money we use, is at least part of the explanation why the economy needs to accelerate just to stand still, and why a drop of a mere 2 per cent in the growth rate, as we saw at the end of 2008, should have such disastrous effects on everybody's lives.

More monopolies

Multinational corporations now account for 28 per cent of all the business done in the world, but they employ less than a quarter of 1 per cent of the world's working population.[18] There are factors that will underestimate their employment – if they employ people on a contract basis, for example – but the basic pattern is clear. As the global economy gets streamlined, it sucks up the available work, streamlines it and puts out of work many of the people who are not central to its business. If this narrow efficiency creates any jobs, this usually happens elsewhere in the wealthier countries, creamed off by the financial services institutions.

Reading the local newspapers of a century ago is like a glimpse at a bustling, diverse local economy that has long since disappeared. There were thousands of local papers in Britain alone, paid for by the diversity of local businesses that advertised in them. But a century of lax monopoly regulation has allowed all this to disappear. In many sectors, like waste disposal, there are only a couple of contractors left in the UK to take on local government contracts. The news that Tesco, for example, the retailer that already has a third of the UK grocery market, is intending to carry on growing is not good news for anybody except Tesco shareholders.

This consolidation over the past century has been encouraged because of the belief that big systems are more efficient, still largely held among policy makers, though there is little evidence that they ask precisely what they are efficient for. But the assumptions of classical economics tend to encourage monoculture, because economics finds it difficult to measure anything except money, and – as we have seen – what does not get measured tends to get forgotten, and then gets concreted over. Monoculture economic measures drive out other cultures, other species, other languages, other opinions and other forms of wealth.

The result is a terrifying consolidation of corporate power, especially in food.[19] Six companies now control 75–80 per cent of the global pesticides market. DuPont and Monsanto together dominate the world seed markets for maize (65 per cent) and soya (44 per cent). Monsanto controlled 91 per cent of the global genetically modified (GM) seed market in 2001 and took over 60 per cent of the Brazilian non-GM maize seed market in the space of two years (1997–99). Two US companies control almost half the world trade in bananas. Four supermarket giants control three quarters of the food sales in the UK. The new economics says that open markets require not just competition, but also competitors – otherwise global competition becomes a narrow battle between a couple of giants, fighting over the heads of the majority of the world's population.

These distortions stem from the lack of competition regulation at global level, but they are also a symptom of the blind eye being turned to monopolies by national regulators, forced to accept them because other countries accept them. Worse, the regulators have castrated themselves because they perceive an unspoken message from their governments that they prefer a handful of whales, which they believe they can influence and draw on for economic muscle, to having to deal with a multiplicity of sprats. Our governments have lost faith in genuinely open markets, while protecting free markets for the wealthy alone. Light touch regulation of the financial sector is now seen as a major factor leading up to the global economic crash of 2008.

But money itself is a measuring tool that also encourages monoculture. Different currencies might measure a variety of assets differently, but since they are all increasingly linked, so the yardstick they use is increasingly the same. The results are everywhere: the impoverished local economies, the emptying of the great harbours and rivers that have bustled for a thousand years, the weed-covered farming communities, even the great corporations – whatever else we may think of them – shedding all the real work until they are just shells that deliver only financial services. It is happening so slowly we can barely recognize it: monocultural measuring sticks are pushing out life.

Less work

Conventional measures suggest that the amount of work in the world is shrinking. Actually there is just as much need as there always was, it is just no longer viable to grow bananas outside the monopolistic system, for example. And much of the need in the world is not capable of being solved in the market system: it is human need. This is the effect of a narrowing in our definition of 'work'. What once meant almost everything we did to develop our lives, improve our surroundings, bring up our families and protect our neighbourhood, now means little more than what we do for money (school 'work' is an exception). There remains a vast amount of work that needs doing that is not 'productive' in the narrow economic sense, but which is absolutely critical to our survival – bringing up children, befriending lonely people, providing support for young and old, making things happen, political campaigning and much else besides. Often this is the kind of 'work' that is far better done by neighbours than by professionals.

But the attitude of conventional economics to this unmarketable, unwaged work is corrosive. Once it drops out of the conventional economic system, it becomes invisible to policy makers, unless it can be sold and commodified. It also leads to a situation where the government believes that 'full employment' – or 80 per cent of the working age population in work – is a valuable objective, when their voluntary work or their work as parents might actually be more valuable to the neighbourhood.

There are costs – social and economic – of everyone being at work.[20] It would mean, for example, that with no one at home except the frail and elderly, there is a gap left among those who socialize our children, look after older people, prevent crime and provide the human face of our neighbourhoods and communities. Some of those gaps include informal childcare. The problem is, under a successful policy of full employment, when all available carers of working age would be at work in the daytime and, in the period after school, the time they have previously spent looking after children will have to be replaced.

The same is true for the people who look after sick or elderly relatives at home. If the full employment policy were successful, these people might no longer be available.

The care they provide includes help with shopping, cleaning, finances, washing, bathing and administering medicine, tube feeding, even occupational therapy. About 890,000 people in the UK over 16 are providing this informally for 50 or more hours a week, at an equivalent cost of £57.4 billion per year, two thirds of what it costs to run the National Health Service.[21]

Full employment would also considerably reduce the amount of time and effort that goes into volunteering. There is also increasing evidence that it is sheer neighbourhood activity, at all times of the day – not just outside working hours – that is the main determinant of crime rates. The major study of Chicago by the Harvard School of Public Health showed that it was the willingness of neighbours to intervene in small ways that was by far the most important factor in reducing crime.[22] Full employment, in other words, is likely to be corrosive of social capital, if it leaves nobody available in communities.

The total costs of benefits are dwarfed by the extra costs that are liable to be caused elsewhere in the system by the savings they make from getting people off benefits and into total employment. But the one-dimensionality of government targets means that they are blind to the problem of costs as externalities elsewhere in the system, even if there are direct causes. Most of the likely costs of full employment will probably not be direct – like the increasing cost of providing basic care to older people – but in less direct ways that are more difficult to quantify, in higher crime and shortfalls in the socialization of children.

One question for policy makers is whether parents have any contribution to make in tackling rates of teenage pregnancy, smoking, truancy, bullying and obesity rates that concern them – and whether getting a job is the best way to help them make it. The danger is that the kind of self-confident parenting that society needs will also be undermined by the kind of low-status, no-prospect, insecure part-time work that policy makers regard as more beneficial than raising the next generation and keeping neighbourhoods crime free.

A new economics way forward

Kelly (not her real name) is a single mother living in a run-down and inaccessible estate in the Welsh Valleys. She is unemployed, but she is not inactive. She helps to run and raise money for the local youth club – the only facility of its kind anywhere near. She has helped to launch a local community garden, and she is among those who run the local adopt-a-railway station scheme. This is worthwhile work. Local police, interviewed as part of a local research project, said that her adopt-a-station project had reduced vandalism and saved them time and money. Yet government policy would very much prefer her to be in paid employment, in one of the few probably dead-end jobs that are available locally. The question is whether, if government policy succeeds in getting Kelly back to work, this will be the success for society that it believes? Would full employment – not in its narrow economic sense, but in the normally understood sense of getting everybody of working age into paid jobs – be helpful given that it would mean removing people like Kelly from their neighbourhoods? Narrow economic assumptions say yes; new economics says no.

What lies behind this confusion is the familiar muddle about the concept of work. As we have seen, the economic assumptions used by politicians regard paid work as the only kind that needs doing, and unpaid work as an infinite resource from somewhere outside the system. The new economics looks at the whole picture, the vital effort that people make bringing up children or making the neighbourhood operate effectively or preventing crime. It may not be appropriate for that work to be paid but, equally, it is certainly not right to ignore it, or pretend that somehow it isn't essential and hugely valuable.

The futurist Alvin Toffler used to ask executives what it would cost in real cash terms if none of their staff members had been toilet trained. The fact that they are is, in effect, a massive subsidy from the informal economy to the formal. The co-production theoretician Edgar Cahn describes this informal economy as 'core' because it is far more important than the money economy.[23] Yet the money economy, and the traditional economic obsession with it, is constantly corroding the core economy, leading to the current problems of crime and alienation.

There is also another, new category of activity – rewarded work, that is not paid with money – that is beginning to emerge, especially for single mothers, or refugees and asylum seekers who are not allowed to work, also for people with mental health problems. This is work that is necessary for the local neighbourhood, good for those doing it – enhancing their abilities as parents and as potential employees – but not coming under the government's category of paid employment.

One organization that recognizes the vital contribution of people outside paid work is Macmillan Cancer Care. Macmillan has been trying to turn its clients into co-workers to help it deliver its services. This is the essence of what is known as 'co-production': Macmillan finds that this contribution is not just important to the services, it is also a crucial part of the cancer recovery process. Many users move through a cycle that starts with being overwhelmed and moves on to joining a support group, then feeling in control of their own treatment – and from there to wanting to give back and share the experience with others whom it might benefit. That involves delivering training, fundraising, volunteering in shops, providing user expertise and much else besides; returning to paid work is often not an option anyway.

The difficulty is that the emphasis on full employment in government policy is undermining Macmillan's attempts to recognize and value this unpaid contribution. It is no longer able to pay honorariums because of the tax and benefit implications, and whilst progression back to work is suitable for some, it is certainly not appropriate for all. Paid work will, in any case, not value their unique perspective: it will be *despite* their status as recovering cancer patients, not because of it.

The point is that, if Macmillan can define its users as vital assets doing useful, valued and rewarded work – though not paid work – then it implies that other organizations and public services could do so as well. The question is whether this kind of work, for which those that are involved will be uniquely suited, might not be more sustainable and more useful than forcing these same people into low-paid jobs.

The bottom line here is the redefinition of work to include the full diversity of what is necessary for life. It requires that we find ways of valuing parenting, caring and community building as much as paid work. That may not mean paying for it directly, but it must mean recognizing or rewarding it in some way – possibly with some kind of credit that is exchangeable for the basic needs of life, perhaps issued through a community time bank.

The question of why we work longer than medieval peasants is a difficult one, and there are no clear answers. One is to redefine work more radically, so that we can shift the mainstream economy into supporting this 'core economy' of family and community, on which we all rely. The new economics regards the concept of 'capital' – traditionally no more than money, land and labour – as far too narrow. It is not alone in recognizing that other kinds of capital are equally fundamental to human development, and often more so, whether it is social capital, intellectual capital (know-how) or human capital. The massive increase in personal debt may have made people wealthier on paper, for example, but it has undermined their time and potential and their 'human capital', the value they would represent if they were working at something they felt they were born to do, rather than something that just pays a massive mortgage bill. Defining objectives too narrowly in terms of money threatens to undermine active communities and their 'social capital'.

The new economics also assumes that economic success is underpinned by environmental capital, the ability of the planet to support life, without which business is impossible. New economics subjects the money economy to all of these: its ability to maintain these different kinds of capital provides its ability to create sustainable wealth – and therefore opens up the possibility of genuine progress in the future, rather than something that claims to be progress but is actually a few steps backwards.

This is a broader understanding of what is most important, and it implies that one of the most urgent tasks of the new economics, and critical to any new economics manifesto, is *major anti-trust and monopoly-busting legislation*. Adam Smith famously argued that, when a couple of business people got together, the conversation invariably turned to devising a conspiracy against the public.[24] Traditional economics is as suspicious of monopoly power as the new economics, but modern economic policy has become lax on the subject, to the extent that there are only a handful of major food companies in the world, only a handful of major supermarket chains, and these titans fight it out – often merging together – in ways that distort our lives and ruin their small competitors. In the end, monopoly means higher prices, ruined suppliers and frustrated customers. Policy makers prefer large multinationals to a multiplicity of enterprising companies, and believe somehow that their market power can be used to the advantage of the state: the evidence suggests otherwise.

We need to break down the big corporations, starting with the banks – splitting their merchant bank functions from their high street bank functions (a repeat of the American Glass-Steagall Act after the Wall Street crash) and then breaking those down into far smaller units to guarantee genuine competition at local level for the basic task of looking after people's money and giving loans to individuals and small businesses. No company, either nationally or locally, should have more than 8 per cent of their market: that is the point where the Office of Fair Trading says that companies can abuse their power along the supply chain, distorting markets. Diversity depends on proper competition, which is increasingly scarce in the feather-bedded, monopolistic corporate world.

In the long term, a key brick in the new economics edifice is going to be provided by *issuing interest-free money* and ending the link between savings and lending, together with adequate safeguards to prevent inflation. The new economics suggests that the way money is created, bearing interest – so that debts have to be paid back in a way that demands unsupportable infinite growth – is a built-in driver of unsustainability in the economic system. We need new methods of issuing money, and making loans, without interest, learning perhaps from Islamic banking. Thomas Edison and Henry Ford teamed up in 1922 to urge the US government to create money for major infrastructure interest free, and then withdraw it from circulation as the loan was paid back (see Chapter 10).[25]

Other alternative economic doctrines, like social credit, suggest that banks should be banned from creating new money in the form of loans, and that it should be issued interest free by governments or their representatives. This is a controversial area, and it is therefore hard to speak for the new economics as a whole. Returning the benefits of money creation to the public would be an improvement. But the idea of nationalizing the money supply fails to adopt the whole new economics critique of money: it still assumes that money is an effective measuring device – and if it is the measurement function of money that is faulty, then we probably need a multiplicity of different kinds of money, operating from the neighbourhood to international level, and operated by different institutions rather than one state-controlled bank (see Chapter 4). Ultimately, to reconnect the money economy to the real world of natural resources, some currencies could be backed by baskets of commodities or carbon, as part of the system to bring climate change under control (see page 61).

Other ways forward include measures to:

Reform the global financial institutions

The IMF and World Bank are caricatures of democratic institutions. The connection between financial stakes and the voting strengths of nations on their boards is reminiscent of governance in pre-Civil War England. They need to be opened up democratically so that they represent the world as a whole, and their decisions made openly where they can be scrutinized. There also need to be institutions, perhaps also attached to the United Nations, that can regulate their decisions: for example, acting as a safe haven for bankrupt nations (see Chapter 10) and acting as arbiters in disputes over intellectual property between impoverished communities and wealthy corporations.

Outlaw ownership of life

Whatever the threat, or otherwise, posed by genetically modified (GM) foods to the environment, they certainly pose a threat to the poor, by making illegal the traditional method of seed saving and seed sharing that has kept poorer farmers alive ever since the dawn of agriculture. Seed contamination is now considered 'counterfeiting' unless farmers can prove otherwise. The main engines for GM, Bt cotton and hybrid rice, have plunged many small farmers using them into debt, because their yields have not justified the loans required to buy them, and in practice they have often needed considerably more inputs than traditional seeds. GM seeds lie behind the terrifying stories of the numerous small farmers who have committed suicide in India. The project to dominate the world's food market is about undermining genetic diversity, reintroducing the Terminator technology to make seed saving impossible – under the guise of a safety feature to prevent contamination – and offering these seeds cheaply at first until their hold on the market is stronger.

Limit the amount people can borrow

It is increasingly clear that using mortgages as the main way we inject money into the financial system has, at the very least, put an incredible strain on house prices. These have certainly risen because of a shortage of homes in places where people want to live and the influx of wealthy people into the UK – especially London – but mainly because of an inflationary increase in the amount of money that people can borrow for a mortgage. Before the credit crunch, this was anything up to six times their salary. It is no coincidence that the country that introduced 'grandparent mortgages', paid off by the generation after next (Japan), also suffers from the highest property prices in the world, and some people in Tokyo are reduced to living in what is little more than a tube. The best way of bringing prices down is credit controls.

Reward people's effort in the community

We need institutions like time banks that are capable of drawing on the assets of other groups – including older people as foster grandparents, for example – to generate better support systems for families and communities. These may not reward people for their effort with money, but they will in some other credit system, perhaps giving them the right to access surpluses elsewhere, because the monetary value of bringing up families and making communities work is extremely low. There is more on this in Chapter 9.

Shorten the working week in the formal economy

If people are working too hard, so hard in fact that it is undermining their ability to bring up children, then we need to share out the paid work better. One way to do that is to shorten the working week in such a way that organizations have to increase the number of people they employ to do the basic work. This reform goes hand in hand with the minimum wage, because it helps to prevent exploitation of the lowest paid.

Other books to read

David Boyle (1999) *Funny Money,* HarperCollins, London
David Boyle, Sherry Clark and Sarah Burns (2006) *Hidden Work*, Joseph Rowntree Foundation, London
Colin Hines (2000) *Localization: A Global Manifesto*, Earthscan, London
Alison Ravetz (2008) 'Is the government trying to abolish illness?', *New Statesman*, 5 May
James Robertson and Joseph Huber (2000) *Creating New Money*, New Economics Foundation, London
Shann Turnbull (1975) *New Money Sources and Profit Motives for Democratising the Wealth of Nations*, Company Directors Association, Sydney

Notes

1   Tim Jackson, Nic Marks, Jon Ralls and S. Strymne (1997) *An Index of Sustainable Economic Welfare for the UK 1950–1996*, Centre for Environmental Strategy, University of Surrey, Guildford.
2   Robert Lacey and Dabby Danziger (1999) *The Year 1000: What Life was Like at the Turn of the Last Millennium*, Little, Brown, London.
3   Jean Gimpel (1977) *The Medieval Machine*, Penguin, New York.
4   Christopher Brooke (1969) *The Twelfth Century Renaissance,* Thames & Hudson, London.
5   James E. Thorold Rogers (1884) *Six Centuries of Work and Wages*, Swan Sonnenschein, London.
6   Andrew Simms, Julian Oram, Alex MacGillivray and Joe Drury (2002) *Ghost Town Britain*, London, New Economics Foundation.
7   Bernard Lietaer and Stephen M. Belgim (2004) *Of Human Wealth: Beyond Greed and Scarcity*, Access Foundation, Boulder, CO.
8   World Bank (2007) *World Development Indicators,* Washington DC.
9   David Woodward (2007) 'Imagine our leaders were chosen on World Bank lines', *Guardian*, 14 June.

10 Richard Douthwaite (1996) *Short Circuit: Strengthening Local Economies for Security in an Unstable World,* Green Books, Totnes.
11 Andrew Simms, Julian Oram, Alex MacGillivray and Joe Drury (2002) *Ghost Town Britain,* New Economics Foundation, London.
12 Juliet Schor (1993) *The Overworked American: The Unexpected Decline of Leisure,* Basic Books, New York.
13 BBC News (2004) 29 July.
14 Michael Rowbotham (1997) *The Grip of Debt,* Charlbury, Jon Carpenter Publishing.
15 *Los Angeles Times* (2003) 7 December.
16 *The Independent* (2008) 6 July.
17 David Boyle (2003) 'The strange rebirth of a forgotten idea', *New Statesman,* 7 April.
18 Jonathon Porritt (2007) *Capitalism as if the World Mattered,* Earthscan, London.
19 Action Aid International (2005) *Power Hungry: Six Reasons to Regulate Global Food Corporations,* Johannesburg.
20 David Boyle (2006) *Aspects of Co-production,* New Economics Foundation, London.
21 Carers UK (2002) *Without Us,* London.
22 R. Sampson, S. Raudenbush and S. Earl (1997) 'Neighbourhoods and violent crime', *Science,* 15 August.
23 Edgar Cahn (2000) *No More Throwaway People: The Co-production Imperative,* Essential Books, Washington DC. The phrase 'core economy' was originated by Neva Goodwin in Neva Goodwin, Julie Nelson, Frank Ackerman and Thomas Weisskopf (2003) *Microeconomics in Context,* Houghton Mifflin, New York.
24 Adam Smith (1976) *An Inquiry into the Nature and Causes of the Wealth of Nations.* Ed. R. H. Campbell and A. S. Skinner. 2 vols, Glasgow Edition of the Works and Correspondence of Adam Smith 2. Oxford University Press, Oxford.
25 *New York Times* (1921) 4 December.

7

Resources: Why are Cuban Mechanics the Best in the World?

Every Cuban is a mechanic.

Cuban proverb, quoted in the film *Yank Tanks*

Money is round and it rolls away.

Confucius

Cuba provokes controversy, friendly, beautiful, strangely ambitious, and caught between the traditional raucous disapproval of the United States government and the yearning hope of the traditional Left. But what is impossible to deny, especially if you wander into Havana's Parque de la Fraternidad, with its cieba trees and its multitude of taxi drivers boasting what are antique jalopies, is the extraordinary skill of Cuban mechanics.

The Parque de la Fraternidad was set out in 1892 as a parade ground for the Capitol building, and is filled with obscure monuments to long dead heroes. But the taxis, and all the other cars that Cubans drive, are not dead by any means. They have had their lives extended long after they have disappeared from the roads anywhere else in the world, by ingenious people working without spares, but a great deal of imagination and an enhanced sense of the possible. Many of the cars are vast Cadillacs, Buicks and Hudsons from the days before the fall of the Batista regime in 1959, corroded but kept alive despite the 40-year trade embargo from their northern neighbour, the USA.

The recent American documentary *Yank Tanks* celebrated their skill, watching the alarming relining of brakes with buckets of old asbestos in the back garden, or the retrofitting of a chainsaw engine onto a bicycle to transform it into a homemade moped. Cuba's extraordinary mechanics have also been credited with keeping the nation's armed forces viable. Cuba bought no new weapons after the Soviet bloc collapsed in 1989 and, for 14 years, they struggled along as best they could without spares. But the economy began to recover a little after 2003, and that meant a little more money for spares and new equipment, in case President Bush took some kind of military action.

Whatever anyone thinks about Fidel Castro's rule, Cuba is a fascinating object lesson in the new economics. Cuba has already lived through the economic and environmental shocks that climate change and peak oil hold in store for the rest of the world. Its sudden loss of access to cheap oil imports and its economic isolation were so extreme in 1990 at the end of the Cold War, and its reaction to the shock was so contrary to orthodox approaches, and so successful, that it was dubbed in Washington the 'anti-model'.[1] Then oil imports dropped by over half. The use of chemical pesticides and fertilizers dropped by 80 per cent. The availability of basic food staples like wheat and other grains fell by half and, overall, the average Cuban's calorie intake fell by over one third in around five years.

But serious and long-term investment in science, engineering, health and education meant the country had a strong social fabric and the capacity to act. Successive reforms, dating back longer, reduced inequality and redistributed land. Before its local oil shock, Cuba had investigated forms of ecological farming far less dependent on fossil fuels, and had in place a system of regional research institutes, training centres and extension services to support farmers. At the heart of the transition was the success of small farms, and urban farms and gardens. State farms later followed their example. Immediate crisis was averted by food programmes that targeted the most vulnerable people – the old, young, pregnant women and young mothers – and a rationing programme that guaranteed a minimum amount of food to everyone.

Soon half the food consumed in Havana was grown in the city's own gardens and, overall, urban gardens provide 60 per cent of the vegetables eaten in Cuba.[2] The threat of serious food shortages was overcome within five years. Interestingly, Cuba's experience echoes what America achieved in a more distant time of hardship during the Second World War, when Eleanor Roosevelt led the 'victory gardening movement' to produce between 30 and 40 per cent of vegetables for domestic consumption.[3]

Cuba demonstrated that it is possible to feed a population under extreme economic stress with very little fossil fuel inputs. Other consequences were also surprising. As calorie intake fell by more than a third, and fuel was unavailable, the proportion of physically active adults more than doubled and obesity halved. Between 1997 and 2002, deaths attributed to diabetes fell by half, coronary heart disease by 35 per cent, strokes and all other causes by around one fifth.[4] But the humble Cuban miracle required between 15 and 24 per cent of the labour force to get involved in growing food. The Soil Association points out that, in the UK, the comparable figure is less than 1 per cent.

The main point is that, by being so unnaturally insulated from the world, the Cubans have been forced to build an economy that values reuse and repair – and recycling if necessary – rather than simply throwing away. It means they have a business infrastructure, such as it is, that can provide those services, and they have the innovative skills necessary to make do and mend at every level of the economy.

The basic problem: Our economy is geared to rubbish

The real question is why don't we? The new economics has three answers to explain how Cuba has brilliant repair skills and a repair infrastructure, but we no longer do. They are as follows:

Because narrow definitions of economics exclude the beginning and end of the product life cycle

Old economics confines its interest to the point where money becomes involved and to the point when a product is thrown away. A forest has no value in old economics – no place at all in fact – until it is cut down and turned into toothpicks or paper, or until it is designated for that.[5] The process that grew it, or which created fossil fuels, for example, is assumed to be infinitely productive. This basic misunderstanding of the world drives the mistake: economics assumes that the resources of the planet are infinite because they are seen as an endless free income stream to the economy; and, because they are incapable of being measured in terms of money, there is no apparent depreciation. As Herman Daly puts it, we end up treating the planet as if it were a business in liquidation.[6] Neither is there much in the way of a feedback mechanism in conventional economics that shows what resources remain, at least until they reach crisis point.

The same process happens at the other end, when products are disposed of. Until recently, conventional economics assumed that nature's capacity to absorb waste was also infinite, but charging for landfill – for example – has begun to shift that old perception. Now that the remaining landfill sites around London have been bought by American hedge funds, we can expect this perception to shift further. Some hedge funds seem particularly blind to the Earth's resources (buying General Motors seems to have been particularly short-sighted), but for some reason others have been able to be more aware of the future, including the scarcity of landfill space and the potential for wind energy.

Conventional economics assumed that economic processes are linear – that they begin with a raw material and end with a disposal. In fact, this process is part of something far larger that has natural resources involved at every stage. In theory, it is part of a natural cycle that starts with raw materials and life and ends with the basic components being turned back into raw materials – either in thousands of years or more quickly, using modern reclamation. The bottom line is that economics is most efficient when it is circular, and closest to the real world where it is a branch of biology and geology, rather than a science in its own right.

Because narrow definitions of value downgrade the worth of what is broken and worn

About 5 million computers are thrown away in the UK every year. Most of them work perfectly well. Those that don't work can be repaired, but they are thrown away because they have no monetary value. The cost of a new model, assembled using slave labour wages and flown across the world using subsidized fuel, is lower than the cost of repair.

Even so, there are at least some remaining computer repair shops. The rest of the sector of the economy devoted to repair and recycling has almost disappeared. There are shoe repairers, washing machine repairers, but they often charge as much or more than buying new. The result is that the skills required for repair, at least repair beyond the simple reassembly of supplied parts, have also all but disappeared.

Because old economics favours built-in obsolescence

It is more profitable to make a washing machine that breaks down after five years, than to make one that will last indefinitely, partly because there is a whole industry that has grown up to service that obsolescence, including extended warranties that rely on products being unreliable. When labour costs are very high, as they are in many developed countries, repair becomes unfeasibly expensive.

The new EU directive known as WEEE (Waste Electrical and Electronic Equipment), has reduced that margin a little, because manufacturers are now liable for the disposal of their old products. Unfortunately, while that may have diverted computers from landfill in the UK, they have still ended up polluting the lives of poor communities in the Far East charged with taking them apart.

New ways to make rubbish into raw materials

This failure of conventional economics to price the natural processes that underpin it has been answered by environmental economists determined to tackle the problem by putting prices onto these aspects of the natural world. By the end of the 1980s, and led by economists like David Pearce in the UK, they were attempting to put a value on elephants, the cash cost of aircraft noise or the Grand Canyon.[7]

These were useful exercises in that they allowed negotiations to take place on the costs of not polluting the air or cutting down forests, or saving the African elephant by paying off ivory traders and equipping game park wardens. But the new economics has always been sceptical of the idea of pricing the environment to make it friendlier to old economics rather than re-thinking economics so that it is friendlier to the environment.

What, for example, are we to make of the attempt by some Washington economists to value the moon at $1 trillion?[8] Or of the whole basis of valuing things by asking people what they would be 'willing to pay' to preserve them (the fact that many people might not be 'able to pay' is considered irrelevant). In the 1990s, people seemed to be prepared to pay $40–48 per person to preserve the entire species of humpback whales, or $49–64 after seeing a video of them.[9] Grizzly bears seemed to be worth $24 per person, under this system. The Grand Canyon's existence was calculated at $4.43 a month, again per person. These might be useful for making arguments, but it is important not to fall for the idea that these are objective values. All you have to do to make this vast bean counting exercise fall apart, is subtly change the question to one that is equally valid but is liable to produce vastly different results. For example, to find the value of a meadow, instead of asking someone how much they are willing to pay to preserve it – the answer to which is constrained by their ability to pay – you could ask them how much compensation they would be willing to accept for it to be built on. Such an exercise could deliver a value that was infinite in monetary terms if they simply didn't want the meadow concreted over. In other ways it can be practically and scientifically impossible to give prices meaningfully.

How, for example, would you calculate the price of the marginal tonne of carbon that, when burned, pushes the climate over the edge into catastrophic, irreversible global warming? The pharmaceutical giant Merck actually bought the rights to Costa Rica's entire genetic diversity – plants, seeds and soil – for $1 million plus royalties. The real question should have been whether such basic aspects of natural capital should have been purchasable at all.

All this demonstrates the very different approach of the new economics. The question is not, as it used to be, how do we make the most profit? It is the broader question of how we create the most human well-being from the least resources whilst living within the thresholds of tolerance of the ecosystems we depend on. The new economics, in other words, stands for a broader definition of efficiency. Conventional economics used to regard financial capital as the only relevant input. The new economics looks at natural capital as well, and how effectively it is used. It regards the loss of raw materials, and repair skills, as basically impoverishing, and any economic measures that fail to recognize that loss as blind.

If the old economic assumptions looked at the whole process as a simple line, then the new economics sees it as a whole system, and asks about reusing – not just materials, but people, energy and money. People are considered in Chapter 9, but re-using resources, energy and money are all considered below.

Reusing resources

In a particularly fearsome mood about the environment some years ago, Prince Charles visited a successful stationery company, and unnerved the chairman by brandishing one of their plastic files. 'Can this be recycled?' he asked.

There was a nervous silence. 'Certainly not,' said the chairman, thinking quickly. 'This file will last you a lifetime.'

In that short exchange lies the bones of some of the contradictions that have bogged down the waste debate. Despite the enormous effort put into increasing recycling rates in recent years – despite the warm glow we get when we put our green box out for collection – recycling is not an end in itself. When it is used at all, most recycled material gets turned into low-value products like cattle bedding, gravel substitute or rubbish bags. Its recovery requires a great deal of carbon-emitting energy. There has to be a better way to tackle what is, after all, quite a new problem. A century ago, three quarters of household waste was ashes from cooking and heating. Only a few decades ago, we still bought biscuits from tins by weight and drank from returnable bottles that carried a deposit.

Why this enormous change? Partly the refrigeration revolution over the past century, which meant that food could be packaged and trucked into cities. Partly because it is cheaper to package products than to employ someone in a shop to weigh them out. Partly because we have been deskilled in the home and kitchen by the mass retailers' peddling of prepared food and ready meals. Partly because rapid technological change has intensified the trend towards in-built obsolescence. Partly, also, because of the extraordinary growth in consumption worldwide. A terrifying 80 per cent of products are thrown away after a single use.

But if we are not yet going to follow the lead of the stationery company chairman, and keep everything for a lifetime – and even then it all gets thrown away – the interim solution means using waste products as raw materials for something else. This was a concept pioneered by green economists – many of them originally engineers, who have a different conception of efficiency to many conventional economists – but taken up in 1989 by two General Motors' researchers in *Scientific American*.[10] It is now beginning to happen.

And if waste is a resource, then that means that – potentially at least – there are by-products that can be sold that might offset the cost of setting up recycling systems. China is already sucking in plastic and paper from the UK. New markets are emerging. But the revolution is not just happening by itself. It is being driven first by tough landfill targets backed by even tougher fines, as well as new regulations that put the responsibility back onto manufacturers.

The much delayed WEEE Directive follows the Packaging, the End-of-life Vehicles and other similar rules emanating out of the European Union. Together they are already changing the way industry thinks. Manufacturers are beginning to design in materials that are easier to reuse, or to create designs that are easier to take apart at the end of their life. Producers will also have to pay for collection and recovery, and there remain some points of conflict about what role local authorities will play in all this, but success or failure in the short term depends on whether manufacturers fight the regulations or embrace the opportunities.

This regime is based on environmental economics. WEEE is a kind of tax on manufacturers – they have to spend money to buy compliance – yet the rewards can be huge. The motor manufacturer Audi has shifted over to aluminium engines, and manages the extra costs because they now recover the metal from their old cars and reuse it in their new ones. The drawback is that WEEE still fails to reward products that last as long as Prince Charles' plastic file, because that is extremely hard to track. Even so, the Energy Using Products Directive is now encouraging business to look at product life cycles, and that could provide the beginning of tackling built-in obsolescence.

But in the meantime, the main effort is focusing on designing products differently. Some manufacturers are redesigning them so that every product has a disassembly manual, and every part has a number, so that they can be taken apart and the various materials sorted easily. That means a shift from the trend that has seen, not just the end of repair skills, but the way that manufacturers have off-shored their design functions, simply demanding that the factories they employ produce things to certain specifications at a certain price.

Waste-free design is some way off. But, in these small shifts, there is a real opportunity emerging to transform waste into something valuable – initially because it costs so much to throw away, but increasingly because it is a raw material in its own right. When all that has been achieved, we still need to create demand for recycled products. As much as half of all construction material is now recycled, which means less quarrying, but that is possible only because purchasers, usually in the public sector, are prepared to buy it.

The last ten years have seen some slow progress as the influence of the new economics becomes felt, largely thanks to the impact of European Union regulations and the creation of a new recycling industry that now dwarfs the waste industry. But recycling is not the objective in itself: we also need the kind of skills and local repair infrastructure that they have in Cuba, so that people can once more make a living out of extending the lives of products almost indefinitely.

Reusing energy

On Christmas Eve 1968, the astronauts on the Apollo 8 spacecraft took a series of pictures of the Earth rising from behind the moon. It was these pictures, rather than the more famous colour snaps of the blue Earth taken by Apollo 17 a decade later, which caused the first shift in awareness of the wholeness and vulnerability of the global systems that sustain life. Now satellite images of the Earth allow us to see closer behind the clouds, and we can see the cities: pulsating with light, spreading out over their suburbs and regions across the known world. Robert Frost would find it much more difficult today to say that he had 'outwalked the furthest city light'. These cities are the world's energy hotspots. Dense or spread out, they pump out the carbon dioxide like giant 24-hour parties. In the UK, they are responsible for about 70 per cent of the nation's energy use.

Yet there is an irony here. Because the actual production of electricity, being used with such abandon in the cities, is generally speaking rural: from great nuclear monsters that are safer on the coast or vast fossil fuel generators attached to the national grid. That distance has consequences for the efficiency of generation. The national grid model loses as much as two thirds of the energy produced, partly in the distribution system but mainly in wasted heat.

This is not a new problem. We have been brought up, at least in the UK, with a grid system that dates back to 1926 and massive energy corporations like the now defunct Central Electricity Generating Board, serviced by equally distant technocrats. But this is not necessarily the way they do things in other parts of Europe, where cities have been handed considerable responsibility for energy. Since its 1980 referendum rejecting nuclear energy, Sweden put its cities in the front line of finding an alternative – seeking out sources of waste heat from industry, building district heating systems linked to power stations and retrofitting homes with small-scale renewable genera-tors. The UK has been extremely slow to learn from the Scandinavian way of doing things, though most of those solutions are open to our cities too, but once more the new economics is beginning to filter through into local practice. London is working on plans to generate its own renewable energy, and an alternative to a centralized grid system – a decentralized system of local generation, where the main responsibility lies with cities – is rising up the political agenda.

The Greenpeace report *Decentralising UK Energy* suggests that turning every building into a mini-power station, providing for as much of its own energy needs as possible and coupled with smaller scale neighbourhood or community grids, would be cheaper – and certainly more sustainable – than a new nuclear option. But it is a slow process.[11] While 98 per cent of Helsinki is heated by local community heat networks, and cities like Vaxjo in Sweden have more than a decade's investment behind them in combined heat and power (CHP) plants – the latest powered by waste straw – British cities are only just looking around for possibilities. Even hospitals in New York are installing CHP plants.

But things are moving. There are more than a thousand homes, leisure centres and hospitals now using decentralized energy generation. There is also one place that is clearly in the lead: Woking in Surrey. The local authority has cut the council's own emissions of carbon by as much as 77 per cent, thanks to their private grid and a range of renewable technologies on council buildings, buses and fleet vehicles. As many as 10 per cent of all the UK's photovoltaic generators – turning sunlight directly into electricity – are now in Woking.

The pioneer there was Allan Jones, a former engineer from the old Inner London Education Authority, who was then appointed to do the same on a bigger scale in London. The difficulty is how cities can make a difference on any scale. They have not been energy innovators since the days of Joseph Chamberlain. And why should energy producers reduce demand when it would mean less revenue?

But a new business model has emerged that is designed to solve both those problems, and it puts cities back in the front line. Escos, or energy service companies, contract with a city, or housing developer or hospital, for example, to install energy efficient technology. The city gets the equipment and the Esco gets paid back from a share of the energy savings that result. The Esco idea was developed mainly in eastern Europe to deal with the need for urgent investment after 1989. And in the UK, once again, it was Woking that took the lead. And once again, it was Danish investors, rather than their conservative equivalents in the City of London, who put up the money.

Woking's Esco began by building a co-generation plant in the town centre – co-generation means combined heat and power – which now powers local businesses, car parks and events centres, as well as the council's offices and leisure centre. Public housing and old people's homes are getting photovoltaic cells and the council's vehicle fleet is being converted to liquid natural gas.

After co-generation comes tri-generation: heating, electricity and cooling. Allan Jones himself is promoting the idea of quad-generation, because one by-product of hydrogen fuel cells is water. In the years to come, British cities will be following suit – encouraging householders to make their homes into power stations, with every lamp-post a net producer of solar energy.

Reusing money

Raw materials and energy are not the only aspect of production that needs to be used more efficiently, and reused if possible. The new economics particularly pinpoints money itself as largely wasted, as it flows to places that are already wealthy and inefficiently rewards investors more than would be necessary to persuade them to make the investment.

For the new economics, it isn't just a matter of how much money there is in your country or neighbourhood, it is a question of where it flows to, how fast, who gets it and whether it stays put – or whether it pops in but seeps out again to be invested in offshore trusts or hedge funds. Money that stays circulating locally is like life blood: it keeps communities alive. It means there is something that can bring together the people who need things doing, with the people who have time on their hands and the raw materials they need. Otherwise everything just grinds to a halt and dies. This is known as the multiplier effect and it was described first by a disciple of Keynes and applied to nations. But conventional economics has yet to understand that the same applies to cities and communities too.

Take two places for example. One has a supermarket, which pays a little of its takings out to local employees, then sends the rest up to London overnight to be invested in the money markets. Studies of very dependent communities, like First Nation American reservations in the USA, have found that 75 per cent of their money leaves again within 48 hours – to pay bills to distant utilities, or to shop in Wal-mart, which sends all its takings every night to Arkansas.[12]

The other place has a range of small shops, and when the shopkeepers need something, they can find it and buy it locally, so what is earned by one shop is used in the next and so on. Not only is their town centre vibrant and alive, but the small businesses are in charge of their own destiny. Both neighbourhoods might have the same amount of money coming in, but one is an economic desert and the other is thriving, sustainable and 'real'.

A study by **nef** in Cornwall found that a pound spent on the local vegetable box scheme multiplied in the local economy nearly twice as far as a pound spent in the local supermarket.[13] When Knowlsey Council in Merseyside measured its local multiplier effect, it found its local economy had become a seriously leaky bucket – only 8 per cent of its expenditure even reached local people. All the rest was siphoned off by consultants, big corporations and outside contractors.

The question then is how you plug the leaks. You make sure that when investment comes to your community, it behaves like a funnel towards local business. You can also take a critical look at investment that might be worth far more, but acts like an umbrella, shooting the money off to outsiders so that it barely reaches local people. The sad fact is that most modern investment is more like an umbrella than a funnel. Once again, the trickle down effect – the idea that money spent on the rich will eventually trickle down to the poor – simply does not work.

We invest vast sums in regeneration schemes or attracting foreign factories that so often just benefit the intermediaries involved, and then – at the first sign of an economic downturn – the investments collapse or the factory owners are off looking for a better deal somewhere else on the globe. A diverse range of local businesses are more likely to stay put, more likely to spread the wealth around, and more likely to create a sense of local well-being, than a couple of large retailers run by a board of directors in London or New York.

The LM3 (see p60) system of tracking local money flows, developed at **nef**, is one way that people can understand the extent to which their local economy is using scarce cash effectively.[14] It can be used to find out where the money is going and to plug the leak, as the people of the Marsh Farm estate in Luton have done, realizing that they were spending a combined £1 million a year on fast food bought from businesses owned outside the neighbourhood and setting up a fast food social enterprise on the spot instead.

It can also be used to evaluate possible plans. Will a large supermarket setting up near the high street bring more money that stays put, or will it suck out people's spending power and decimate the local shops? Measuring this reuse of money – just like we measure the efficiency of energy use or raw material use – is a vital part of the new economics approach to regeneration.

A new economics way forward

The new economics regards this wasted stuff, energy and money as forgotten assets, the loss of which impacts partly on the environment but also on the lives of the poorest. Because, although old computers and white goods might have no value, and all the energy spent locally is gone for good the moment it is used, they all represent potential resources that can be reused to keep local economies going. The computers and white goods can be repaired or their raw materials resold, the wasted energy can be reused and the money leaks can be plugged. All of these can provide home-grown assets that poorer neighbourhoods can draw on, rather than remaining so dependent on central handouts. In themselves, none of those three may be enough to revive an impoverished neighbourhood, but they are resources nonetheless – and using them can only increase local independence in a way that begging for grants will not.

The reason why Cuba has managed to develop such expertise in repair is because of the long drawn out economic blockade it has endured. We need to find ways of developing these skills and this infrastructure without such a harsh driver, and while we can still draw on products and skills from further afield.

There are also implications here for the kind of places we live in. Since Ebenezer Howard first staked out the site for Letchworth Garden City on his bicycle a century ago and, with his revolutionary diagrams, sketched out towns where functions were separate from each other, we have been busily building different parts of our communities that 'specialize'. That was important when we had heavy industry. The race for the suburbs was largely a race to get away from the smell and pollution. When the pollution from cars became too much for us, then the process of separation continued further. An alliance of green campaigners, architects and transport experts have pushed a model of cities that is dense, often high-rise, but which still imagines that food will be trucked or trained in from outside cities.

The new economics suggests a different shape for the future. The new recycling industries require space in cities. So does the business of food production – there is no reason why cities should not produce food, as they increasingly do in developing countries, as well as providing the related employment. The business of re-using resources, recycling energy and recirculating money, requires places that have space for such activities, which means greener, more bustling places of mixed use – not low-density suburbs at all, but not high-density specialized living quarters either.

Those new spaces have yet to emerge though some are already partially visible in the growth of urban agriculture. But the future seems likely to encourage towns and cities to be increasingly interdependent, to use their waste as their raw materials, to provide as far as possible for their own food – and to use waste also to help in this process – to share tools to prevent unnecessary initial production, and to reuse waste energy. All of those imply that successful places will be those that can reuse best, and that means those that are most mixed.

Probably the most important items on any new economics manifesto would be energy conservation, demand management and a *systematic programme of decentralized energy*. The Greenpeace report *Decentralising UK Energy* proposes that buildings, anything from terraced homes to factories, should use a mixture of solar panels, small wind turbines and combined heat and power units, and be net producers of electricity.[15] It also wants a network of local energy networks producing heat and energy. About half the annual investment in energy in the UK at the moment is going on costs associated with transmission, so local energy would clearly represent some substantial cost savings. It would also avoid the dead end of nuclear energy and avoid having to replace, at enormous cost, the ailing grid system.

The added benefits of this programme would be that it would involve an enormous influx of 'green collar' jobs into the economy, while providing very low cost energy and insulation too (energy saving is itself an energy source). It would mean that small generation capacity, local wind and solar installations, could be locally owned and fund community trusts or time banks. Energy will increasingly underpin the new economics as an asset that drives the local community and funds it as well.

Taken together, the following policies would also be important:

Reward people for recycling and reusing

Rotterdam's experimental Nu-Spaarpas 'green' smartcard paid points for recycling, or buying green, all funded by savings in the bulky waste collection budget.[16] Cardholders could spend their points on local buses or cinema tickets. The alternative – fining people for not recycling – had been less successful. When Dublin started charging for rubbish collection along these lines, they ended up by gaoling three councillors who refused to pay. The Rotterdam NuSpaarpas experiment, which paid people in exchangeable credits for behaving in a sustainable way, is at an end, but it will return in some guise or other.

Invest in recycling intermediaries

We need new intermediaries that can take products apart, collect waste and find the markets for it, as well as new manufacturers that can use it. The EnvironCom assembly line in Grantham, for example, now takes fridges apart automatically – only the doors are removed by hand – and sells on the metals. They will soon be doing the same with televisions. All these intermediaries and manufacturers need financing, but often they are social enterprises that combine collection or sorting with providing training, like the pioneering Bulky Bob's in Liverpool, which collects and restores furniture or household goods.

Invest in a new repair infrastructure

We need to use the income from landfill, and from companies that do not otherwise pay for the repair and recycling of their products, to pay for a new repair infrastructure of small craftspeople, maybe working from home for extra cash, who can get our equipment repaired, or our shoes and clothes, and keep money circulating locally at the same time.

Evaluate new projects by their impact on money flows

How much will a new supermarket or regeneration scheme keep money circulating locally? That is the key question, rarely asked, that decision makers need to answer before giving the go-ahead or not. Instead they look at the bottom line figure for investment, assuming it will somehow stay put. But what happens to the money after it is invested, whether it stays put or seeps away, is a key factor in the success or failure of the regeneration.

Other books to read

John Adams (1995) *Cost-Benefit Analysis: Part of the Problem, not the Solution*, Green College Centre for Environmental Policy and Understanding, Oxford

Tim Cooper (1994) *Beyond Recycling*, New Economics Foundation, London

Herman Daly and Joshua Farley (2004) *Ecological Economics: Principles and Applications*, Island Press, Washington DC

Greenpeace UK (2007) *What are we waiting for?* (online film)

Andrew Simms (2009) *Ecological Debt: Global Warming and the Wealth of Nations*, Pluto Books, London

Notes

1   Green New Deal Group (2008) *The Green New Deal*, New Economics Foundation, London.
2   G. M. Novo and C. Murphy (2001) 'Urban agriculture in the city of Havana: A popular response to a crisis' in *Growing Cities Growing Food: Urban Agriculture on the Policy Agenda: A Reader on Urban Agriculture*, Resource Centres on Urban Agriculture and Food Security, The Hague.
3   S. Hylton (2001) *Their Darkest Hour: The Hidden History of the Home Front 1939–1945*, History Press, Stroud, UK.

4   M. Franco, P. Ordunez, B. Cabillaro, J. A. Granados, M. Lazo, J. L. Bernal, E. Guallar
     and R. S. Cooper (2007) 'Impact of energy intake, physical activity, and population-wide
     weight loss on cardiovascular disease and diabetes mortality in Cuba, 1980–2005',
     American Journal of Epidemiology, Vol 166, No 12.
5   Marilyn Waring (1988) *If Women Counted*, Macmillan, London.
6   Herman Daly and John Cobb (1989) *For the Common Good*, Beacon Press, Boston.
7   See for example David Pearce, Anil Markandya and Edward Barbier (1989) *Blueprint for
     a Green Economy*, Earthscan, London.
8   This was based on the idea that the value of land on the moon was $100 an acre.
9   V. H. Heywood and R. T. Watson (eds) (1995) *Global Biodiversity Assessment*, United
     Nations Environment Programme, Cambridge University Press, Cambridge.
10   Frosch and Gallopoulos (1989) 'Strategies for manufacturing', *Scientific American*,
     September.
11   Greenpeace (2005) *Decentralising UK Energy*, London.
12   Bernie Ward and Julie Lewis (2002) *Plugging the Leaks*, New Economics Foundation,
     London.
13   Bernie Ward and Julie Lewis (2002) *Plugging the Leaks*, New Economics Foundation,
     London.
14   Justin Sacks (2002) *The Money Trail: Measuring Your Impact on the Local Economy
     Using LM3*, New Economics Foundation, London.
15   Greenpeace (2005) *Decentralising UK Energy*, London.
16   Maxine Holdsworth and David Boyle (2004) *Carrots not Sticks: The Possibilities of
     Sustainable Consumption*, National Consumer Council, London.

8

Trade: Why Does Britain Import the Same Number of Chocolate Waffles as it Exports?

I sympathize with those who would minimize, rather than those who would maximize economic entanglements among nations. Ideas, knowledge, science, hospitality, travel — these are things that of their nature should be international. But let goods be homespun wherever it is reasonable and conveniently possible, and above all, let finance be primarily national.

John Maynard Keynes

Before you finish eating breakfast this morning, you've depended on more than half the world.

Martin Luther King

The figures add up, but bizarrely so. In one year, we imported 465 tonnes of gingerbread into the UK and we exported 460 tonnes. Ships and lorries pass each other in the night carrying virtually identical goods back and forth between countries. Perhaps it would be easier to eat our own or email the recipes of those that are slightly different.[1]

It is the same story with boneless chicken: 44,000 tonnes in and 51,000 tonnes out. And chocolate covered waffles: 17,200 tonnes in and 17,600 tonnes out. Jelly sweets back and forth to Italy, and ice cream from the UK to Sweden and back. So much for the efficiency of modern international trade built on the old economic theory of countries enjoying comparative advantages. We have enough chocolate waffles in the UK, but we have to take the trouble of shipping and trucking ours somewhere else and then bringing containers of the stuff back again from somewhere else.

The visionary new economist Jane Jacobs demonstrated how cities have traditionally developed economically by replacing imports and producing their own local replacements.[2] Modern laws about intellectual property (IP) undermine this process, but this is how cities and nations have dragged themselves up through the centuries. Even so, IP regulations are not enough to explain entirely why we are dragging in imports at such a rate when we produce the same stuff ourselves.

When John Maynard Keynes spoke to the Irish government in 1933, he set out a theory of 'national self-sufficiency' where he distinguished between different kinds of interdependence – globalization as we would call it now – to explain why worrying about trade for its own sake is not the same as small-minded isolationism:

> *Ideas, knowledge, science, hospitality, travel – these are things that of their nature should be international. But let goods be homespun wherever it is reasonable and conveniently possible, and above all, let finance be primarily national.*[3]

This lecture, a classic exposition of the new economics before its time, has been conveniently sidelined by his more conventional colleagues. But this passage has often been quoted by critics of globalization to explain their worry about too great an interdependence of the wrong kind with the rest of the world.

Of course, interdependence is neither a bad thing in itself – quite the reverse – nor is it anything new. When Russia threatened to turn the gas off from the Ukraine pipeline if it joined Nato, that was one of the problems of interdependence. But the cultural awareness of interdependence can be traced back at least as far as the depiction of city life depending on its rural hinterland in Virgil's *Eclogues*, written over 2000 years ago. More recently, during India's struggle to escape British colonial rule in the first half of the 20th century, Gandhi went to great lengths to demonstrate the simultaneous importance of interdependence. In 1929, he said:

> *Interdependence is and ought to be as much the ideal of man as self-sufficiency. Man is a social being... If man were so placed or could so place himself as to be absolutely above all dependence on his fellow beings, he would become so proud and arrogant as to be a veritable burden and nuisance to the world.*[4]

The UN conference on human rights in 1993, which produced the Vienna Declaration and Programme of Action, said that: 'All human rights are universal, indivisible, interdependent and interrelated.' UN Secretary-General Kofi Annan, speaking in 2004, said:

Today, no nation or group of nations, not even the most powerful, can protect itself from threats by turning itself into an impregnable military fortress. No army can prevent capital movements, stop the spread of AIDS, reduce the impact of global warming, halt the flow of information, or reverse the spread of radical violent ideologies which threaten us all… For good or ill, we live in an age of interdependence, and we must manage it collectively.[5]

That is the issue about interdependence. Interdependence is human and natural, but when that interdependence fails to meet basic human needs, becomes exploitative or too divorced from natural systems – for example, because energy costs discount the impact of energy intensive transport – then there is a problem, because the systems behind it start to distort reality in a dangerous way. The truth is that trade has always been double-edged. We need exchange, like we need human conversation, but it has side effects that make much of it dangerous: the spread of AIDS in southern Africa is at its height on the routes used by lorry drivers. The demand for hamburgers by Americans, and soya by the Chinese, is accelerating the loss of rainforest in the Amazon. These things matter, but they are also side effects of an unbalanced trading system that causes poverty.

The basic problem: The wrong kind of interdependence leads to poverty

There is no reason why nations should be entirely autonomous. Too much autonomy, for example, might mean neglecting the vulnerability of the global commons. Total autonomy is not the ideal, but then neither is it physically possible.

Take the question of food. Without even considering our great Mediterranean imports, pizza and pasta, the UK has thousands of restaurants selling global cuisine and enriching the way we eat. There are more than 10,000 Indian and 8000 Chinese restaurants in the UK and hundreds of others serving Thai, Mexican, Caribbean, Japanese, Korean and Middle Eastern food. In fact, 38 per cent of the UK fast food market is ethnically non-European in origin.[6] You might argue about the quality from certain food outlets sometimes, but international cuisine can demonstrate the wonderful cultural enrichment brought by interdependence. Yet, conversely, the massive loss of orchards in England has not only deprived us of a glorious variety of different apples, displaced by vast inflows from abroad of bland, uniform varieties, it also impoverishes our food culture, identity and the landscape. On the other hand, the flow of cultural products from the worlds of art, literature, film, fashion and television across national borders also stimulates our senses, brings pleasure and excites curiosity. Without it, the dynamic creative exchange necessary for a culture to flourish and develop would probably be lost.

The problem with these exchanges is when they undermine aspects of planet or community, as is the case with the humble apple, either because they have to come by airfreight or lorry – undermining the climate as they come – or because they replace productive capacity nearer home. In both cases this can happen because of failures by the economic system to put realistic prices on aspects of production: energy is too cheap to prevent lorry loads of biscuits trucking from Glasgow to Italy just for packaging, or labour is too cheap elsewhere to prevent the grubbing up of the vast majority of English orchards.

'I do not want my house to be walled in or my windows blocked,' said Gandhi on just this issue. 'I want the cultures of all lands to be blown about the house as freely as possible. But also I refuse to be blown off my feet by any.'

Take a look, for example, at one ecologically significant product that is invisible to most consumers: palm oil.[7] The UK imported over 700,000 tonnes of it in 2004. It is grown to earn foreign currency, traded internationally and needs energy throughout its production cycle. Palm oil is a key ingredient in inexpensive chocolate, and oil and wax from the palm kernel tree are used to add bulk and shelf life to a variety of products from food to cosmetics. Palm tree plantations make good economic sense in Southeast Asia, where the tree grows quickly. Fuelled by increasing demand from abroad, these plantations are expanding rapidly. But quick expansion and a monoculture approach are creating serious problems, including destruction of the rainforest and other unique ecosystems, local pollution and social conflicts rooted in the increasing power of agribusiness.

Understanding the impact of ecological footprints sometimes means having to visualize long and complex supply chains. For example, a thread connects chocolate to palm trees to shrinking rainforests in Southeast Asia, but it is not easy to see. It is just as difficult to visualize the links between a shrimp salad served in London and the loss of mangrove forests in Bangladesh, which once provided valuable buffers against storms and floods. But these, and many other environmental connections like them, are growing in size, number and complexity as the world becomes ever more interdependent.

Unbalanced trade

The trouble with this complexity is that it is difficult to see immediately how unbalanced the trading patterns of the world have become. International trade rules skew the benefits in favour of the richest companies and nations: that is probably why the last decade has reduced the real income of the poorest 5 per cent of the world by a quarter and raised the income of the richest 5 per cent by 12 per cent. That is another reason why inequality in the world has been rising, driven by the trade barriers in the developed countries, their subsidies to their own industries and dumping of cheap subsidized products in foreign markets. It is being driven by the forcing open of the markets of developed countries, the Trade-Related Aspects of Intellectual Property (TRIPS) agreement that prices basic drugs out of the hands of the poorest, the absence of proper competition regulation and the massive inequalities in know-how, education and training.

The most insidious aspect of this is the tariff imbalance. The average tariff for most goods traded between countries is 2–3 per cent. But if a developing country exports the same goods to a developed country, those tariffs rise fourfold to reduce demand. Sometimes they rise much more. Japan imposes a tariff of 26 per cent on Kenyan footwear. Some imports of rice, sugar or fruit from developing countries to the European Union or the USA face tariffs of over 100 per cent. Vietnam pays $470 million in taxes for exports to the USA that are worth $4.7 billion, while the UK pays about the same on exports worth $50 billion.[8]

There is particular pressure on exports that are processed, forcing developed countries to remain in the least valuable sectors where they have the least market advantage. Tariffs for goods to the European Union go from 0 per cent on cocoa beans to 9 per cent on cocoa paste and 50 per cent on chocolate.

Developing country exporters also have to compete with the subsidies. About 25,000 American farmers got $4 billion in subsidies in 2002, which was three times the total US aid budget for Africa. By 2005, the total had risen to $4.7 billion for 20,000 farmers. One estimate suggests that these subsidies cost $200 million a year to West African cotton farmers in lost business and low prices.[9]

Ecological debt

Another problem with the wrong kind of interdependence comes when trade masks corporate or national abuse of the global commons, using an unfair share of resources like fossil fuels and open sea fisheries. Using ecological accounting makes it possible to find the shadowy boundaries of the global commons, and makes them visible on the otherwise misleading spreadsheets of the market economy. It can also help reveal how ecologically unequal exchange can be neither socially nor economically sustainable.

In extreme cases, major reliance on ecological imports can undermine a country's economic viability and sovereignty, leaving it politically fragile, and even resented by the other nations who supply it. Fossil fuels and water are two obvious cases in point. Trade, of course, has many benefits if it is voluntary. Every nation is increasingly interdependent on traded goods, but ecologically imbalanced trade, coupled with over-consumption in some places and subsistence in others, is a recipe for breakdown. Just as nations closely monitor their financial balance of trade and debt to keep healthy and stave off the threat of economic collapse, they might also benefit by measuring their ecological balance of trade to make sure their ecological self-sufficiency doesn't fall to critically low levels, or provoke social unrest and political conflict.

If the UK consumes more than its fair share of the world's resources, or if it exports its sweatshops or the dangerous disassembly of its asbestos-ridden ships or its chemical-ridden computers, then that interdependence becomes a concern. It becomes a type of exploitation of its superior economic might, distorting power relationships with suppliers. The clearest demonstration of this comes from looking at the day in a typical calendar year when, in effect, the UK stops relying on our own natural resources to support ourselves, and starts to live off the rest of the world. The moment we begin living beyond our environmental means is what we call our Ecological Debt Day. At current levels of natural resource use in the UK, the country as whole went into ecological debt in 2009 on 12 April.[10] As our total consumption grows, it moves ever earlier in the year. In 1961, it was 9 July, advancing to 14 May in 1981. The world as a whole is also living beyond its ecosystems' capacity to regenerate and now goes into debt around 23 September.

If the whole world had wanted to share UK lifestyles back in 1961, the Earth would just have managed with its available resources – one planet would have been enough. But today, if the whole world wanted lifestyles like those enjoyed in the UK, we would need 3.1 planets. These are all conservative measures because, relying on the Ecological footprint measure, they assume that all the Earth's biocapacity is there for human use. But, for the healthy functioning of ecosystems, ecology and biology suggest that a significant proportion needs to be allowed to lie fallow. Exactly how much is hard to say, but it could be anything from a quarter to a third. This would mean that the global economy is far more unsustainable than previously thought – and urgently needs further research.

The side effect of this is that, while we are using superior economic resources to drag in food and energy from around the world – not to mention nurses and doctors to keep our National Health Service functioning – our own domestic production of indigenous food in the UK now appears to have hit one of its lowest points for half a century, making us increasingly dependent on imports.

The UK also has huge untapped renewable energy sources, and a shift to more decentralized energy generation (see Chapter 7) – coupled with other efficiency measures – could radically reduce the amount of energy needed and imported. But because of its continuing dependence on fossil fuels, rising demand and inefficient supply, the UK lost its energy independence in 2004, and came to rely on imports to balance supply and demand, which will rise steeply in the coming years.

Energy costs

Schumacher talked about the ludicrous situation of lorries taking biscuits from Glasgow to London, passing lorries taking biscuits the other way.[11] If energy is limitless, and the planet has capacity to absorb all the carbon and pollution, perhaps this kind of interdependence would not matter. But neither of those is the case. Economies, like everything else, are subject to the laws of physics and thermodynamics. Against a background of volatile rising oil prices and pressure to reduce greenhouse gas emissions because of climate change, much of this trade becomes dangerously inefficient.

If we are buying and selling specialized products around the world, to the benefit of both sides, then that can be largely enriching. If, on the other hand, identical products like chocolate waffles are being shipped backwards and forwards with heavy environmental costs, then that is another example of the blindness at the heart of the old economic assumptions – the assumption that price is somehow an objective measure of value.

The real reason the chocolate waffles are undertaking their wasteful journeys, and that much of the similarly unnecessary trade is taking place, is that energy costs do not cover the damage to the future of the planet. The real cost of road transport, for example, is subject to the same qualifications as other prices – it is a translation of real effects into current prices. It has been some time since the calculation was last done, but when it was, by the environmental economist David Pearce in 1996, it covered assumptions for the true costs of environmental damage, child asthma, polluted air and road deaths. In the UK, that then came to between £45.9 and £52.9 billion (1996 prices). The petrol tax then raised about £22 billion.[12] But, once again, how do you price the gallon of petrol or diesel that, when burned, pushes the climate system over the edge?

The problem with narrow economics that ignores these externalities – and the far greater costs of global warming that we now understand – is that it distorts what the economy is doing. This happens at great cost, not just to future generations, but to productive resources that are nearer home: skilled people, orchards, farms and workshops. They are blown out of the way by a hurricane fuelled by energy sources that are, in effect, subsidized by the future.

The task of the new economics is to make sure these costs are identified, reflected clearly and are paid, but also to create a different kind of interdependence – using human and ecological resources more effectively.

New economics solutions

The new economics looks at global interdependence rather as Keynes did. Ideas, morality, human values, art and culture are rightly global. They are international now because information technology makes that possible. International trade in what is unique is the stuff of culture, but human well-being and wealth might be better served by trying to provide for what is not unique without wasteful transport around the globe, using up local resources. We might also have a better chance of feeding the world if people's basic needs were met as close to home as possible, rather than forcing people to rely on unstable delivery systems dependent on dwindling supplies of cheap energy. Where we do trade, and we should be free to do so within those ecological constraints, then the rules have got to be equal. Neither enforced compulsory trade, as the global regulators want, nor trade between sharks and minnows, is free trade at all.

Trade, in short, has to be sustainable. It has to generate economic value, reduce poverty and inequality, regenerate the environment and be governed by an open and accountable set of rules. It has to operate in a system that is underpinned by the duties every nation, organization and individual has under the United Nations Declaration of Human Rights to make sure that all Earth's citizens have enough to eat, that they are educated, have access to health care and are paid fairly for what they do. If the trading system fails to bring us closer to that point, then it is not working.

Conventional economics suggests that the law of comparative advantage drives economic development. Places specialize, or they use what price differential they have, to intervene in trade. But the opposite economic doctrine also applies: throughout history, cities have also competed by replacing their imports with locally produced alternatives. Even if intellectual property laws limit their ability to do this now, the same basic idea applies – not just to cities, but to any community – that it makes long-term economic sense to plug the leaks in local spending by producing the same waffles locally. Conventional old-fashioned economics is also bad at dealing with the dynamics of beggar-thy-neighbour trade, both between rich and poor countries, and between poor countries. It also has little to say about handling the emergence of 'absolute' advantage in trade, which many increasingly see as the reality about China.

It is hardly surprising that the big corporations battle against this idea of wealth building through plugging the leaks or producing locally. They do what they can, for example, to prevent generic versions of patent drugs. But that is the way forward, both under open trade and the new economics, and especially when energy prices are rising.

There are four key political objectives to underpin this kind of economics:

1 *Major global anti-trust legislation*, repeated at a local level, to prevent the wasteful concentration of power (see Chapter 6). The UK Office of Fair Trading says that any more than 8 per cent of any market can mean that anti-competitive distortions can occur along the supply chain (though it has allowed Tesco to build up a national share of over 30 per cent of the grocery market, rising to very much more than that in some towns). That figure should be enforced at every level, to boost local enterprise and innovation. We will also have to make sure governments are still allowed to discriminate in favour of local suppliers if they want to.
2 *Taxation* or other measures to make sure that the price of energy reflects the true costs involved, including air fuel (currently untaxed). Trade should not be subsi-

dized by those who have to pick up the tab because it does not reflect the environmental costs or health costs that it imposes on other people, or on the next generation. The most effective way of achieving this is by capping global carbon emissions and then trading, whose mutually advantageous, the right to emit carbon, as long as those permits are allocated in a way that progressively removes the inequalities across the world.

3   *Measures to roll back the spread of intellectual property legislation*, especially when it uses indigenous knowledge or genetic understanding to increase the dependence of ordinary people on corporate monopolies. It means altering the TRIPS regime to let southern countries make generic versions of life-saving drugs. GM food is unproven in its impact on the environment, but it has a devastating impact on farmers who are banned from the ancient practice of saving seeds, or who are unfortunate enough to be prosecuted because GM genes have migrated onto their land. It also drives out the plurality of different varieties that are so vital for sustainable food systems.

4   *An end to subsidies* to unsustainable energy production, fisheries, agriculture and transport. The green economist Norman Myers calculated that these are worth more than twice global military spending every year, and there are 40,000 corporate lobbyists in Brussels making sure the gravy train continues.[13]

An overarching principle for the movement of goods and services was described by E. F. Schumacher as 'subsidiarity'. It is an idea he took from the Catholic church that means things should be done at the lowest, or most local, practicable level with the aim of maximizing social, economic and environmental benefits, and minimizing costs. Hence every neighbourhood might have a bakery, but not every town would have a factory manufacturing trains. The fact that energy looks set to rise considerably in price as this book goes to press – either because of political considerations in the Middle East, or because global oil production is reaching its peak, the point when prices are set to start rising rapidly – means that it is much more likely that the following new economic patterns are going to emerge. Probably the only way of getting the prices of goods and services to reflect their impact on the planet is to *cap emissions and institute a carbon tax*. It makes no sense to zero rate air fuel either: the use of fossil fuels must pay for the effect it has on people and planet, and that will itself cause a major shift to local distribution and production.

We will probably need *a system of personal carbon allowances, an equitable carbon ration or entitlement*. Imagine, said the policy analyst David Fleming, that carbon emissions permits are not just credited towards nations, and traded by them, but credited to all of us as individuals and ordinary businesses, rather like wartime ration coupons.[14] In fact it was his childhood experiences with sweet rations that gave him the idea that the permits or coupons could be held on a personal smartcard and either spent or traded, just as nations do. The idea of 'domestic tradable quotas' (DTQs) – now tradeable emissions quotas (TEQs) – was introduced for the first time in an article in *Country Life* in 1996, and immediately caught the attention of the European Commission. They were then developed further by Richard Starkey of the Centre for Corporate Environmental Management at the University of Huddersfield. They would, after all, provide a kind of basic income to every individual, as of right.

Other new economic policies might lead us to:

Impose duties on inward investors

All inward investment needs to make sure there are advantages to local people. There need to be requirements for local procurement, local training and local ownership. The new economics suggests that these are final elements in rebuilding local economies, which provide an underpinning to everything else. Conventional wisdom suggests that this would deter investors. In practice, it would be welcomed by companies that genuinely want to invest in a community for the long term, as long as it also applies to all their competitors. The idea that inward investment should revert to local ownership after 20 years, beyond the normal time horizon of investment, would probably be welcomed too, but for the opposite reason. Most investors look no further than 20 years; providing them with perpetual ownership because they provided the capital and initial management is therefore overpaying them.

Increase local production

When the Apollo 11 spacecraft landed on the moon in 1969, the astronauts carried with them a much publicized series of meals in tubes and plastic wrappers – to which you added water – which became iconic images of the future. The fact that we have in some ways gone in the opposite direction – huge kitchens, bestselling cooks and TV cookery programmes, foodie magazines and organic supermarkets – demonstrates that the technocratic vision of the big food companies may already be going into reverse. Just as the Campaign for Real Ale has begun to transform our drinking habits, so the rise of Slow Food and its equivalents has begun to rebuild local food economies everywhere, though the poorer sections of the population still exist mainly on processed, unhealthy, expensive food. It is not that the market for fast food has somehow disappeared – it clearly hasn't – but there is a growing demand for what is authentic, local and trustworthy. There is a rising demand for healthy local food, which is very slowly beginning to produce the local businesses and infrastructure capable of providing it, and very slowly encouraging local government to buy it for schools and hospitals.

Fair trade for local agriculture

American farmers now get just 9 cents in every dollar spent on agricultural produce by consumers, with 24 cents going on seeds, energy, fertilizer and other inputs, and 67 cents going to marketeers, middlemen, transport and supermarkets. Half a century ago, they used to get 41 cents. Desperate farmers in India have been committing suicide to get out of debt to the seed companies. Food is an absolutely critical component in the new economics, not supported by central grants but by providing effective local markets that are not undercut by subsidized products dumped from the other side of the world. The rise of farmers' markets is one sign that they may survive after all. So is community-supported agriculture, a Japanese idea that has been taken up in the USA and the UK, whereby people support a local farm with a subscription and receive a guaranteed box of vegetables at their door every week.

Take the corporate ownership and control out of the food chain

Over 90 per cent of consumers rejected GM food in the last poll in the UK, and many farmers in developing countries are suffering from the heavy cost and poor-to-average yields of GM seeds. Bizarrely, the GM debate in the UK has still not progressed beyond the issue – important as it is – of how GM genes can escape to pollute other crops. The new economics objection is not so much against GM because it is inherently unsafe and unstable, though it may be, but because it is 'owned' technology that further reduces farmers to being supplicants to a few mighty corporations. It tightens the grip of a handful of seed companies on the global market, leading to abominations like the prosecution of indigenous farmers for carrying out the traditional practice of keeping and sharing seeds. GM may be an environmental issue; it is definitely an economic and competition issue.

Shift to Slow Food

Carlo Petrini launched his Slow Food campaign because of the arrival of McDonald's in Rome's Piazza di Spagna in 1986. It is now a sophisticated campaign that has 65,000 members in 42 countries, an office in Brussels for lobbying the Eurocrats and another one in New York for organizing trade fairs. From their headquarters in Bra in Piedmont, at the foot of the Alps – a region known for its truffles and red wine – Petrini and the Slow Food movement have since taken up the cause of the long-tailed sheep of Laticauda, Siennese pigs, Vesuvian apricots and many other half-forgotten foods. They have a publishing house, a programme to protect endangered food, and about 500 local organizations known as *convivia*, where they meet to eat. He describes his campaign as a defence of what is ordinary and ubiquitous, a repeated new economics theme:

We want to extend the kind of attention that environmentalism has dedicated to the panda and the tiger to domesticated plants and animals. A hundred years ago, people ate between 100 and 120 different species of food. Now our diet is made up of at most ten or twelve species.[15]

Any kind of future for local food, and food diversity, is going to depend on the survival of small farmers and artisan food-makers. Otherwise the diversity of food is going to carry on giving way to those that just grow fast and travel well.

Other books to read

Jane Jacobs (1986) *The Economy of Cities*, Penguin, London
Jeffrey Sachs (2005) *The End of Poverty: How We Can Make It Happen in Our Lifetime*, Penguin, London
Amartya Sen (1999) *Development as Freedom*, OUP, Oxford
Andrew Simms (2007) *Tescopoly*, Constable, London
Andrew Simms (2009) *Ecological Debt*, Second Edition, Pluto, London
Andrew Simms, Peter Chowla and Dan Moran (2006) *The Interdependence Report*, New Economics Foundation, London
Jeffrey M. Smith (2003) *Seeds of Deception*, Green Books, Totnes, UK
K. Watkins and P. Fowler (2003) *Rigged Rules and Double Standards*, Oxfam International, Oxford

Websites

www.capandshare.org
www.dtqs.org

Notes

1   Andrew Simms, Dan Moran and Peter Chowla (2006) *The UK Interdependence Report*, New Economics Foundation, London.
2   Jane Jacobs (1970) *The Economy of Cities*, Vintage, New York.
3   John Maynard Keynes (1933) 'National self-sufficiency', *The Yale Review*, Vol 22, No 4, June.
4   *Young India* (1929) 21 March.
5   Quoted in Sondra Myers and Benjamin R. Barber (2004) *The Interdependence Handbook*, International Debate Education Association, New York.
6   Leisure Intelligence (2002) *Ethnic Takeaway and Other Fast Food*, Mintel International Group, London.
7   See www.sustainable-palmoil.org.
8   UNDP (2005) *Human Development Report 2005*, New York.
9   Oxfam America (2007) *Paying the Price*, Boston.

10 See www.neweconomics.org.
11 E. F. Schumacher (1973) *Small is Beautiful: Economics as if People Mattered*, Anthony Blond, London.
12 Olaf Johanssen, David Pearce and David Maddison (1996) *Blueprint 5: The True Costs of Road Transport*, Earthscan, London.
13 Norman Myers and Jennifer Kent (2001) *Perverse Subsidies*, Island Press Washington DC.
14 David Fleming (2005) *Energy and Commons Purpose*, David Fleming, London.
15 Quoted in Alexander Stille (2001) 'Slow Food: An Italian answer to globalization', *The Nation*, 20 August.

9
Community: Why Do Fewer People Vote when there is a Wal-mart Nearby?

Market economics values what is scarce – not the real work of society, which is caring, loving, being a citizen, a neighbour and a human being. That work will, I hope, never be so scarce that the market value goes high, so we have to find a way of rewarding contributions to it.

Edgar Cahn on time banks

The worst enemy of life, freedom and the common decencies is total anarchy; their second worst enemy is total efficiency.

Aldous Huxley

The phenomenal growth of 'big box' hypermarket retailing is a feature of the modern landscape. Vast, unlovely piles of metal, glass and plastic loom on the outskirts of our towns and cities, surrounded by prairies of asphalt that are home to herds of dozing sports utility vehicles. The cars in turn double as oversized, petrol-hungry shopping trollies. Places like this have become known as 'dead zones' in the USA, the nation that largely invented this retail lifestyle. The model is also reaching an apotheosis there, where town centres have become ghost towns, and even some Wal-mart stores are being closed and replaced with giant 'supercenters' that have parking spaces for 26,000 cars.

The new economics criticizes how this style of shopping offers superficially attractive, apparently cheap products, which are in reality bought at high cost to the real local economy, jobs, community life, local distinctiveness and the environment. The retail model depends on enormous hidden subsidies, like transport infrastructure and cheap fuel to bring the customers in and to operate its just-in-time distribution systems, without which these technocratic retailers could not survive. It also relies on a wholly unbalanced and frequently abusive power relationship between the retailer and its producers and suppliers. To understand why we have lost most of Britain's orchards and why our farmers are suffering economically, look no further than the silver spoon, in terms of planning and legislation, used to feed the ever growing major supermarkets.

We know that subsidies to Wal-mart in the USA (its UK arm is the supermarket Asda), for example, go a long way further than cheap fuel. Their employees receive an estimated \$2 billion in income support, and there are tax breaks on both sides of the Atlantic, as well as actual subsidies. Due to an old-fashioned and discredited idea that such stores are the best route to bring regeneration, local and national government are often prepared to subsidize them directly to set up in the more marginal areas.[1] They can even be directly favoured over smaller, more local stores, whose deeper connections to the local economy typically mean that dollar for dollar, a larger proportion of customer spending stays and recirculates in the local economy.

But the real question at the heart of this chapter is not so much the economic corrosion brought by subsidized large-scale retail. It is the impact on the social fabric. Day-to-day experience at least suggests that big stores do not provide the kind of complex community services that small shops manage, but recent research in the USA suggests the problem is bigger than that. All the research suggests that communities with higher levels of social capital are healthier and more resilient, and their members are more engaged and better able to work together to solve problems – and this contributes to thriving economic life and helps reduce poverty. But the evidence is that Wal-mart in particular also seems to make people vote less, a clear sign of disengagement.

When two economists, Stephan Goetz and Anil Rupasingha, carried out a detailed study of the links between Wal-mart and dwindling 'social capital' – the community cohesion and mutual support that makes neighbourhoods work – they got more than they bargained for. They looked at communities in which new Wal-mart stores were built in the 1990s and those that already had a Wal-mart at the beginning of the decade. The study controlled for other variables known to affect the stocks of social capital in a community, such as educational attainment. And, strikingly, if there was a Wal-mart nearby all the measures of social capital went down over the decade.[2]

They found that communities that gained a Wal-mart during the decade had fewer local charities and local associations like churches, campaign groups and business groups per capita than those that did not. They also found that Wal-mart's presence actually depresses civic participation. Communities that had or gained a Wal-mart store in the 1990s had lower voter turnout in the 2000 presidential election.

Goetz and Rupasingha came to the conclusion that Wal-mart's negative effect on social capital was partly a result of its impact on locally owned businesses.

Supermarkets can harm not only local retailers, but also a wide variety of other businesses and professionals that serve local retailers, such as banks and accountants. 'The social capital they embody is destroyed, and their entrepreneurial skills and other forms of location-specific human capital are forever lost to the community,' they wrote in the *American Journal of Agricultural Economics*.[3] But why not vote? What is it about the dominance of invasive chain retailers, who measure everything by a technocratic bottom line, and something that corrodes people's belief in the possibility of change? Are people simply too busy because they are shopping? This chapter looks at the phenomenon of social capital and its role in the new economics, but also at the corrosive effect of supermarkets.

Problems with supermarkets

Britain's most successful organic farmer doesn't deal with the big supermarkets. He doesn't because of his first phone conversation with one of their purchasing departments. He asked if he could shift their meeting to a day later than the date they had suggested, when he would be in London – and the phone went dead. Thinking this was accidental, he called back, only to find the buyer he had been talking to had cut him off deliberately.

'Listen,' he was told. 'When we say jump, you jump!'

The current debate about supermarket monopoly power dates back to a pioneering report written by South East Cornwall MP Colin Breed in 1994.[4] There have been several Competition Commission inquiries since then, which uncovered a range of abuses, but which failed to steel themselves to do much about them. None of this is to suggest that supermarkets should somehow be abolished. The problem is that Britain's sleepy competition watchdogs have allowed four of them to build up a distorting position of power over farmers, communities, suppliers and us, their customers.[5]

They have so much power, in fact, that they can insist that suppliers give them 90 days to pay their bills, rather than the normal 30 days that their smaller competitors have to work with. This gives them a rolling interest-free loan equal to their entire stock over two months – again not open to their smaller competitors – enough to fund the massive expansion that Tesco has been driving (six stores alone in one small town, Bicester, and just see what's happening in the Scottish borders where they have been shown to take over half of all spending on groceries).[6] It's a self-reinforcing unfair advantage that comes predominantly from size alone, a distortion to the market that regulators are supposed to prevent.

So if anyone tells you they are big because people use them, that is only partly true. They are big because they are now semi-monopolies, and can enforce massively lucrative deals at the expense of farmers and others. Although often presented as opportunities for job creation, most superstore developments are, in fact, net destroy-ers of jobs, and those replacement jobs they provide are less well paid and less flexible.[7]

The truth is that we don't just have problems with supermarket monopoly, we have a problem with our competition regulators (see Chapter 6). They are charged with protecting the future interests of consumers – and all consumers, not just those with cars who can drive to retail parks – yet seem prepared to preside over this damaging monopoly, where 2000 small shops are going under every year (up from 500 a year in 2005).[8] The failure to take monopoly seriously, because of a naive conviction that large structures are somehow efficient and that consumers must somehow have chosen them, is having devastating effects on enterprise all over the UK, but one of the effects of the squeezing of local enterprise and local retailing is the reduction of social capital and everything that goes with it.

When Jane Jacobs was writing her ground-breaking *The Death and Life of the Great American Cities* in the 1960s, she was inspired by an ebullient man called Bernie Jaffe who ran the sweet shop on the ground floor of her apartment building.[9] On a typical day, she wrote, he could be counted on to lend a dollar or an umbrella, safeguard a neighbour's keys, offer directions, and advise a mother not to buy a ship-model kit because another child going to the same birthday party was giving the same present, and much else besides. Local stores were part of the social glue, a communal memory and consciousness. They watched the street, knew everyone and played a major role in reducing crime. Not all small shops played a role in this – some were depressing and inefficient – but many did, and the supermarkets now free ride on this social capital that lends community cohesion and resilience, and they undermine it.

The basic problem: Efficiency is not the same as effectiveness

This chapter has concentrated on the impact of supermarkets, and of technocratic systems on local neighbourhoods: another example of how narrow interpretations of efficiency have a wider and disastrously corrosive effect on the wider networks around them. But it is worth asking more broadly what has happened in the devel-oped world to undermine these social networks that we know as 'social capital'. The phrase has only been used since the 1960s, coined originally by the pioneering new economist Jane Jacobs but brought into the mainstream by the communitarian writers in the 1990s. The social theorist Robert Putnam described a visit to a bowling alley in Connecticut in his book *Bowling Alone*, with giant TV screens above each lane, where the solo players never talked to each other between turns, but just stared sadly upwards.[10]

He also talked about some of the reasons for this collapse in social engagement in that period. Some of it is clearly the wider effects of house prices and both partners working full-time. Some of it is the effects of television and other technological invasions of our leisure time. Some of it may be, at least in the USA, an increasingly footloose population, though the latest census results in the UK show that half of us – and rising – now live within half an hour of where we were born.

The corrosion of culture and values is a serious problem, partly driven by welfare policies, partly perhaps driven by rising divorce rates and the absence of fathers. But the evidence of the American research about Wal-mart suggests that the corrosion of the human interaction that happens in more vibrant, diverse and local shopping networks also has something to do with the devastating atomization of society.

None of this is relevant to conventional economics, which is mainly concerned with money. But the new economics recognizes the importance that social networks have for money wealth. They provide the trust necessary to do business, keep down crime and provide the confidence that things are possible. The truth is that the social economy of networks, neighbourhoods and families provides the equivalent of an enormous subsidy to the business world, largely unrecognized, taken for granted and certainly not paid for. The new economist and civil rights leader Edgar Cahn describes this as the 'core' economy and says that it works like a computer operating system, which must be maintained before anything else can work.[11] When that core economy fails, everything else unravels. Perhaps on the way towards unravelling, people lose faith in voting.

New economics solutions

Edgar Cahn goes further, pointing to the corrosion of this core economy as the key to the problem of why so much else fails to work properly. To explain this, he developed and deepened a concept coined by Elinor Ostrom from Indiana University, who used the term 'co-production' to explain why crime rose in Chicago in the 1970s when the police started using patrol cars.[12] Co-production describes the way that people work together with public services, not just being consulted about how they should be run, but helping to deliver broader, human services to rebuild our fractured neighbourhoods. When people work alongside doctors, for example, to visit their sick neighbours, or teach English to a new arrival, then those services are being used as a base to reach out and knit the neighbourhood back together again.

Co-production provides a critique of aspects of welfare and other institutions, and an explanation of why we still suffer from poverty, ignorance and disease and the other giants named by Sir William Beveridge in his famous 1942 report.[13] Because, although the communitarian writers of the 1990s, like Amitai Etzioni and Robert Putnam, set out the problem, they failed to come up with a prescription about what could be done about the social problems they had identified; Etzioni because he thought the situation was almost hopeless, and Putnam because he thought it would right itself automatically. But now 'co-production' – the way that professionals rely on clients to help others – is providing the first glimmer of a solution emerging, and doing so simultaneously on both sides of the Atlantic.

Policy makers often assume that social collapse is an intractable and inevitable symptom of modern life, just as they assume now that welfare and social programmes will not work beyond providing a desperate sticking plaster over a deteriorating situation. But co-production is beginning to emerge as the missing factor, both practical and coherent, to provide a new agenda for social policy. And it builds on experience as diverse as the drop in crime in New York City and the aftermath of a major Japanese earthquake.

The key is to substitute 'reciprocity' for 'entitlements'. Co-production means that people cease to be passive recipients of services that are provided impersonally by remote professionals. Instead, they enter into a relationship in which their abilities get recognized, and in which they also help to deliver the service itself, according to what they have to offer. That controversial shift creates a reciprocal relationship that turns welfare beneficiaries from dependent supplicants to partners who are earning what they need by doing the vital work society needs. In the process, a sense of personal usefulness and self-worth can be built alongside the strengthening of neighbourhood relationships. There is urgent work that needs to be done. While we might not always have the money to pay for it, we do have people able to do it. And, they must be rewarded in such a way that they can buy the services and necessities they need. It is a fundamental shift, and it should raise the status of beneficiaries and enormously improve their lives.

Co-production isn't an ideal that professionals are supposed to aspire to. Nor is it simple consultation with clients, or asking people's opinion, or even basic participation in decision making. All that has been tried and it either isn't enough, or it is used as a method of further coercing the ultimate clients – or to tick the box on the funder's report that says 'user involvement'. Co-production means that clients and beneficiaries have to be equal partners in the business of their own regeneration, and equal partners in the delivery of care – in such a way that they and others can be embedded into a new community that will be there when they need it, and insulate them from further harm.

Co-production gives responsibility to people who are regarded as 'the problem', and makes people feel useful when they had been condemned as useless – and by so doing, transforms their lives. Old economics forgets that people are an asset, however poor they are. They may be too young, too damaged, too old or too unstable to get a job in the market, but that doesn't – whatever conventional economics says – mean that they are not needed and can't play a useful role. People have a serious and largely unrecognized need – unrecognized at least by politicians – to make a contribution. To find what Kennedy called 'a cause beyond self'. What we urgently need is some kind of infrastructure that allows anyone, whoever they are, to do the work that neighbourhoods need.

There is a divisiveness built into much organized welfare and many charities. When you ask for nothing back from the person being helped, maybe for their entire lives, you give a damaging and erroneous message: that the person has nothing whatever to offer that society needs. 'Charity wounds,' said the anthropologist Margaret Mead, and this is what she meant. That is emphatically not to say, of course, that vital services should ever be withheld from someone in need if they cannot, for whatever reason, contribute in return. The point is that practically everybody does have something to give and both they, and the community around them, are better for the giving.

The new economics approach suggests first that nothing the government can do, with its regulations and targets, is able to make things happen without the active involvement of ordinary people who are giving their time and effort at a local level. And second that this involvement is not something they can demand or impose, or even simply cajole, but must be part of a series of reciprocal relationships between service users and professionals. When the Lehigh Hospital outside Philadelphia promises patients being sent home that someone will visit them and make sure they are all right, or shop for them, they also say that – when they are fully recovered – they will be asked to do the same. Many of them carry on doing so for years afterwards. The hospital readmission rate goes down, and there is also an active and supportive local network that exists around the hospital.

In fact, it is precisely those reciprocal relationships in the local high street that monopolistic supermarkets are breaking down. All this might mean that recipients of public services were asked to pay back in some way in their local community – by passing on what they have learned or providing some kind of mutual support. That was not how the Welfare State was intended to work, but it might also boost the status of claimants, improve both their health and social cohesion, and also make services more robust against the threat of cost cutters.

The co-production agenda suggests that the practical way to restore this trust is to rebuild the reciprocal links between people and professionals, and between people and each other. Consequently, what started as a simple critique of public institutions often ends up somewhere rather more surprising. Like the poorest neighbourhoods in downtown Boston working alongside Harvard professors to eliminate drug resistant diseases. Or 16 year olds from some of the most notorious housing estates in Washington running their own courts, under licence from the District of Columbia.[14] It means that 'consumers' of justice, mental health services or health care are involved with professionals in a whole new series of reciprocal partnerships, which are also more effective at guaranteeing welfare.

If this idea becomes mainstream, co-production means an end to the old familiar formulae of philanthropy. No more giving as convenient absolution by the wealthy, no more *noblesse oblige* and grateful recipients. Instead, it means giving but asking for something in return, to turn those grateful but passive recipients into active, equal participants in the business of regeneration. That is why the proponents of co-production hope it might mean that, for the first time since the emergence of the gigantic public institutions across the Western world, they don't appear to be permanently stressed and struggling. It could even bring about the elusive holy grail of public policy: real change.

The underlying message behind this and other findings was the vital importance of extended relationships, trust and informal networks. And even more important: that patients, old people, neighbours, busybodies, are also all vital assets – necessary to preventing crime, keeping people well, bringing up children and all the other tasks that society currently has trouble with. The difficulty is that our welfare systems and philanthropic bodies are geared in the opposite direction – defining clients primarily by what they lack.

This is an agenda that is sceptical about the over-weening power of professionals, which is why American professionals who flirt with co-production are often treated with suspicion by their colleagues. The founder of the charity Homebuilders is child psychologist Jill Kinney, who had built an organization devoted to sending professionals to work with at-risk families rather than take children into care. When she publicly questioned whether the permanent neighbourhood support that families needed might be provided by neighbours once the professionals had gone – as they have to go eventually – plus other lay people who had faced similar problems themselves, she was banished by her own organization. Her new organization Home, Safe does just that.

But sometimes the issues are so intractable that there is really no alternative to getting ordinary people to do what had once seemed the sacred preserve of professionals. In 1994, one of the local workers employed by the US charity Partners in Health in Lima died from multi-drug resistant tuberculosis (MDR-TB).[15] It soon became clear that hundreds of locals were also suffering from MDR-TB, thanks to disastrous treatment programmes in the late 1980s. Medical opinion now says that MDR-TB requires such expensive drugs – and such complicated safeguards to make sure that courses of the few powerful antibiotics are completed – that only the very wealthiest communities can afford to start. Health agencies advise developing countries not even to try. But against their advice, Partners in Health solved the monitoring problem by training the local community to supervise the drugs in patients' homes.

Local people also designed individual treatments to suit each patient, with great success. Partners in Health is now achieving cure rates of 80 per cent – as good as anything achieved in the USA but at a fraction of the cost – and has brought the lessons home to Boston.

Time banks

Cahn himself first used the 'co-production' phrase to explain his approach to training lawyers. Students at the District of Columbia School of Law are trained on the job by providing legal support for people and communities who need it but can't afford it – and this is where co-production comes in, because they don't do it for free. They charge out their time in a currency of Cahn's invention that he calls 'time dollars' or 'time credits'. The recipients of legal advice pay off their bill either by passing on what they have learned to somebody else or by helping out in the community in some other way.

Time banks are not new: there are now over 100 of them in the UK alone. But systems like these that measure and reward people's contributions are increasingly now being adapted to use inside public services. That is why Chicago schools now run a peer-tutoring programme in 20 or more failing schools, funded by recycling donated computers that pupils can earn by tutoring younger ones – plus ten hours contributed by a parent. The result has been a consistent average gain in maths and reading, by pupils who normally fell behind further and further each year. Similar projects have gone ahead in three Tower Hamlets schools in London.

In St Louis, a regeneration programme has put a similar principle to work, so that locals earn time credits for each hour of mutual support. These are then used to buy help from other neighbours, to pay doctors' fees, to take courses in the local college or to buy basic food. In the same way, a UK time bank in the Rushey Green GP surgery in Catford, London, has resulted in health improvements for those taking part – both as givers and receivers – befriending, visiting or doing small repairs through its do-it-yourself (DIY) scheme. This is a whole new conception of the NHS, for example, so that it recognizes patients are vital and wasted assets that can make all the difference between illness and recovery for neighbours.[16]

Smart commissioning

The same narrow thinking that has caused so much damage via retailing is very obvious in the business of public sector commissioning. The frontline reality is that many commissioners are under pressure to make savings. Such pressure is often more keenly felt than the need to create positive outcomes for people's well-being. The unintended consequences for many public services, particularly social care that supports the most vulnerable members of society, are very worrying. It is too easy for the holistic, human aspects simply to go missing from the outcomes demanded in the commissioning contracts.

The 2007 **nef** report *Unintended Consequences* showed some of the perverse outcomes.[17] These include reductions in preventive services and cuts that fall hardest on small and medium-sized community and voluntary sector providers, simply because commissioners reduce their definition of the service to units and take no account of the wider impact of building relationships and rebuilding community. A recent National Audit Office report also showed commissioners are increasingly focusing on the price per 'unit' of caring for people as their basis for decision making, rather than on the quality or effectiveness of care.[18]

Unless we want to sleepwalk towards 'total efficiency', where we look at units rather than people, we need a new approach that puts public benefit at the heart of what local authorities and government buy on our behalf. *Slow Tech*, a book by Andrew Price, a scientist and professorial fellow at Warwick University, makes the case that in countless walks of life, from agriculture to fisheries, business and finance, the pursuit of narrowly defined efficiency has one consistently negative consequence: it undermines the robustness, or resilience of the systems, often vital life supporting ones, where it is applied.[19]

If social networks and social capital underpin everything else, then we need to find ways of rebuilding them from the damage left by consumer culture, technocratic or out-of-town retailing and the breakdown of families. We also need to hold back narrow technocratic measurements of what is important. These, as we have seen, are the main problems that the new economics identifies about the old.

That means we are going to have to move towards *developing systems that can reward and use local skills and time, and then embed them in public services*. None of our major social problems, from mental ill health to truancy are going to be solved without massive volunteer involvement on a scale way beyond anything that the current volunteering infrastructure can deal with. We need to harness the skills and assets of local people, rather than purely relying on market-based contracting of professionals to 'do' services 'to' people. That means experiments like the youth courts in Washington DC, which now try half the first time non-violent offences in juries of teenagers who earn credits for being there to spend on computers and training. We also need a network of systems of give and take in every public institution from doctor's surgeries to schools and housing estates, that are able to measure and reward the small efforts people make. That means time banking in every school, surgery, hospital, housing estate and community centre in the country – making sure they are affiliated locally but not run centrally – as a way of creating that new volunteering infrastructure that involves everybody.

In the long run, it means turning public services on their head so that they seek out what people *can* do rather than simply concentrating on 'units of care' based on perceived need. That is the *co-production approach to public services* that would mean that, as far as possible, public services are managed locally and have as their core task building a supportive and active community around them. Beyond that, any new economics manifesto will need to:

Launch radical anti-trust action at every level

Semi-monopolies that allow retailers a third of the UK market and very much more in some cities, towns and regions, may appear to suit some consumers now, but they certainly don't suit all consumers – like those without access to cars – and nor are they likely to suit consumers in the future, where the pressure they bear on UK farms and suppliers undermines our national ability to feed ourselves. We need rigorous local competition policies aimed at encouraging local enterprise, as well as better resourced competition watchdogs at national level that are prepared to break up companies that have built up an abusive position.

Change the way public sector commissioning is done to look at broader effects

We need to start commissioning for real, positive social and human results rather than process-driven targets and outputs. This means making sure that both commissioners and providers of services are able to measure what adds up to a successful outcome. We must also redefine what we mean by value for money in terms of those outcomes – what is the broader 'social return'? It also means that commissioners will know what they are buying and why. Ultimately, their job is to make sure their services are effective and to enhance the well-being of the communities they serve.

Make philanthropy reciprocal

We need an understanding by funders that any grant must be matched by time put into mutual support by local beneficiaries. If people benefit from the money, then they will be asked to give back in some way, not to the funder but to each other, and to be rewarded for doing so, preferably by being given the basic requirements of a civilized life. That means that grants should all include a proportion that goes on the rewards to engage the beneficiaries. It means that local projects should, as far as possible, be handed over to local control and informal delivery systems. It also means that grants are less likely to be siphoned off by middle class professionals, convinced that it is simply too dangerous to allow the ultimate beneficiaries to do any of the work. It means that the relationship between funders and funded is more equal.

Other books to read

David Boyle, Sherry Clark and Sarah Burns (2006) *Hidden Work*, Joseph Rowntree Foundation, York
Stacey Mitchell (2006) *Big Box Swindle*, Beacon Press, Boston
Julian Tudor Hart (2006) *The Political Economy of Healthcare*, Policy Press, London

Notes

1   Philip Mattera and Anna Purinton (2004) *Shopping for Subsidies*, Good Jobs First, Washington DC.

2   Stephan J. Goetz and Anil Rupasingha (2006) 'Wal-mart and social capital', *American Journal of Agricultural Economics,* Vol 88, No 5.
3   Stephan J. Goetz and Anil Rupasingha (2006) 'Wal-mart and social capital', *American Journal of Agricultural Economics,* Vol 88, No 5.
4   Colin Breed (1994) *Checking out the Supermarkets,* Breed.
5   Josh Ryan-Collins, Lisa Sanfilippo and Stephen Spratt (2007) *Unintended Consequences: How the Efficiency Agenda Erodes Local Public Services and a New Public Benefit Model to Restore Them,* New Economics Foundation, London.
6   Andrew Simms (2007) *Tescopoly,* Constable & Robinson, London.
7   H. Barton, M. Grant and R. Guise (2002) *Shaping Neighbourhoods: A Sustainable Settlements Desktop Guide for Health, Sustainability and Vitality,* University of the West of England.
8   All-Party Small Shops Group (2006) *High Street 2015,* London.
9   Jane Jacobs (1961) *The Death and Life of the Great American Cities,* New York, Random House.
10 Robert Putnam (2001) *Bowling Alone: The Collapse and Revival of American Community,* Simon & Schuster, New York.
11 Edgar Cahn (2000) *No More Throwaway People: The Co-production Imperative,* Essential Books, Washington DC.
12 Elinor Ostrom (1973) *Community Organization and the Provision of Police Services,* Sage Publications, Beverly Hills.
13 William Beveridge (1942) *Social Insurance and Allied Services,* HMSO, London.
14 Time Dollar Institute (2003) *Time Dollar Youth Court Annual Report 2003,* Washington DC.
15 Sarah Burns (2004) *Elements of Co-production,* New Economics Foundation, London.
16 Lucie Stephens, Josh Ryan-Collins and David Boyle (2008) *Co-production: A Manifesto for Growing the Core Economy,* New Economics Foundation, London.
17 Ryan-Collins, Sanfilippo and Spratt (2007) op. cit.
18 National Audit Office (2007) *The Efficiency Programme: A Second Review of Progress,* London.
19 Andrew Price (2009) *Slow Tech: Manifesto for an Over-wound World,* Atlantic Books, London.

10
Debt: Why are Malawi Villagers Paying the Mortgages of Surbiton Stockbrokers?

280 million Americans are bingeing on Toyota Land Cruisers, Sony video players and Cartier watches – and are doing so by raiding the piggy bank savings of five billion people in developing countries. It's time the rich financed the poor, instead of filching from them.

Ann Pettifor

I think greed is healthy. You can be greedy and still feel good about yourself.

Ivan Boesky, 1986, a few months before he was indicted on insider trading charges

Malawi is one of the most beautiful countries in sub-Saharan Africa, clustered around the long lake that gives the country its name – Malawi means 'the glitter of the sun rising across the lake'. It has faced serious problems in recent years, partly because more than 14 per cent of the population lives with HIV or AIDS, and partly because – like so many other countries – it has struggled to get out of debt.

Those debt repayments have been massively reduced – from £60 million a year to £5 million – but only as a result of debt-reduction urged on the world's governments over the years by vociferous Jubilee Debt campaigners. The process of getting there was also traumatic. Malawi was approved for debt reduction in 2000, and a number of conditions were imposed by the International Monetary Fund (IMF). One of these was that many of the state functions should be privatized. This caused agricultural commodity markets to collapse because the state withdrew from commodity marketing, removed farm subsidies and sold off their state-run banks. The Malawi Commercial Bank, which had been set up specifically to help Malawi's small farmers, was sold and immediately closed many small accounts, ending the access to loans of hundreds of small farmers.

Part of the IMF's advice was that the Malawi government should sell off two thirds of its grain reserves. In fact, the Malawi government went further and sold them all, and the country was almost immediately hit by a serious famine in 2003. The government responded by borrowing heavily to buy in grain to feed its starving people, and was punished by the IMF suspending the little debt relief it was receiving. Malawi is now receiving more than £300 million in aid a year, but in those difficult periods – when concern about corruption was also leading to the suspension of much of its foreign government aid – as much as £60 million a year was flowing straight back from Malawi to the rich countries of the north.[1]

One of the peculiar things about aid is that we fondly imagine help flowing from the wealthy north to the poor south. In practice, the situation is much stranger. For one thing, despite the UK's increase in annual aid, a quarter of that rise has gone to just three countries – rather predictably, Iraq, Afghanistan and Pakistan. Another issue is the difference between the popular idea of aid – all selfless donations to health and education – and the reality that much is poorly disguised export subsidy for rich countries whilst only small proportions actually pay for obvious measures to reduce poverty.

When you look at money flows, the picture is complicated too. Money deposited in UK banks from developing countries has risen fast. While much of the money coming into the UK comes from countries that are not as financially poor as Malawi, some of it does. And even then, intriguing questions hover above this quite dramatic increase in deposits to UK banks. In 2005 alone, the amount surged by well over $115 billion to reach a total of $385 billion. Deposits from several African nations rose noticeably in the first half of this decade: Cameroon by 516 per cent, Ethiopia by 103 per cent and Nigeria by 47 per cent (£5 billion in the UK).[2] The stories from India and South Africa are even more striking. In the same period, Indian deposits in UK banks went from $8 billion to $30 billion, and South African deposits from $5 billion to $21 billion. Both India and South Africa have been making it easier for domestic finances to leave the country.

The last three decades witnessed a growing deregulation of the way money moves around the world. As international financial interdependence has grown, an increasingly large amount of money due to governments in tax to pay for public services has gone missing. Both at global and national levels, sums of money that dwarf spending on the Millennium Development Goals are avoiding legitimate tax authorities through a network of tax havens, complex accounting manoeuvres, and with the advice and support of the major accountancy firms. According to research by campaign group the Tax Justice Network, approximately $11.5 trillion of assets are held offshore by wealthy individuals.[3] It estimates that the annual income from these assets could be $860 billion, and the tax lost because they are held offshore could exceed $255 billion each year. Other estimates put the total at between a third and a sixth of the world's assets.

The same group has also measured the UK's corporation tax gap – the difference between the expected rates of tax that UK companies should pay and the tax that those companies have actually paid. The gap between the expected and actual amounts has been rising slowly by about 1 per cent every year. Looking across all UK companies, it may now equal £9.2 billion per year – between a quarter and a third of income from corporation tax in 2004/5.[4]

During the early 1990s, the flow of money from developing countries to developed countries in debt repayments dwarfed the flow of aid the other way around. The fact that this is not the case now is partly because of the limited success of debt cancellation, and partly because of the millions of tiny remittances sent back home from wealthy cities by people from developing countries – from office cleaners to undocumented fruit pickers or dish washers in restaurants. The World Bank took a second look at these flows in 2003 and defined some of them differently, and found they were six times bigger than they had estimated before. That year, they worked out that a total of over £220 billion was going home in tiny amounts in this way, and that takes no account of informal methods of transferring money using cash, or – more recently – phonecards.[5] It may be twice as much.

In some ways this is an example of self-help, but in others it is rather tragic. These foreign workers are doing the jobs nobody in London wants to do because they can't get work near their families, and live in constant fear of the immigration authorities. To do so, they have to move at great risk half way across the world to earn the equivalent of a pittance and send some of it home. 'Poor countries can't earn decent revenues by exporting coffee or cocoa,' said Ann Pettifor, who led the Jubilee Debt campaign, 'so they export people instead.'[6] These servants and cleaners could be skilled workers back home, and – because they are forced to migrate for work – they are not available to build their home economies. It isn't development; it's desperation.

All these factors complicate the issue of where the money is flowing to and from. But what really unbalances everything, and explains why the ubiquitous Surbiton stockbroker has been doing so well, is that these net capital inflows to countries like Malawi are more than outweighed by interest payments on debt and profit remittances from foreign-owned companies back to their international headquarters in London or other big cities. While there is a small net *capital* flow from developed to developing countries, there is a much larger net *financial* transfer when you include interest and profit payments in the opposite direction. In fact, *the net financial transfers between developing and developed countries have shifted from a balance of $46* *billion in favour of developing countries in 1995 to an estimated outflow of $683 billion in 2006*: about 5 per cent of their gross national income, and it gets worse every year.[7]

Conventional mainstream thinking suggests that foreign direct investment is always a good thing for developing countries. The truth is that it is only good for them if the resources it generates stay put, and usually they do not: the capital is footloose and will set out across the globe again in search of greater profits, and the profits and the interest payments also go home again. The reality is less like investment and more like foreign direct extraction. That is why the ubiquitous Surbiton stockbroker, like the Docklands trader working for a multinational bank, is being paid out of these widow's mites, recirculated backwards and forwards across the globe.

The basic problem: The barriers to development

There is a core paradox here, not just about development, but about whether the majority of people in the world can better themselves under the current economic system. Conventional economics, as wielded by powerful Western policy makers, sets out a process whereby nations, neighbourhoods and nobodies can drag themselves up by borrowing money, to make investments that will eventually pay off the loans and live off the human and physical infrastructure that is left behind. That is the conventional answer to the critique of 'trickle-down' development set out in Chapter 4. But there is a flaw at the heart of it, which stems partly from the modern design of money, which is largely conjured into existence by commercial banks in the form of interest-bearing loans (see Chapter 4). The money must eventually be paid back plus interest, and the poorest usually pay the most interest. The kind of economic activity that goes on in developing countries, often agriculture, can only provide the kind of returns that the planet can provide. But investing in financial services and money markets can go way beyond that.

There is a second, related, problem. Being the lender gives the northern banks enormous privileges. These advantages are, of course, at the heart of the long struggle between lenders and borrowers that stretches back through the history of money, and underpins so much else. In fact, the privileges given to the lenders are so powerful that, as monetary historians have pointed out, the banking infrastructure of northern Italy and The Netherlands lasted for centuries after the economic forces had moved away.[8]

Small-scale debts that can be paid off quickly are absolutely vital to underpinning people's economic freedom. But big debts are corrosive, and the way the economic system depends on these debts to keep going – yet finds it can also no longer sustain them – is one of the biggest accusations against it.

National debt

There is no better example of the way debt entrenches the power differences between people and between nations as the debt crisis in Argentina. As Argentina ratcheted up its indebtedness during the 1990s, encouraged by the IMF and other advisors, those who benefited were the British, Spanish and German banks and multinational companies involved in its flirtation with global turbo-capitalism. Winners included the Spanish companies like Telefonica and Repsol, 60 per cent of whose profits came from Argentina, and who benefited enormously from the privatization of Argentina's assets. They also included the wealthiest Argentines who, helped by foreign banks, managed to export $130bn over 10 years through the capital flight mechanisms that both foreign and local banks provided.[9] Some of the biggest banks in Europe and the USA colluded with the desperate Argentine government in the infamous 'mega swap', which restructured the national debt and raised it by another $55bn, earning $150m in commissions for the bankers involved.

Despite the limited success of debt reduction, the poorest 53 countries still have debts totalling between $290 and $380 billion; for the poorest 149 countries, it is over $2.6 trillion. During 2005, the poorest countries paid nearly $43 billion to the rich world in debt service (payments of interest and principal), or about $118 million every day.[10] When Honduras was hit by Hurricane Mitch in 1998, its creditors moved in, represented by the IMF and World Bank, and took over the shop. There was no standstill allowed on debt repayments until the nation had recovered, even though its crucial banana plantations – which earned the revenues for debt repayments – had been devastated.

In fact, much of the debt of poor countries is left over from the 1970s – and often arose through reckless or self-interested lending by the rich world banks that then had large sums available (mainly oil revenue) to lend, and were prepared to use it as a weapon in the Cold War. The oil crisis meant that interest rates rose and the debts grew. The prices of the kinds of products produced by the poorest countries fell, often because they followed the advice of the World Bank and IMF to produce and export identical primary commodities. That meant they had less hard currency available to pay the interest. The result was that many countries ended up owing huge amounts, even after repaying far more than they, or their former regimes, had originally borrowed.

Manipulated debt

The historic resentment between creditors and debtors has been exploited dangerously over the centuries by politicians and imperialists. When Columbus sought a way to control a population of Tainos he considered were dangerously lazy, he taxed them: he imposed an annual debt of a hawk's bell – like a thimbleful – of gold. When the British were determined to find better ways of controlling the populations in the villages of India, they imposed a tax to force them to work to pay it. In our own day, the extraordinary debt that many households face – just to get a mortgage – forces both partners to work full time for a quarter of a century at least, when they might otherwise have preferred a different, less well-paid career.

The manipulation of debt reached notorious levels where it came closest to slavery. The share croppers of the American South after the end of slavery in 1865 were forced to buy their plot of land and equipment and pay it off with the crops they grew, but at such ruinous rates of interest that they never escaped. They lived in a state of debt bondage. Most examples of slavery in the world today are related to debt in some way.

The truth is that it isn't just the old imperialists and slave owners who prefer those they rule to be controlled by debt, it is our modern rulers today. Because we need to pay off mortgages, we are more docile, more economically productive – but in the narrowest terms – and more exhausted, than we would be otherwise.

Debt can be found, for example, lurking behind the coercion of some in developing countries who are persuaded to plant commercial genetically modified (GM) crops, when they drive out hardy, local varieties and leave farmers indebted and dependent on seeds they have to buy every year, rather than using traditional seed sharing techniques. The environmental impact of GM food technology is beyond the scope of this book, but the economic impact can be profound (see Chapter 6). Farmers, particularly in India, have been persuaded by the promises of GM seeds to borrow the money to invest in them, only to find themselves heavily in debt. Monsanto now dominates the market for Bt cotton, which kills some of the most threatening pests when they eat it and theoretically reduces the need for fertilizers. In practice, the targeted pests can be replaced by other kinds, and the seeds themselves can be up to three times as expensive, leaving farmers worse off. Alternative projects where farmers share sustainable farming techniques for reducing pests have been able to eliminate pesticides without becoming dependent on a single corporation.

GM corporations have presided over a situation that has often seen seeds accidentally released, where they rapidly infect the surrounding crops, making farmers liable for punitive damages for infringing patents. Something similar seems to be happening with animals: Monsanto has been seeking patents on actual herds of pigs and their offspring, which would give them huge rights over any farmer breeding pigs with the characteristics described in the patents. The relative failure of Bt cotton and other GM seeds is partly to do with disappointing yields, partly also – at least until recently – to do with low prices because of western food subsidies to their own farmers, but the result is visible in a wave of Indian small farmers committing suicide between 2002 and 2006.[11]

It is this shift in the power balance between small farmers and the economic infrastructure they need to succeed that is the real price of commercially controlled GM seeds. Not only are the seeds patented, but some employing the so-called 'terminator technology' engineered to be sterile, which makes the traditional practice among small farmers to save seeds from one year to the next impossible. Debt changes us from independent economic players to indentured supplicants, and nowhere more so than in the commercial GM food chain.

First world debt

The most indebted county on Earth is actually the USA (see Chapter 4), creating a state of economic affairs that has unpredictable consequences for the global economy. In fact, it owes about the same as the whole developing world combined. But when you also factor in the indebtedness of people in developed countries, then the scale of the problem becomes clearer. Around the world, there is now $100 trillion in debt outstanding, but only half that in money circulating (GDP) with which to repay those debts.[12]

This is a major problem in the UK, where people are borrowing almost twice as much as in other western European countries. Informal or 'unsecured' UK lending, such as credit cards and overdrafts, was £216 billion in 2005, more than a third of all new non-mortgage borrowing in Europe. The average British resident owes £3175, according to the business research firm Datamonitor. Total UK personal debt, including mortgages, is about £1.2 trillion, which again is more money than is in circulation in the UK to pay it off.[13] The UK national debt following the bank bail out, owed by the government, now amounts to over £22,000 per man, woman and child.

All this underpins an economy where the creditors – and those masters of the universe who control them – take nearly everything (see Chapter 4). Partly the vast wealth has been driven by insane pay packages for the chief executives of some of the world's leading businesses – often no matter how unsuccessful they are. Disney's chief executive officer (CEO) Michael Eisner was among the first to be notorious for this, when he was paid a package worth $575 million in 1998 – about 25,070 times the average Disney worker's pay (and far more than that if you count the pathetic sums paid in factories in Honduras or Bangladesh that make Disney shirts and bags). Of all the wealthy individuals, the most outrageous has been Microsoft founder Bill Gates. When Windows 2000 was launched, Gates' personal stock of Microsoft shares rose in value by more than $130 billion – or 12 times more than the entire shares and investments owned by the whole population of African-Americans.

Yet many super managers were also being rewarded for driving down the wages of those at the bottom end, increasingly seeking out immigrants who were ignorant of their rights. The question is whether democracy can survive these gigantic disparities in wealth and power, or whether, as the economist Jeff Gates puts it, the system is 'making the world safe for plutocracy'.[14] He uses the following examples:

- Nearly 3 billion of the world's population live on less than $2 a day.
- The world's 200 biggest corporations account for 28 per cent of world economic activity but employ less than 0.25 per cent of the global workforce.
- The world's 200 wealthiest people – who doubled their net worth between 1994 and 1999 – own the same amount of wealth as the combined annual income of the world's 2.5 billion poorest people.
- African-Americans owned 0.5 per cent of the net worth of the USA in 1865, the year that slavery was finally abolished. By 1990, their net worth had crawled up to 1 per cent.

Corporate debt

Fred Goodwin, the former chief executive of the failed bank RBS, whose decisions lost billions and led the bank to be nationalized in all but name, walked away from his job with millions and a pension of £703,000 per year, begrudgingly later lowered but only after relentless public vilification. For a moment the old assumptions of economics seemed not quite as much like the rational, mathematical science it claims to be – more like a rather colourless and grubby version of Alice in Wonderland. A nonsense world ruled over by capricious, self-absorbed financial royalty who were careless about the consequences of their actions on the rest of the world.

The vast rewards for those in charge of the system have often been belied by their miserably indebted companies. This is partly a side effect of the junk bond revolution in the 1980s, which fuelled the activities of corporate raiders like T. Boone Pickens and Sir James Goldsmith. The main complaint by critics was that these takeover ventures, tailored to reap short-term profits for high rollers, left many companies deeply in debt or dismembered. If a company had been prudent and paid off too much debt, then a raider could potentially use that as their own asset for grabbing control of the company, loading it with debt to pay for the takeover, stripping it of saleable assets and then selling the remains on.

That was the role of the junk bonds, which offered high yields because of the high risk involved. The junk bond revolution was led by a California company called Drexel Burnham Lambert, whose senior executive vice president, Michael Milkin, was the so-called 'junk bond king'. Evidence obtained from the insider trader Ivan Boesky led to Wall Street's biggest criminal prosecution ever (at least until the Bernard Madoff affair in 2008), after which 98 indictments of fraud and racketeering were brought against Milkin. He was sentenced to ten years in jail and agreed to pay $600 million in fines. Without his leadership, the junk bonds faltered. It is widely believed that the temporary decline of the junk bond market led to a credit crunch that contributed to the 1990 recession. Milken was released from prison early because he had been given only 18 months to live, and now runs his own economic think tank. But one of the legacies of those years has been the defensive loading of companies with debt in order to stave off hostile takeovers, while those that have been success-fully seized are anyway loaded with vast debt.[15] Debt has, in short, become a way of life for corporations.

This private debt is often miraculously transferred to the struggling developing countries, via the export credit agencies in Paris, London or Washington. The agencies agree to compensate the company if their foreign partner defaults on an export deal. But when that happens, most agreements include a stipulation that the credit agency will be recompensed by the developing country involved. Not only does debt become a way of life for corporations, it is often not the corporation that ends up having to pay it.

A new economics approach

The core new economics critique is that money is not a good measure of wealth (see Chapter 3). It is not the one, indivisible, totemic, semi-divine, golden truth issued from on high by an infallible central bank and handed down to a grateful populace. The gold standard disappeared completely from the world in 1971 when Richard Nixon accepted the inevitable, but gold standard thinking is still with us, and – because this kind of narrow measurement leaves out most of what is valuable – we are blinded to our own wealth.

Instead, we have a situation where gold standard thinking is applied to the poor. They are the ones who are kept in the rigid straitjacket of 'sound money', where money means something reliable and debts are paid back. Yet those involved in finan-cial services or multinational business, especially in Tokyo, London and New York, are able to benefit from almost complete flexibility. If they want to buy a company, they can conjure the wealth as if from nowhere in the form of debt – load it onto somebody else – and reap the benefits. When Robert Maxwell died, he owed twice as much as Zimbabwe, but he still managed to keep a luxury yacht from which to fall. This is not to criticize the idea that money should be reliable, but to suggest that we need more measuring sticks and many kinds of money to do justice to ourselves. Some of it must be sound: we will rely on that for savings. Some of it will be based on something else – but that flexibility needs to be extended to the poor as well.

In the same way, globalization, which can – as Keynes explained – cover anything from hospitality and culture to money, has been reduced to one narrow interpreta-tion, peddled by international institutions like the IMF and World Bank, and one rather fundamentalist approach to the market and to money, linked to some dubious, misrepresented Darwinian ideology about the survival of the economically fittest. The first thing we need, therefore, is a range of other institutions that can make available the benefits of sensible, small-scale debt to help the poorest.

That was what Mohammed Yunus, the Bangladeshi banking professor, managed with the Grameen Bank. He was at a conference of New York bankers in 1976 when he realized that at least 80 per cent of his country would be turned down for loans by almost everyone else in the room.[16] He went home and founded the micro-lending institution that has become the model for micro-lending and small-scale banking all over the world. It lends very small amounts – enough for a hen or a cow, or more recently a mobile phone that can be used by a whole village ('a mobile phone is a cow,' they say at Grameen). The money is lent almost entirely to women, because they were found to manage money better than men, and each loan is rooted in support groups of other women.

Grameen operated originally from motor scooters, around some of the poorest villages in the world. 'Your bank just rushed past in a cloud of dust,' said the headline of the first article about them in *Christian Science Monitor*. It was also enormously successful. Not only did they reduce bad debts to just 1 per cent, they also set out a whole new model of development that could genuinely help the poorest people stay independent. Grameen was also about allowing people to find the investment they needed to make a major difference to people's lives, by providing the services or food neighbours needed in the poorest places, rather than waiting hopelessly for big corporations to provide anything along the same lines.

It has spawned thousands of similar micro-credit projects all over the world, one of the major ways that the first world is learning about development from the third world. Micro-credit reached its apotheosis with the UN Micro-Credit summit in 1996, hosted in Washington by Hillary Clinton. Some of the other models include:

- **Grameenphone:** providing phone services in Bangladesh where they are otherwise non-existent, and redressing the anomaly that Bangladeshis who wanted a mobile had to wait ten years and pay $500, whereas New Yorkers could get one immediately, free and over the counter.
- **Credit unions:** the small community-controlled savings and loan schemes that have spread from Ireland to the UK, giving the poorest people some more financial clout – when they otherwise have to rely on loan sharks charging the equivalent of anything up to 5000 per cent APR.
- **Social banks:** like the pioneering South Shore Bank in Chicago, that lend money to social enterprises – profit-making companies with social objectives – providing services to inner city areas.

The business of lending money to poorer people is the challenge that caused the credit crunch in 2008. Yunus and other pioneers have found other models than the sub-prime lending that promised to deliver risk-free home loans in an inflated market to people who couldn't afford them. Grameen and micro-lending provide an infrastructure that lends small amounts to people who can afford it, but who are otherwise sidelined or charged huge sums. The UK only abandoned a usury interest rate in

1977. The previous top rate of interest was 48 per cent. In many EU countries, half this level is the ceiling today. Britain is unique as a developed country in having no cap on interest. In 2002, a **nef** report revealed the scale of sub-prime lending with a yearly turnover then of £16 billion and charges to low-income households from 160 to 500 per cent APR.[17]

In 1987, **nef** founder James Robertson forecast the emergence of 'enterprises with mixed economic and social objectives ... as a major feature of the 21st century economy, and that with it will evolve a "financial third sector".'[18] This prediction has come true. The barriers to expansion faced by voluntary sector finance providers are formidable and similar to those of fair trade goods a decade ago. The good news is that a shift of the fair trade idea into financial services has just begun. Triodos Bank has launched a fair trade account. Unlike mainstream banking, fair trade bank accounts are transparent about where the funds are going, what the charges are and what social enterprises, just causes or local communities are being financed.

The government responded in 2005 with reforms to credit union legislation and by setting up a Financial Inclusion Fund to tackle the problem of debt and lack of access to affordable credit. This initiative has supported about 100 credit unions and community development finance institutions to access £40 million of investment capital and revenue to provide affordable credit. Thanks to this investment, micro-credit loans of over £21 million have been advanced. An extension of this programme to 2011 was agreed.

Bill Clinton targeted the development of 100 community development banks. The social investment programme he implemented has borne fruit. From invisible players in 1992, by March 2007 community development credit unions (CDCUs) had attracted over 1 million low and moderate income members, were mobilizing savings of over $4 billion and were advancing new loans of over $3 billion annually. CDCUs are the Grameen bankers of the USA.

With help from the USA, a new business model has been launched in the UK called a community banking partnership, a social cooperative network among credit unions, a community development finance institution and money advice agency.[19] Seven of these partnerships are operating in east London, mid-Wales, Coventry and Warwickshire, Devon, Portsmouth and Southampton, Merseyside and Sheffield. They provide debt advice, banking and affordable credit. They are also, to some extent, re-inventing the parallel institutions of friendly societies that grew up in the UK in the 19th century.

One of these, Fair Finance in east London, has stopped over 100 evictions, rescheduled £500,000 of household debt and provided over 400 micro-loans a year to households otherwise paying 160 per cent plus. Those 2 million people in the UK without a bank account don't just pay more for services than rich people, they pay vastly more. Energy costs are typically £195 per year extra because many low-income households use prepayment meters to avoid debt. Shop credit used to buy a cooker with an extended guarantee for repairs will be charged at over 50 per cent APR.

It may not bridge the growing gulf between creditors and debtors, between rich and poor, but building a new infrastructure to help the specific financial needs of poorer people will at least provide a lifeline for them when none currently exists. It will also provide some watertight doors to keep the ordinary economy running when there are global financial problems.

Any more fundamental solution is going to have to include a far bigger and more *powerful network of small-scale banks and micro-lenders* that can provide for people's credit needs at reasonable interest. Providing alternative sources for people is at least half the battle of undermining the monopoly power of the current system. To do that, we will have to break up the banks into far smaller, more specialized units, so that the greed of the merchant bankers and speculators has less power to undermine our lives. We need to support the growth of local credit unions and a range of other kinds of infrastructure and social banking to underpin our lives. It means providing an infrastructure that can lend poorer people amounts they can afford – rather than the sub-prime trick of lending them 'risk-free' sums in an inflated market that they patently cannot afford.

In the long run, we will have to *learn from Islamic banking* to find ways of providing credit without charging interest, and creating money without interest. Some aspects of Islamic banking are indistinguishable from Western banking – car loans, for example – but some of it, where lenders take a stake in the business rather than charging interest, provides important lessons for economics, and at the very least a way of injecting diversity into the business of lending and borrowing.

Any new economics manifesto will also have to:

Develop a concept of odious debt

A new concept of 'odious debt' is required that can protect the innocent citizens of a nation ruled over by corrupt governments and dictators, who load the country with international debt for their arms and palaces, which then have to be paid off by the people who live there, long after the dictator has escaped to tax exile elsewhere.[20] The possibility of odious debt means that lenders are just as responsible as borrowers if the debt is wrong, or corrupt or damaging. If an international bank lends money to a dictator for missiles, or to a company involved in a massive and damaging dam project, it is no less responsible for the damage. It also means that those left to pay back the loan afterwards should be able to have it cancelled on the grounds that it was 'odious', at the risk of the lender. It is adolescent to imagine that somehow the bankers who make these loans are not morally responsible for the result of their action, especially as they are making considerable amounts of money in commission. Odious debts should not stand.

Develop an international bankruptcy process for nations

Since the late 19th century, we have recognized that human rights take precedence over debts and the rights of creditors: we no longer lock up defaulting debtors and let their families starve, partly because we also know this makes it next to impossible that the debts will be paid. That is why bankruptcy law was introduced. It was a legal framework whereby debtors could have a line drawn under their debts, and spiralling debts brought to an end, and get legal protection from creditors. This subordinates the rights of money to the rights of individuals. But in the international sphere, it is the other way around. In the absence of such a legal framework of justice, international creditors play the role of witness, plaintiff, judge and jury in the court of international finance. The IMF plays the role of receiver – and moves in on a country as soon as it is unable to find the foreign reserves to finance debt service.

But the IMF is not only the agent of all international creditors – public and private – it is a major creditor in its own right coupled to a governance structure in which voting power is related to wealth that is closer to pre-Civil War England than a modern democracy. Poor countries are obliged by the IMF to prioritize payment of debt service to rich western creditors, starting with the IMF and World Bank, and in descending order to private creditors and finally western government creditors, and to prioritize repayments to these rich creditors over spending on health, clean water and sanitation for their own people. We need to correct the profound injustice of this with an international bankruptcy law for sovereign governments.[21]

Create low-interest loans for vital projects

There may be better ways of producing the finance that governments need, at least for capital projects, than by borrowing it from banks where it is created by the banking system, with interest attached. All but 3 per cent of the money in circulation is created in this way; a generation ago, the amount of money minted or printed by the government and spent into circulation (without interest or debt) was as high as 20 per cent. Back in 1922, Henry Ford and Thomas Edison teamed up to propose a more sophisticated system for financing projects in the public interest, whereby the Federal Reserve should create the money themselves, pay it back, and withdraw it from circulation as the loan was paid off.[22] A third of the money to pay for the controversial public–private partnership to refurbish the London Underground in 2001 went to financial intermediaries, so this would make an immediate difference. The World Bank might also be more effective if it helped countries create their own money, sustainably and in their own currency, to finance projects, rather than by lending them money in foreign currency that inevitably seeps out of their economy again.

Create new international currencies

The creation of a new international currency called special drawing rights (SDRs) was agreed at the Rio de Janeiro meeting of the IMF Board of Governors in September 1967. The IMF was given the authority to create more reserve assets through general allocations of SDRs to its members in proportion to their quotas. The SDRs are then exchangeable for other countries' currencies that can be used as an international means of payment. There have been several proposals for reinvigorating SDRs in recent years for various purposes that range from reserve allocation to poverty reduction and the provision of global public goods. The financier George Soros has suggested that SDR allocations be used to provide global public goods, in particular for the fight against communicable disease, especially AIDS and TB, for education, judicial reform and initiatives to close the digital divide. Other commentators have suggested that the IMF use SDR allocations to cancel some of the debt owed by poor countries.

Create a new currency based on emissions rights

Instead of being linked to gold, currencies could be linked to carbon emission entitlements under a global system that sets a safe cap on emissions. This idea implies moving toward issuing equal emission permits to every adult in the world. These permits, called special emission rights (SERs), would be rationing coupons equivalent to an international citizens' income and be based on the recognition of emissions entitlements as the only logical way to manage the global commons of the atmosphere, and one that recognizes basic human rights and equity in international law. This would help reduce some of the inequality that is endemic in the current monetary system and also help cut greenhouse gas emission. The SERs would be issued every year and producers of fossil fuels would be allowed to sell only as much fossil fuel as there are emission rights for. The SERs would expire and be reissued annually in decreasing quantities and hence cap greenhouse emissions at decreasing levels. The green economist Richard Douthwaite has suggested that this also be linked with a new international currency called EBCU (emissions-backed currency unit) that could be used for all international trade, not just for buying permits.[23] Like SERs, EBCUs would be issued to each country on the basis of its population but, unlike the SERs, they would be given to each country's central bank rather than to individuals. The system would be similar to the Bretton Woods system except that the right to burn fossil fuels replaces gold and EBCUs play the role of the US dollar. Its introduction would make sure that the level of economic activity around the world was always consistent with the ability of the Earth to cope with it, at least as far as greenhouse emissions were concerned. It would re-link the monetary system to reality and the world, though it may require a global re-negotiation akin to the original Bretton Woods conference to achieve.

Other books to read

Richard Douthwaite (2006) *The Ecology of* Money, Green Books, Totnes, UK
Jubilee Plus (2000) *It Takes Two to Tango*, New Economics Foundation, London
Paul Krugman (1994) *Peddling Prosperity,* W. W. Norton, New York
Ann Pettifor (ed.) (2004) *Real World Economic Outlook*, Palgrave Macmillan, London
Ann Pettifor (2006) *The Coming First World Debt Crisis*, Palgrave Macmillan, London

Notes

1   OECD (2008) 4 April.
2   Andrew Simms, Dan Moran and Peter Chowla (2006) *The UK Interdependence Report*,
     New Economics Foundation, London.
3   Tax Justice Network (2005) *The Price of Offshore*, London.
4   Tax Justice Network (2006) *Mind the Tax Gap*, London.
5   Richard Adams and John Page (2003) *International Migration, Remittances, and Poverty
     in Developing Countries,* World Bank, Washington DC.
6   BBC news (2004) 18 March.
7   Susanna Mitchell (2006) *Migration and Remittance Euphoria*, New Economics
     Foundation, London.
8   Peter Spufford (2005) 'From Antwerp to London: The decline of European financial
     centres', *Ortelius Lecture*, Netherlands Institute for Advanced Study, The Hague.
9   Ann Pettifor, Liana Cisneros and Alejandro Olmos Gaona (2001) *It Takes Two to Tango*,
     Jubilee Research, New Economics Foundation, London.
10   See www.jubileedebtcampaign.org.uk.
11   Walden Bello (2007) 'Free trade versus small farmers', *Global Asia*, April.
12   Ann Pettifor (2006) *The Coming First World Debt Crisis,* Palgrave Macmillan,
     Basingstoke.
13   *The Independent* (2006) 28 September.
14   *The Independent* (2006) 28 September.
15   See for example James Grant (1994) *Money of the Mind*, Farrar, Strauss and Giroux, New
     York.
16   Mohammed Yunus (2004) *Banker to the Poor*, PublicAffairs, New York.
17   Henry Palmer and Pat Conaty (2003) *Profiting from Poverty: Why Debt is Big Business
     in Britain*, New Economics Foundation, London.
18   James Robertson (1998) *Beyond the Dependency Culture*, Adamantine Press, London.
19   Pat Conaty, Mick Brown and Bob Paterson (2004) *Community Banking Partnership*,
     New Economics Foundation, London.
20   New Economics Foundation (2006) *Odious Lending: Debt Relief as if Morals Mattered*,
     London.
21   Ann Pettifor (2002) *Chapter 9/11: Resolving International Debt Crises*, New Economics
     Foundation, London.
22   *New York Times* (1921) 8 December.
23   Richard Douthwaite (1999) *The Ecology of Money*, Green Books, Totnes.

11
The Future

But while I pondered all these things, and how men fight and lose the battle, and the thing that they fought for comes about in spite of their defeat, and when it comes turns out not to be what they meant, and other men have to fight for what they meant under another name.
William Morris, *A Dream of John Ball* (1988)

Great Barrington in western Massachusetts is one of those small American towns that has bucked the trend. It still has a high street full of locally owned shops and a thriving network of local banks. It has access to a range of local food, which is fresh and healthy. There is life in Great Barrington, when – in thousands of other places from there to the Pacific – town centres are windswept places devoid of life, business or people.

What makes Great Barrington interesting is that it seems to carry within it some of the elusive answers that economics has been missing. It has become a test bed for the new economics, led by the nearby E. F. Schumacher Society, one of the most inspirational think tanks in the USA. The Schumacher Society is the creation of the pacifist pioneer and carpenter Bob Swann and his partner Susan Witt, and it is behind the community land trusts that are keeping housing affordable. They have their own pioneering micro-credit schemes, to help launch people into enterprising careers, even when the conventional banks won't touch them. And they are behind the berkshares currency, nearly $2 million of which has been issued in and around Great Barrington to keep the wheels of the local economy turning, and to maximize the way that it engages local people, food and resources where possible.[1]

Berkshares was launched in 2006 as a series of beautiful notes, which can be bought at a 10 per cent discount and spent and circulated around Great Barrington, and banked in many of the local banks – unlike the UK, Americans have managed to retain their local banking network. The notes are designed by local artists and include pictures of local heroes, an unintentional consequence of which is that some are snapped up by collectors. But most berkshares stay circulating locally. They don't get sucked out of the local economy in the way that money tends to be when communities lack a diverse mix of businesses, a healthy share of which are locally owned, and source and sell a good proportion of local products and services. They make sure local resources are used effectively, whether they are material or human. The fact that they are used quite so widely is a testament partly to the design of the currency, and the understanding and commitment of local people, but also to the need for something that keeps the local human, distinctive and alive.

Contrast Great Barrington with another small American town, some 2000 miles away in the foothills of the Rocky Mountains (see Chapter 1). You could choose a million different impoverished towns, empty former agricultural belts, empty docks that had bustled for centuries until now, but – in conventional terms at least – Black Hawk, Colorado is nominally a success. It has money rolling through it, but there is almost no economic activity apart from gambling, and the local website warns people not to bring children to the town.

Great Barrington is different because its wealth is inclusive. It builds diversity and resilience. It makes the town safer from the cold winds of economic change. All three of these values are the precise opposite of the wider effects of conventional economic success, which tends to breed division, monoculture and economic dependence. The prevailing economic view, which still has the decision makers of the world in its grip, is an ideology dressed up as a science that creates billionaires, yet which also accelerates poverty, financial and spiritual.

Great Barrington is not alone. The Marsh Farm estate outside Luton, UK, which was one of the pioneers of **nef**'s Local Alchemy programme, was one of those places that have suffered from the way conventional regeneration tends to vacuum life and finance out of outlying places. The local shops had closed, even the employer at the heart of the estate had gone. In conventional terms, the people there were economically powerless, supplicants to big agencies and big business. But the new economics analyses these situations differently. It denies that money is the only possible asset. The empty building on the estate was an asset, and that has now been refurbished, with the help of the government's New Deal for Communities programme, and will eventually be the base for a series of new enterprises on the estate. But through the work of **nef**, the local organizations on Marsh Farm also carried out a survey to find out what money they had actually spent, and where it leaked out of the local economy. They found that, between them, they were spending over £1 million on fast food takeaways every year, all outside the estate. As a result, they are now setting up a healthy fast food business on the estate, employing local people. They have also leased one of the nearby unused fields in order to provide food for the business, and employ more local people.

More radically, they have begun to turn globalization on its head by linking up with an impoverished community of tea growers in south India, who sell them cut price fair trade tea direct – avoiding all the middlemen and supermarkets – and selling it on at low cost on the estate. They have recently received their first consignment of a tonne of tea. It is a whole new dimension to fair trade, which is not just fair to the impoverished growers but to the impoverished consumers. It means the final decision about price is made at a very late stage, when it is clear – within the constraints of the cost of production – what the receiving community can afford.

These are not just a series of bright ideas. They are putting some of the principles of the new economics into practice – a broader idea of assets, using the people, land and buildings that are wasted by the conventional economy, and putting them to use in fair and ethical trade. They dovetail with the principles behind the success of Great Barrington. They are also among a growing list of places that have used those new economic principles to change the way the system works.

These include the Grameen Bank (see Chapter 10), which was the original model of micro-credit. They include the network of cooperatives in Mondragon in Spain, which successfully began substituting their imports with food and products made locally by local people, using local resources after the Second World War, and guided by their local Roman Catholic priest. There are a whole range of innovative local banks, local currencies, food cooperatives and networks that are putting similar ideas into practice.

The new economics is still feeling its way towards many of the answers, but it asks challenging questions of the status quo – the ruling elites with their creaking economic ideas – and those questions imply something about where the answers might lie. People are poor because the assets they need have been taken from them, or simply devalued, leaving them impoverished. It implies that, if we can recognize those assets, measure them and put them to use, we might begin to make real, unambiguous progress. If the legal and organizational economic institutions of the world are weighted in favour of the rich, then we need to reform and reorganize those institutions. Out of these questions, new directions and concepts begin to emerge – together with a whole raft of new, more difficult questions. How do we provide resources for welfare in a dynamic equilibrium economy? How do we sell the new economics to those whose privileges will be undermined? But the beginnings of the answers are there, in a series of building blocks and techniques (see Appendix B), which amount to a work in progress.

Many of the original campaigning demands of the new economics, as set out in the 1980s, are also now mainstream. Green taxation is limited but is on the political agenda all over the world. The ideas behind environmental and social auditing of companies are widely accepted, and many companies produce reports even though their variable quality merely highlights the limits of voluntary approaches to corporate responsibility. Around £10 billion is invested ethically in the UK alone.[2] New ways of measuring that reveal the true environmental and social success or failure of the economy are starting to push older, cruder measures aside. There are anything up to 9000 complementary currencies in the world, though this is still primarily a technique used by mainstream business in the barter and reward points industries.[3]

Here is the rub. Simply because these new economic techniques have not been stitched together as an underlying philosophy, there has been a tendency for the mainstream to pick and choose a few ideas and bend them to their own purposes. That is the danger. If the mainstream economy has become a machine for creating poverty in both the direct and broader sense of the word – and it has – then failing to stitch the new economics together into a seamless challenge means that it is liable to be used partly in order to maintain the status quo. The old economic institutions are still in place and there is a tendency for the most enlightened reforms to find themselves co-opted by the status quo in return for small, temporary local effects.

There is a bigger problem. Ever since money was invented 6000 years ago – as a method for renting out women – it has carried within it this same damaging disconnect from real life and underlying, intrinsic value. That gap, between the narrowness and blindness of money and the realities it fails to measure, can seem impossible to bridge. But this is precisely the gap that new economics is designed to narrow. When it is stitched together, the new economics works, and is doing so on every continent, from the micro-hydro systems in the mountains of Nepal to the pocket parks of New York City, from the food co-ops of Tokyo to the complementary currencies of Thailand, Argentina and Japan.

* * *

The final words for this book have been written in the midst of the extraordinary events of the autumn of 2008, as – one by one – the great names of Wall Street investment banking disappeared into bankruptcy, state ownership or different regulatory regimes. Meanwhile, on this side of the Atlantic, the former mutual building societies, turned into banks with such a trumpet from policy makers a decade go, have one by one disappeared into a similar abyss. President George W. Bush found himself presiding over the biggest socialist-style nationalization in American history. His successor, Barack Obama, has set out a parallel bail out, even more spectacular.

The significance is enormous. Not only are those who have advised us about our finances, personally and politically, been revealed as incompetent and self-deluding, but many of the predictions and warnings by the new economics tradition over the past quarter of a century seem to be coming to pass. The sadness is that they do so in the most uncomfortable way for those most affected, who are often the least equipped to cope. The American model of economics has failed as finally and spectacularly as the Soviet model did in 1989. Ironically, the era of triumphal, finance-driven turbo-capitalism that once was acclaimed as the background scenery to the end of history lasted a shorter time than the bleak and brutal Russian communism whose failure it gloated over. But it is by no means clear yet either whether politicians have recognized this or whether they are aware of the risk of some of the alternatives. Chinese capitalism is a potential dark night of totalitarianism. It is by no means clear that the humane, human-scale open markets of the new economics will be able to flower in the face of that kind of centralization in a country that enjoys potentially absolute advantage in all spheres of economic life, not just comparative advantage in a few.

The hurricane of change through the financial markets has been so overwhelming that there is another bizarre conundrum that might have made a chapter title, and based on the American insurance giant's sponsorship of a major UK football team: why are American taxpayers sponsoring Manchester United? The answer is that they nationalized the football club's sponsor, the insurance giant AIG.

Add to this crisis the increasing failure of the great bureaucracies of state, struggling under the weight of their own complexity, the rise of externalities capable of crushing the basic tasks of welfare, health and education, the pensions time bomb and other crises outlined in Chapter 1, and you have the background to the rise of the new economics – and a handful of reasons why it will become increasingly prominent. The emerging crisis is, in its own way, speeding the adoption of new economics solutions.

But the crisis that is driving change most immediately apart from that is probably about our energy and climate. The Stern report finally brought the business of global warming into the remit of old economists.[4] As we reach the peak of oil production, we can almost certainly expect enormous hikes in the price of oil, combined with enormous and unpredictable dips. This last crisis is the most important as far as the new economics is concerned, because it turns on its head all the assumptions of recent generations about the economics of local production. We have developed many of our institutions in a period where energy was so cheap that it was worthwhile to truck a consignment of beans grown in The Netherlands down to Italy – or further afield – just for packaging, and then send it all the way back again. Our just-in-time distribution systems depend on cheap energy. If energy becomes expensive, none of that works any more. We need to find not just decentralized sources of energy that no longer waste a third in transmission, but decentralized food production systems too – and those are likely to include very small family production as well, which will increase access to land for the poorest.

The question is no longer whether aspects of this massive localization are going to happen, with the accompanying reskilling of local people to deal with the new local tasks and roles, but – as fossil fuels become expensive – *when* it will happen.

What this change means is that the real cost of energy is finally being reflected in the price of everything. This will make renewable energy investment immediately economic, as well as local food production, and a range of other changes. But to reap the benefits, and build a new economics on the back of that shift, we will need a more fundamental change in the way success and failure – nationally, locally, institutionally and individually – are measured in economics. Once again, the first signs of this are emerging already, but we have yet to see the new measurements linked properly to decisions about funding and investment in the way that they need to be – and will be once the mainstream understands that these are ways of measuring future risk and success.

Changes in measurement, and shifts in the cost of energy, are the twin changes that are driving the new economics. These will represent a shift in the basic engines of the world as fundamental as the Copernican revolution in science. If Copernicus discovered that the Earth actually revolves around the sun, rather than the other way around, the new economics insists that the economy exists to serve people rather than the other way around – and not just a tiny elite.

Both these imply a third vital change, this time in the nature of business, away from the idea that businesses are amoral entities that occasionally fling a little largesse on the community around them, so that businesses become primarily drivers that improve the world. There are dangers in this, of course. We do not want to confine imagination and innovation to a narrowly puritanical approach to human utility. On the other hand, the current situation, which massively favours the useless and damaging over the useful and creative, is no longer defensible. This is an important institutional shift, and requires a whole new generation of financial services that will make it happen. These changes are again in their earliest stages, though there are already major businesses that have, as their main purpose, creative and profit-making solutions to human and planetary problems.

They require a range of different institutional changes, including new models of financing, prices that genuinely reflect the impact of human and environmental costs, and a new kind of ownership structure that no longer overpays investors. These are beginning to emerge. They need to be joined by a new global network of regulations and institutions to replace the creaking network we now have, which is little better than medieval, in the worst sense of the word.

***

In the summer of 2007, before the full storm clouds of financial crisis gathered, a group of green economists met in the upstairs room of a small café in the backstreets of Vauxhall in London. They set about pulling together a set of solutions that could tackle the three climate, credit and oil-related crunches together. The group eventually included the *Guardian* economics editor, two former directors of Friends of the Earth, one of the authors of this book, and a number of other well-known names. What they published in July 2008 was known as the 'Green New Deal', launched 75 years after President Roosevelt launched a New Deal to rescue the USA from financial crisis.[5]

The Green New Deal urged governments to embrace a comprehensive, self-reinforcing programme including to:

- invest in a major programme of renewable energy and wider environmental transformation that would create thousands of new green collar jobs;
- build a new alliance between environmentalists, industry, agriculture and unions to put the interests of the real economy ahead of those of footloose finance;
- set up an Oil Legacy Fund, paid for by a windfall tax on the profits of oil and gas companies, as part of a wide-ranging package of financial innovations and incentives to assemble the tens of billions of pounds that need to be spent, including local authority green bonds, green gilts and green family savings bonds;
- make sure fossil fuel prices include the cost to the environment, and are high enough to tackle climate change by creating economic incentives to drive efficiency and bring alternative fuels to market;
- cut corporate tax evasion by clamping down on tax havens and corporate financial reporting;
- re-regulate the domestic financial system, inspired by reforms implemented in the 1930s, including cutting interest and much tighter regulation of the wider financial environment;
- break up the discredited financial institutions that have needed so much public money to prop them up in the latest credit crunch.

Taken together, the Green New Deal urged a programme of re-regulating finance and taxation plus a huge transformational programme aimed at substantially reducing the use of fossil fuels and, in the process, tackling the unemployment and decline in demand caused by the credit crunch. It involved policies and new funding mechanisms that will reduce emissions and allow us to cope better with the coming energy shortages caused by peak oil. The importance was not so much the details of the plan, but its pattern. What the Green New Deal understood was that these crises needed to be tackled together, in a way that modern government finds difficulty doing. There is no point in tackling the crises alone, nor is it possible. Tackling climate change needs to be done alongside redistributing the wealth of the planet. Tackling energy poverty needs to be done alongside investing in a new kind of workforce. All these shifts will move the new economics a little further from theory to action.

Aspects of the Green New Deal have been taken up and copied from the United Nations to Barack Obama's administration in the USA. It is a means to a series of ends that are at the heart of the new economics, the characteristics of which are set out at the ends of these chapters, but which includes the following principles:

- changing the nature of corporations so that they are legally accountable to society at large, and are structured in such a way that their prime purpose is to tackle the basic problems of humanity;
- making sure that the scale of the economy and our levels of consumption within it, respect environmental limits – the planet's biocapacity to provide resources and absorb waste safely;
- rebuilding the financial sector from below so that productive enterprise can get the sustainable funding it needs, and financial services return to providing the basic plumbing to achieve this;
- creating open markets, kept free of the distorting power of large corporations, that prioritize local trade and culture over speculation;
- reorganizing the way we measure success in economics so that prices reflect their full costs and decisions are based on human well-being rather than the false progress of fluctuating money growth;
- re-forging local democracy in its broadest sense, to revitalize public services with an influx of citizens, and to revitalize local life by reasserting local control and deliberative decision making;
- rebuilding the core economies of community and family.

There are undoubtedly major barriers to the emergence of this, because the status quo has the most enormous ability to survive. Using modern communications, it is endlessly possible to subvert new ideas and just use those aspects of them that benefit the elite. If the new economics is going to successfully transform the way the economic system works, its proponents might be well advised to follow the advice of Jesus Christ, that – to be effective – you have to be as wise as serpents and as harmless as doves.

Harmless in the sense that a revolutionary overthrow of the status quo is vulnerable to a brutal and counterproductive backlash and may, in any case, be unnecessary. What the new economics has to do instead is to provide an alternative to the system that works better and is more attractive for people and planet, especially as solutions for the crises. Nor is it sensible for the proponents of a new economics to wait around until the system and its institutions are completely transformed by international treaty and legislation. If you wait for the government to do it, said Ebenezer Howard – urging the creation of a series of new garden cities a century ago – 'you will be as old as Methuselah'.[6] The new economics is also a series of techniques that amount to a massive change in themselves, and people can set them to work and – by doing so – find themselves relying less on a mainstream system that starves them of what they need. They can use the lifeboats and reduce the power of the system that assumes they don't have any.

But we need to be as wise as serpents too. The new economics therefore requires a parallel new politics. This is partly because the old assumptions of economics – though they have long since been superseded by imaginative new approaches – remain alive and, unfortunately, well in the political system. Remember, again, Keynes' warning on the apparently independent 'practical men' who were slaves of some 'defunct economists'. The same is true of the corridors of power. We need a politics capable of forging the framework for a new economics.

But there is another sense in which we need a new politics, because the massive re-localization of the economy leaves politicians with an embarrassing dilemma. And a question as well: what are they for in this new local world? They are trapped in a role that assumes they must be the great providers, sitting on top of a giant and dysfunctional government machine, receiving the supplications of grateful constituents and distributing largesse.

It is a role that is rapidly disappearing, because the levers of change that Sir Keith Joseph warned a generation ago were not connected to anything, are often local. Just as professionals are increasingly coming to terms with their own powerlessness, unless – as the new economics explains – they are working alongside their clients and their neighbours, the same is now true of politicians. They need a new role as local catalysts and leaders, and the best ones are now playing that role – without pretending to have a finger on levers of power that are increasingly delusory. But we need alongside that some sense of the grammar of change, how to make things happen sustainably – not just until the next swing of political fashion.

* * *

Will the new economics become mainstream? You could say that the original sin at the heart of economics – the 6000-year-old disconnect between money and life – is just too ancient to be healed. You could also say that whatever the system is, it will be used for their own ends by the rich and powerful. The new economics is sceptical about solutions that pose as a single magic bullet, whether they are interest-free money or land tax, important as they may be to the eventual solution.

Yet it is still possible to organize new institutions – social, administrative and economic – that can force our economic systems to make life thrive rather than stifling it. Beyond that, the new economics tradition has emerged from a range of influences, some mainstream, some emphatically not, to offer a more fundamental approach, and a set of solutions that are already at work all over the world and with increasing success.

Some of those solutions are radical and dramatically effective, at least potentially so. Some of them are the kind of thing that anyone can do, and millions are doing around the world, insisting that their values, ethics and morality have an impact on the way they spend their money. Some of them are already mainstream, having floated up through mixed market economies. But the basic problems that new economics is emerging to solve are horribly with us, and the solutions are increasingly urgent. The new economics is a challenge and an opportunity to those who run the world, and they are already adopting some of the assumptions that lie behind this book. Without any fanfare or announcement, and barely perceptibly, the 'practical men' that Keynes lambasted are taking on the mores and methods of the new economics.

But we can't wait for them to do so. We can't just wait until we wake up and find either that the crises of people and planet have overwhelmed us, or that the existing establishment has seamlessly accepted the ideas they so ridiculed a generation ago. We can't wait for human evolution to move slowly forward again. We have to use some of the ideas in this book, both in our lives and in the institutions we work in, and put the new economics to work.

Notes

1   See www.smallisbeautiful.org.
2   See www.eiris.org.
3   Peter North (2007) *Money and Liberation*, University of Minesota Press, Minneapolis.
4   Nicholas Stern (2006) *The Economics of Climate Change*, HM Treasury, London.
5   Green New Deal Group (2008) *A Green New Deal*, New Economics Foundation, London.
6   Quoted in Dennis Hardy (1991) *From Garden Cities to New Towns*, Routledge, London.

Appendix A
From the Ashes of the Crash:
20 First Steps from New Economics
to Rebuild a Better Economy

This programme was published in November 2008, during the banking crisis. It assumes a UK audience, but can be applied in other countries too. It claims that the crisis in the global system that was both predictable and, in fact, predicted, was the most important sign yet that a new economics is emerging. The tragedy is that the crisis-ridden financial system has long since failed to do the basic job required of it – which is to underpin the productive economy and the fundamental natural and social operating systems upon which we all depend. These have been variously neglected, taken for granted or cannibalized by finance. They include the core economy of family, neighbourhood, community and society, and the natural economy of the biosphere, our oceans, forests and fields.

Worse, even when the financial system is working at full throttle, it corrodes the real economy – by its sheer profitability and faulty measuring – and dominates the policy priorities of politicians.

If nothing else, the crisis provides an opportunity to rebuild a financial infrastructure that actually works for people and the planet. This means investing – not just bailing out failed banks – but in loan facilities that support an interdependent network of productive local economies, which genuinely underpin life, and work within the tolerance levels of the natural environment. This doesn't mean starting from scratch. Just beneath the surface is the sleeping architecture of a new, diverse and resilient local financial system. As the fissures in the old system threaten to crack open with potentially devastating consequences the good news is that those living on the economic front line have been developing and building alternative methods of saving, exchanging and lending that we can learn from, and multiply to create a thriving, resilient network able to fill the gaps left by the collapse of the old order.

We make a number of proposals that include measures both for immediate stabilization of the economy and for long-term restructuring. Here are several short- to long-term steps that, in the midst of the crisis, we believe will breathe life into a phoenix-like new economy.

What is new is that these are no longer distant dreams on a hopeful wish list. Because the state now owns a large slice of the financial system these are things we can do now. Measures can be put directly into place. The argument that they are impossible because the state cannot intervene directly to shape the financial system has fallen. Massive intervention has already occurred.

But as we aim for recovery, we shouldn't simply try to get back to how things were before. That was unsustainable for many reasons. We must make sure that the means by which we find our way out of the crisis – through injecting liquidity into the system, and looking for signs of recovery in the return of consumer binge spending on the high street – don't, perversely, build a larger crisis for the future. Done well, responding to the triple crunch of the credit, climate and natural resources crises provides the opportunity for transformational change.

* * *

1 Demerge banks that are 'too big to fail' – to reduce the risks of systemic failure

Instead of further consolidation, the discredited financial institutions that have needed so much public money to prop them up during the credit crisis should be reduced to a size whereby their failure would not jeopardize the system itself. We are calling for the forced demerger of large banking and finance groups. Retail banking should be split from both corporate finance (merchant banking) and from securities dealing. The demerged units should then be split into smaller banks. Mega-banks make mega-mistakes that affect us all. Instead of institutions that are 'too big to fail', we need institutions that are small enough to fail without creating problems for depositors and the wider public.

In the rush to nationalize and force 'shotgun weddings' on the banks, we are storing up worse crises for the future. A major cause of the meltdown has been unchecked consolidation of the banking sector. The latest planned merger, Lloyds TSB with Halifax Bank of Scotland, is not just a messy name; it reveals regulatory short sightedness. A truly resilient financial system has a multitude of financial actors, making diverse investments and taking different kinds of risks so that if one is hit by crisis, the others aren't dragged down with it. It is no accident that the safest UK bank according to its safe financial reserves (so-called Tier 1 capital) is the Nationwide – a mutually owned building society. The government is set to own great swathes of our financial system: Northern Rock, RBS, Lloyds TSB, HBOS. It should take the chance to demerge these behemoths that grew so complicated that they couldn't keep track of our money or their own money. A rich, diverse ecology of different economic systems is needed, not a banking monoculture of giant actors which, when they topple, threaten us all.

2 Segregate financial markets – by separating activities such as trading and retail banking

A central plank of the process of financial de-regulation has been the removal of restrictions on what activities different institutions can undertake. It took more than 50 years for policy makers to forget the lessons of the Wall Street crash of 1929, which led to the Glass-Steagal Act in the USA to prevent financial institutions exploiting their market position and power and profiting from conflicts of interest. Segregation was seen as 'inefficient' and was swept away by liberalization. As institutions ceased to specialize and became financial 'conglomerates', they converged on the most profitable activities. During the boom this was largely trading (or speculative) activities, which paid handsome rewards, but also fuelled the boom itself. The flipside was that less profitable activities – such as maintaining a branch network and providing financial services for low-income people – became ever more marginalized. We need financial institutions to focus on specific functions and to do these well, not to chase the latest bandwagon. Formally segmenting the system by function ensures this diversity, but also allows appropriate regulation of each sector.

3 Bring onto the balance sheet, rigorously check and officially license all 'exotic' financial instruments

All such instruments should be brought onto the balance sheet and be subjected to the same regulatory capital requirements as other activities. They should also be properly licensed. All derivative products and other exotic instruments should be subjected to official inspection. Only those approved should be permitted to be traded. Anyone trying to circumvent the rules by going offshore or onto the internet should face the simple and effective sanction of 'negative enforcement' – their contracts would be made unenforceable in law. Ultimately our aim is an orderly downsizing of the financial sector in relation to the rest of the economy.

4 Create a secure, accessible local banking system for people by growing the role of post offices

Following on from the reforms above, and in the context of building new, stable, secure financial institutions to meet local economic needs, such as mutuals, credit unions and cooperatives, the Post Office should be grown into a national banking system that delivers stable, accessible and dependable services to the public and businesses. It stands to be one of the best guarantees underpinning economic resilience, promoting financial inclusion and allowing people to invest and save with confidence and security. But, more than that, deposits made through the Post Office Bank could play a vital role in reconnecting the banking system with the productive economy. As a trusted source of information and advice, and a vital part of the social fabric, the Post Office's role as a shopfront for the state should be expanded, providing direct, local access to a range of government services. Local and national government should be encouraged to direct services through the network. The government should halt the closure programme targeting 2500 local post offices and abandon plans to break up Royal Mail. Instead, it should build it up as both financially viable and as a cohesive social and economic institution. And, as an essential component, Royal Mail must be retained as a powerful national network and not cherry-picked by competitors and run down by a government and a regulator that have put too much faith in the deregulated market.

5 Enhance economic support for the local economy by expanding the range of smaller-scale 'friendly' sources of finance

For years, a network of alternative financial institutions has operated alongside conventional banks. They range from the well-known credit unions to the less-known community reinvestment trusts and community development finance institutions (CDFIs). Together they offer finance to both individuals and small enterprises, performing an especially important role in disadvantaged communities. They provide alternative sources for small-scale financial services, including savings, affordable loans, debt advice and financial literacy. Innovative approaches like the community banking partnership, already active in seven areas of the UK, connect these services together to provide a one-stop-shop alternative to the high street banks and predatory lenders. Government should invest in, scale up, and strengthen this network. CDFIs, in particular, provide vital consumer credit and finance for small businesses, including social enterprises, using the personal, supportive and advisory approach that banks once provided. In the current crisis, community lenders are reporting an increase in applications and enquiries. The current financial crisis leaves CDFIs vulnerable if banks cease lending to them, while at the same time demand for affordable credit increases. Government support has been short term and inadequate, leaving the sector without adequate funding to cover a gap created by banks. But the crisis could be an opportunity to use the leverage of public ownership to improve support to the sector. First, banks should disclose their lending patterns, revealing where there is systemic financial exclusion and provide information to rectify the situation. Banks could also work with CDFIs by referring clients and providing loan capital, receiving tax breaks or other incentives to do so. To help underpin the sector, government could use unclaimed assets to fund a social investment wholesaler.

6 Encourage the introduction of complementary, multilevel currencies to provide credit in tune with the needs of regions, towns, cities and neighbourhoods, whilst helping to inoculate the economy from financial shocks

Complementary currencies have a successful track record of providing local means of exchange, when money is running short in the local economy. Successful models are now running all over the world, keeping local resources circulating locally and providing independence for impoverished communities from government largesse. They can provide low-cost or free credit, and – in some countries – they underpin whole sectors of the economy. But they also do much more than that. Because they often require face-to-face exchange, they build the relationships and understanding that productive economic and social life depends on. This close connection also means that they help to create responsive local economic ecosystems that are better able to predict and respond to shocks. Many of them are modelled on the life-saving complementary currencies that grew up on both sides of the Atlantic during the Great Depression. Policy needs to be directed at encouraging a multiplicity of experiments, and providing an explicit legal power to local authorities to set up currencies systems – regulated by a new e-money regulator – and to accept them for local taxes and fines. At the international level, the global financial system needs to be underpinned by a new global reference currency, along the lines of the bancor proposed by Keynes at the Bretton Woods summit, and backed by a basket of commodities. This will make currencies safer from sudden collapse, and will also provide an added underpinning to economies in developing countries that are wealthier in raw materials.

7 Create new public money, free of interest, where necessary to cope with unprecedented financial emergencies, and as the basis for loans to rebuild the infrastructure of productive local economies

During the financial crisis of July 1914, David Lloyd George did this to underpin the banks. We should not make the mistake that the creation of money in other ways – in the form of bank lending – is somehow the only authentic way of doing it. Private banks have enjoyed a sizable, indirect subsidy through being allowed to create money, and there is no reason why money creation should not happen in the name of direct public benefit. The Bank of England should, for example, exercise its power to create money to provide the loan finance for the new local lending infrastructure. This should be repaid, free of interest, when the task is complete, and then withdrawn from circulation. (*Note: this proposal has been put into practice in a basic form by the UK government and is known as 'quantitative easing'.*)

8 Innovations for productive and secure savings (a): Introduce a 'People's Pension' to provide secure savings vehicles for retirement

Attempts to leverage private sector cash to pay for schools and hospitals have repeatedly been exposed as bad deals for the public. At the same time we now have a pension crisis. People in Britain are seeing their life savings destroyed by the fallout from the credit crisis. In 2003, **nef** proposed the idea of a 'People's Pension'; its approach gives people more control over where their savings go and what they are invested in. It proposes an adaptable model more insulated from market turbulence than orthodox pensions schemes. As such, it will be more attractive to the millions of people seeking financial security in old age. It will be capable of raising large sums of money to invest in necessary public services and can easily be adapted to invest in immediate local priorities. The People's Pension would be backed by People's Pension Funds. These entirely new funds will be created to provide a way in which pension contributions can be invested in building new public infrastructure projects, such as schools and universities, hospitals and other health facilities, transport systems (including railways, trams and bus networks), social housing and sustainable energy systems.

9 Innovations for productive and secure savings (b): Enable 'local bonds' as a secure investment vehicle for savers that also helps to finance essential investment and new infrastructure for a more environmentally sustainable Britain

The scope for innovation is broad. A range of products could be introduced, connected to the stronger local financial infrastructure discussed above. These could include local authority green bonds, green gilts and green family savings bonds and publicly approved enterprises, all of which could help deliver the mass transition to a cleaner more environmentally sustainable Britain on a path of low-carbon economic transition, whilst creating more secure vehicles for savings. These investments would also stimulate productive local economic activity, and yield rich rewards through job creation – critical as our service-based economy shored up by unsustainable credit feels the effect of the economic slowdown.

10 Housing

(a) Introduce a moratorium on home evictions related to the crash and reckless lending

The credit crisis is inseparable from distortions in the housing market. To prevent the current misery of those who can no longer afford their mortgages and to prevent a future recurrence, we make three proposals. First, to deal with the immediate crisis, there should be a moratorium on credit-crisis-related home repossessions. While the banks, which are at fault, have been bailed out to a previously unimaginable degree by the taxpayer, thousands of hard-working homeowners face the daily insecurity of potential eviction as the recession makes it harder to meet repayments. This is deeply unjust, destabilizing and imposes a huge burden on society. Evictions could be stopped and in their place could be put long-term plans for restructuring householders' mortgage debts.

(b) Use this chance to rebuild the UK's stock of social housing
Following on from the above, in the event of homeowners defaulting to one of the newly nationalized banks and mortgage providers, another option is open to government. Houses facing repossession could be taken into the stock of public housing. Under careful negotiation this would prevent a rise in homelessness and help reverse the decline of social housing in Britain. It would head off a potential future social problem and add to the taxpayers assets.

(c) Implement radical innovations to prevent a repeat of destructive house price inflation
Thirdly, there is an opportunity to introduce and increase in scale new forms of 'mutual' home ownership – separating the cost of the land from the purchase price of the housing on it. This is achievable in practice by taking the land out of the marketplace through a Community Land Trust. This innovative American mechanism can make housing much more affordable and keep the cost of home ownership in a closer relationship with average earnings in perpetuity. Such an approach would end the extreme and unsustainable ratio of house prices to income. Like other owner–occupiers, mutual homeowners will have the opportunity to invest in their home and the incentive to look after and improve it. At the same time, the land can be held in trust for the benefit of future generations and the community as a whole. Successful examples already exist but there is now a role of more ambitious community land banks that would create scope to find a match with new municipal bonds or other forms of targeted, low-interest capital.

11 Take a 'social investment approach' to public services, measure and reward broader value creation
Unprecedented investment in banking stability has been justified on the lines that the cost of doing nothing would be far greater. The same logic can be applied to public services, when the cost of failing to deliver effective services is often far greater than the cost of ensuring them. Recent **nef** research found that for every £1 spent on alternatives to prison that reduce reoffending, an additional £14 worth of social value is generated. Also, when we value the long-term benefits of sound relationships and stable homes for children in care, we could see returns of up to £6. These savings over 20 years could pay for the entire annual care bill each year. If measured properly,

investment in public services can have returns that demonstrate their 'worth'. While they may not yield immediate financial returns, they can nonetheless generate substantial social value. We've learnt to our cost how hard it is to define 'real value'. Banks with balance sheets that looked healthy to regulators and rating agencies six months ago were brought to the brink, or tipped over the edge of bankruptcy. Some 'assets' became worthless. At **nef** we have been developing a methodology called social return on investment (SROI), which allows a comparison of the value created by a given investment in social, environmental and financial terms – the triple bottom line. Now that the government is the largest shareholder in UK banks, it can redefine value creation in the financial system, and introduce incentives that reward the production of broader social, economic and environmental value.

12 Tap into the hidden value of time banking and grow the 'core economy'

As communities and local economies face the stress of recession, time banking should be promoted as an exchange that can knit communities together and reduce financial pressure on public services. Time banking allows more human assets, including those of people who are underemployed or unemployed, to be usefully engaged in the local economy. As faith in the money-based economy collapses, the value of time as an alternative means of exchange should be recognized and embedded into public services to increase individual and community resilience and reduce demand on hard-pressed resources. Time banking – a practical tool for enabling people to be involved in producing public services – can revitalize schools, hospitals, public housing and even the youth justice system. Time banking is a tried and tested way of growing the 'core economy' – the abundant wealth of human assets that are largely neglected by the machinery of state and eroded by the market system. These assets are embedded in the everyday lives of every individual (time, wisdom, experience, energy, knowledge, skills) and in the relationships between them (love, empathy, watchfulness, care, reciprocity, teaching and learning). Another way of doing this is to make sure that the public services that depend on the financial resources drawn from taxation and professional expertise work in equal partnership with the people they are supposed to serve. Doing so would dramatically increase their resource base and radically transform the way they operate, creating a positive upward spiral.

13 Improve checks and balances by introducing capital controls

Re-regulating the international finance sector is an urgent priority, as is reducing its size in relation to the real economy, to prevent a repeat of the recent destructive distortions. This is a precondition to transforming both national economies and the global economy. Finance will have to be returned to its role as servant, not master, of the global economy, to dealing prudently with people's savings and providing regular capital for productive and sustainable investment. Regulation of finance, and the restoration of policy autonomy to democratic government, implies the reintroduction of capital controls. Governments need the freedom to use capital control as an active component of economic policy, to encourage certain types of capital flow and to discourage others. The Asian financial crisis of the late 1990s made it very clear that countries with capital controls were both insulated from the crisis and retained policy autonomy to pursue their national economic priorities. The current crisis drives the final nail in the coffin of the idea that countries should simply abandon all interference with international financial markets. The logic for doing so is that allowing completely open access would bring major economic benefits – there is no evidence at all that this is what has happened, but plenty of evidence that the opposite is true.

14 Make taxation work

In the new period of public resources being enormously stretched by support given to the banks, it will be vital to minimize corporate tax evasion by clamping down on tax havens and corporate financial reporting. Tax should be deducted at source (from the country from which payment is made) for all income paid to financial institutions in tax havens. International accounting rules should be changed to eliminate transfer mispricing by requiring corporations to report on a country-by-country basis. These measures will provide much-needed sources of public finance at a time when economic contraction is reducing conventional tax receipts. As an organizing principle, we should also move towards taxing more what we want less of, such as pollution and unsustainable consumption of natural resources, and taxing less what we want more of, such as those activities needed for the environmental transformation of the economy. This transition should be managed not only to just protect the poor, but so that it reduces inequality, just as Roosevelt's original New Deal did in the 1930s (see point 16). For example, pensions could be adjusted to enable people to save energy rather than just pay for more fuel.

15 Increase stability and raise resources with currency and financial transaction taxes

Financial flows play a vital role in local, national and international economies, but too little of the vast edifice we have created has any relation to the real economy. Rather than a means to an end, finance has become the end in itself, with short-term, high-frequency trading strategies turning over trillions of dollars every day in global markets, often for no public benefit but – as we see all too clearly today – at a huge cost. We need to discourage the short-term, speculative moving of paper assets but to encourage long-term, sustainable investment. A small tax on international currency transactions would discourage short-term, high-frequency trading (you pay the tax every time you trade) but leave longer-term, real investment unaffected. It is estimated that, globally, a tax of just 0.005 per cent would raise billions of dollars annually, while also 'throwing sand in the wheels' of the global currency markets and reconnecting the financial and real economies.

16 Launch a Green New Deal to fight the recession whilst tackling energy insecurity and climate change

The UK needs a Green New Deal, taking inspiration from Roosevelt's New Deal of 1933. It will address the triple crunch of the credit crisis, high oil prices and global warming. Such a plan would rein in reckless financial institutions and use a range of fiscal tools, new measures and reforms to the tax system, such as a windfall tax on oil companies. The resources raised would then be invested in a massive environmental transformation programme that could insulate the economy from recession, create countless new jobs and allow the UK to play its part in meeting the climate change challenge. A key test is how, in economically stressed times, affordable finance can be made available in a targeted way to kick-start new, low-carbon, energy, transport, food and housing sectors. One useful precedent is the example of South Korea. Over years it channelled lines of low-cost credit to key parts of its economy. The success of this, policy can be measured in the fact that the sections of South Korea's industry that benefited are now 'world leaders'.

17 Pay for energy transition and fuel poverty: a windfall tax on the unearned profits of the fossil fuel companies to provide a safety net for those in fuel poverty, and to help finance the UK's transition to clean energy

Fossil fuels are an unrepeatable windfall from nature, yet the UK government has so far failed adequately to take advantage of its income from oil to prepare for a low-carbon future. Norway, by contrast, has used its oil surpluses to help create a safety net for future generations that is today worth around €260 billion (£198 billion). This amounts to €75,000 (£57,000) for every man, woman and child in the country. The UK could follow Norway's lead and set up an Oil Legacy Fund, paid for primarily by a windfall tax on oil and gas company profits. Before North Sea oil is exhausted, introducing a windfall tax on oil and gas companies would be a significant funding source. Part of these increased revenues would be used to protect low-income households subject to fuel poverty and who would otherwise be too adversely affected by fossil fuel price rises during the transition to a low-carbon future.

18 Hold accountancy firms accountable

Now there is an opportunity to reshape the world of auditing so that it reflects new expectations of transparency, prudence and responsibility in the modern global economy. The cosy world of the big professional services firms needs new measures to counter cronyism, re-regulate, improve auditor self-governance, and more broadly redefine the legal reporting duties of the finance sector. Ultimately, more radical and creative solutions may be needed. For example, the market domination of the Big Four could be broken up. But the outstanding question is how to give real ownership of such a vital public interest function back to its diverse stakeholders, for example by taking on a new, not-for-profit form. With fewer distractions, perhaps the accountants will be able to concentrate more on counting what matters, such as systemic risks posed to the economic architecture and productive economy. A parallel calling-to-account should be applied to the ratings agencies who chronically failed to assess true risk in the financial markets.

19 Introduce a maximum pay differential, or maximum wage

The distorting effect on the economy of massive city bonuses is now painfully obvious. The justification for high executive pay was always that the motivational effect on the senior executive and the aspirational impact on mid-level executives were greater than the demotivational impact on other employees. Not only has this been revealed to have serious unintended consequences, but the academic research to justify it is extremely patchy, and the empirical evidence is even less convincing. A study by a UK management consultancy, Kepler Associates, even found that in 2000 there was an inverse relationship between pay and performance in the FTSE 100. Ironically, more than 100 years ago, business guru J. P. Morgan said no company should have a differential between highest paid and lowest paid greater than ten. He thought that enough to create motivation. The Royal Navy, for example, has had a de facto differential of eight. Some Japanese firms voluntarily impose pay ratios limiting the gap between top and bottom pay. US basketball teams take a total remuneration package and pool it between players, with limits on any individual's pay. A minimum wage was one of the key achievements of New Labour's first term. Now it could tackle income inequality from the other end and propose a maximum wage. It matters both because the economic case for high executive pay in terms of company performance doesn't hold up, and because highly unequal societies have a habit of falling apart.

20 Take a 'five-a-day' approach to well-being to help beat the negative psychological effects of recession and build resilience

In the midst of the current economic gloom, the five ways to well-being recommendations, based on current well-being research, and developed by **nef** for the government's Foresight Programme's Mental Capital and Well-being Project, provide a range of simple steps that have nothing to do with spending money or consuming goods. They are oriented toward enhancing community, rather than materialistic and individualistic. They have been proved, when practised, to significantly add to people's well-being. Yet they are also the very things that the old economic system actively limits. Alongside other interventions they are one of the ways in which we can strengthen the invisible heart of the core economy – family, neighbourhood, community and civil society. The well-being five-a-day are:

- **Connect…** With the people around you, with family, friends, colleagues and neighbours, at home, work, school or in your local community.
- **Be active…** Go for a walk or run. Step outside. Cycle. Play a game. Garden. Dance. Most importantly, discover a physical activity you enjoy; one that suits your level of mobility and fitness.
- **Take notice…** This involves being curious, or remarking on the unusual or beautiful, such as noticing the changing seasons. Being aware of the world around you and what you are feeling, and reflecting on your experiences will help you appreciate what matters to you.
- **Keep learning…** Try something new. Rediscover an old interest. Sign up for that course. Take on a different responsibility at work. Fix a bike. Learn to play an instrument or how to cook your favourite food.
- **Give…** Do something for a friend, or a stranger. Thank someone. Smile. Volunteer your time. Join a community group. Look out, as well as in. Seeing yourself, and your happiness, linked to the wider community can be incredibly rewarding and will create connections with the people around you.

Appendix B
New Economics Tools and Techniques

The new economics is about changing the rules by which economics works, but it is also about making things happen locally – even under the current rules. The new economics recognizes that a neighbourhood's non-monetary assets – its diversity, history, distinctiveness, neighbourliness, know-how, enthusiasm – are as important as money to its economic success. The way that money flows around the local economy, and whether it stays circulating or flows away, is as important as the total amount of money.

Diverse ecosystems are more resilient to shocks in just the same way as diverse local economies, and people also want to invest and live in places that are 'real', not the bland identikit products of much of the regeneration industry. This appendix sets out some new economics ways forward:

BizFizz

BizFizz is an innovative programme for entrepreneurs, developed between **nef** and the Civic Trust, coaching local people to launch start-ups, micro and small enterprises, in areas experiencing economic disadvantage. It turns the passion and enthusiasm of individuals into a driving force for local economic renewal by mobilizing the skills and resources within communities. BizFizz works with passionate people in relatively small and defined communities where there is some level of economic disadvantage, using an innovative, individual approach based on coaching people to achieve their dreams – and backed by a local panel of key advisors and local business people. BizFizz has a proven record of increasing business start-up and survival, but also increases the confidence and sense of self-reliance among the community as a whole. **www.bizfizz.org.uk**

Community finance

Community development finance plays a vital role in the UK to address financial exclusion and underinvestment in disadvantaged areas through provision of finance

and money advice to individuals and enterprises. **nef** was instrumental in setting up the Social Investment Task Force, and introducing the idea of Community Investment Tax Relief, helped found the Community Development Finance Association, incubated the London Rebuilding Society, and is a founding partner in the Adventure Capital Fund, as well as of the European Microfinance Network. **nef** was involved in researching and assisting in the development of seven community banking partnerships in England and Wales, which partner credit unions, community development finance institutions and money advice agencies in the co-delivery of community finance services to low and moderate income households.
www.cdfa.org.uk

Community land trusts
Land trusts were developed at the Institute of Community Economics as a way of dividing the property, which can be owned outright, from the land it stands on, which is owned by a trust. This keeps property prices down and provides greater control over local land use. By separating the land costs from the building costs, community land trusts can reduce the cost of housing by half. They trace their roots to the cooperative land reform efforts of Robert Owen, the Chartists, John Ruskin and the garden cities movement, but the model was forgotten. **nef** worked with Community Finance Solutions at the University of Salford to lead research to help reintroduce community land trusts to England and Wales. **nef** has also developed with CDS Co-operatives a new model called Mutual Homeownership.
www.communitylandtrust.org.uk

Community reinvestment
Banks have a moral obligation – and in the USA this is a legal obligation – to lend money in places they are prepared to accept deposits from. The 1977 Act in the USA requires banks to reveal these patterns, in order to root out red-lining, and has levered considerable investment funds as a result. In the UK, banks are not compelled to disclose their lending patterns, and are increasingly withdrawing from deprived communities. The Community Reinvestment Act was updated under President Clinton in the early 1990s and it has generated billions of new investment for affordable housing and businesses in low and moderate income communities across the USA.
www.ncrc.org

Complementary currencies
When money runs short locally, it gets more difficult to link up those who want work done with those who want to do it. The solution is sometimes to launch a local currency that stays circulating locally, and has different rules attached.
www.smallisbeautiful.org

Co-production

Co-production is an approach to public service reform – and the reform of charity and philanthropy – which involves beneficiaries and their skills and time as a critical part of the success of any project. It is also a critique of public services, explaining why they fail to make sustainable change in individuals or neighbourhoods, and why there remains so much ill health, school failure and collapsing social fabric. It offers an approach that goes beyond simple representation on boards, and focuses on clients as vital assets that professionals need to engage if they are going to make long-term, sustainable progress – and which can weave neighbourhoods (what Cahn calls the core economy) back together again to underpin everything else.
www.timedollar.org

Democs

Democs (deliberative meeting of citizens) is part card game, part policy-making tool, allowing small groups of people to engage with complex public policy issues. Playing with Democs helps people find out about a topic, express their views, seek common ground with the other participants, and state their preferred policy position from a given choice of four. They can also add their own policy positions. The game is a simple way to help people identify and absorb the basic information they need to discuss an issue that may be complex and that they may not have discussed before, and has been used to tackle difficult issues like nuclear energy, climate change and medical ethics.
www.neweconomics.org/gen/democs.aspx

Ecological debt

Ecological debt is **nef**'s concept, which applies the language of international debt to the equitable sharing of global resources, where people in wealthy nations are using up far more than their fair share. In doing so, and by not paying for the consequences of global warming, rich countries are running up huge ecological debts to the poor, majority world. So far, the international response to climate change has failed to fully account for this ecological debt. Action has been confined by the limited ambitions of the Kyoto Protocol and the failure of governments to even stick to that. The policy implications of ecological debt suggest a fundamental realignment of power and responsibility between nations. The concept turns upside down both the debates on poor country debt and global warming. It puts poor people and poor countries on the international moral high ground, and in a stronger position to argue for a better deal.
www.footprintnetwork.org/overshoot

Ethical investment

Why invest for the future with companies that are also undermining it? People are increasingly shifting their investment money to places that have a clear ethical position, and £10 billion is now invested in this way in the UK.
www.eiris.org

Future search

Future search allows communities or organizations to create a shared vision for their future, by bringing together over two or three days a large group of people (usually 64) who are affected by the outcomes or have power or information on the topic at hand. The idea is to get the 'whole system' into the room, including everyone with a stake in the issue. This produces a rich mixture of information and ideas. Proposals are also more likely to be acted upon if all stakeholders feel committed to them.
www.futuresearch.net

Happy Planet Index

The Happy Planet Index is a study of human well-being and environmental impact, comparing the performance of each nation in helping people achieve long and happy lives. The index brings together **nef**'s work on well-being, social justice and environmental sustainability to take a very different look at the wealth and poverty of nations. The index – known as HPI – is a completely new metric that measures the ecological efficiency with which each country provides for its people's well-being. When it was first published in 2006, it was downloaded from the **nef** website over a million times. HPI strips the view of the economy back to its absolute basics: what we put in (resources), and what comes out (human lives of different length and happiness). The resulting index of the 178 nations for which data are available, reveals that the world as a whole has a long way to go.
www.happyplanetindex.org

Imagine

Imagine uses questions that focus local people's attention on success and encourages them to tell stories from their own experience of what works and, by doing so, helps them imagine a vision of the future that is created with a firm basis in reality. Imagine is an energizing and enjoyable UK adaptation of an American approach called Appreciative Inquiry, pioneered by Imagine Chicago, which helped draw people into planning a different future for their city. **nef** has used Imagine in a range of sectors, including recent work for the Four Squares Housing Estate in Bermondsey, Ryedale District Council's community strategy, Watford and Three Rivers Primary Care Trust, and a range of other organizations, services and towns.
en.wikipedia.org/wiki/Appreciative_Inquiry

Index of Sustainable Economic Welfare

The Index of Sustainable Economic Welfare (ISEW) is an indicator that aims to compensate for the inadequacies of GDP as a measure of national progress. It is an economic measure, which adjusts our overall economic welfare (as measured in terms of spending), by taking into account social and environmental costs, as well as forgotten social benefits such as the core economy. The ISEW, also known as the Genuine Progress Indicator (GPI) or Measure of Domestic Progress (MDP) was first developed in the USA, and developed for the UK by **nef** working in partnership with Professor Tim Jackson, Director of RESOLVE (the Research Group on Lifestyles Values and Environment). As well as calculating the ISEW for the UK as a whole, **nef** is in the second year of calculating annual updates of regional ISEWs on behalf of the English Regional Development Agencies.

http://community.foe.co.uk/tools/isew/

Local Alchemy

Local Alchemy is a programme of local economic transformation that starts with what neighbourhoods already have: the natural resourcefulness, skills and passions of the local people. The principle behind Local Alchemy, developed with the East Midlands Development Agency, is that the people who live and work in a place, and others who care about its future, are best positioned to find solutions, implement them and reap the rewards. It is designed to avoid the pitfalls of large-scale regeneration initiatives, which fail to meet local needs or aspirations or address the underlying causes of economic disadvantage. Local Alchemy supports individuals and groups to challenge the economic status quo in their local communities, using an economic toolkit to help them understand better about their local economy and what it could be if they worked together.

www.localalchemy.org.uk

Local distinctiveness

Local distinctiveness studies are a pioneering methodology to help local authorities and developers gather a clearer picture of what makes places distinctive – and hammer out a programme for making them more so. There is increasing evidence, not just that distinctiveness is important to the people who live somewhere, but that it is also important economically. Towns that look and feel different tend to have an energy and enterprise lacking in the others. They also often have a greater proportion of business that is owned locally – which means their income stays circulating locally for longer. Distinctiveness studies are not conventional marketing exercises. They assume that branding for towns must be underpinned by a distinct sense of place, rather than simply having some marketing message imposed from above.

www.commonground.org.uk

LM3

LM3 allows community organizations, business leaders or government agencies to measure how much their spending impacts on the local economy – and work out how they can change to improve that impact. LM3 adapts for local use the Keynesian multiplier, which has been used for nearly 80 years, to measure how income entering an economy then circulates within it. The theory is that a change in income has a multiplied impact on that economy. LM3 measures three rounds of local spending, and where the money goes. Organizations are increasingly using LM3 as a regeneration tool, to see the real effects of spending, and planning for new social enterprises to plug the leaks. See also Bernie Ward and Julie Lewis (2002) *Plugging the Leaks*, New Economics Foundation, London.
www.lm3online.org

Prove and improve

The new economics is, at its heart, a new approach to measuring success. That means we need to redefine the way we understand and measure progress, finding ways to make the invisible value of things – essential to our well-being – visible and measurable. The problem is that what gets counted, counts – but what is most important is the hardest to measure. Our approach focuses on engaging people and building capacity. Whether we are measuring trust or local money flows, we know that involving local people and working with their strengths, not their deficits, is vital to making sure that measuring leads to action and improving people's well-being.
www.proveandimprove.org

Prove it!

Prove it! is a method of evaluating community regeneration projects for anyone who wants to improve their surroundings, developed together with Groundwork and Barclays. Like advertising – as Lord Leverhulme famously expressed it – we know that some neighbourhood improvement projects work, but we don't know which ones. Prove it! is designed to help people find out. The principle is to make data collection part of the process of regeneration itself. People choose indicators from a core set designed to get beyond measuring just the inputs and outputs of projects. Many of the overriding aims of a project are achieved by involving local people in its evaluation as well as its delivery. The spirit of Prove it! is about keeping evaluation fun, simple, manageable and possible within the limited resources that small-scale projects have available to them.
www.neweconomics.org

Social accounting and social auditing

Social accounting and auditing is a way of measuring and reporting on an organization's social and ethical performance. Organizations that take on social auditors make themselves accountable to stakeholders and commit themselves to following the audit's recommendations. **nef** helped to make this a mainstream approach and demonstrated how these approaches enable companies to manage more effectively. From 1995 to 2000, we carried out a series of pioneering social audits of companies (Camelot, The Body Shop, Traidcraft, the Co-operative Wholesale Society, Ben and Jerry's) as well as international public and voluntary sector organizations. Having led the development of the method with these organizations, we helped to form the Institute of Social and Ethical Accountability to promote professional standards. We have also criticized the misuse of social auditing in our 2000 report *Corporate Spin*. **www.AccountAbility.org**

Social investment

Innovative social enterprises often fall between two stools when it comes to financing. They find it hard to get grants because they are working in the market, but banks don't understand them either. The new economics requires a whole new raft of structures that can lend and mainstream these critical organizations. **www.uksif.org**

Social return on investment

Every day our actions and activities create and destroy value; they change the world around us. Although the value we create goes far beyond what can be captured in financial terms, this is, for the most part, the only type of value that is measured and accounted for. As a result, things that can be bought and sold take on a greater significance and many important things get left out. Decisions made like this may not be as good as they could be as they are based on incomplete information about their full impacts. Social Return on Investment (SROI) is an alternative to cost–benefit Analysis that has been developed in the UK by **nef**. It is a framework for measuring and accounting for this much broader concept of value; one that seeks to reduce inequality and environmental degradation and improve well being by incorporating social, environmental and economic costs and benefits. SROI measures change in ways that are relevant to the people or organisations that experience or contribute to it. It tells the story of how change is being created by measuring social, environmental and economic outcomes and uses monetary values to represent them. This enables a ratio of benefits to costs to be calculated. For example, a ratio of 3:1 indicates that an investment of £1 delivers £3 of social value. An SROI report will contain financial information. However, in the same way that a business plan contains much more information than the financial projections, SROI is much more than just a number. It

is a story about change that includes case studies, qualitative, quantitative and financial information on which to base decisions. **nef** is working with a consortium of organizations for the Cabinet Office to develop and disseminate SROI. It is now widely used by social economy organizations, and increasingly by policy makers and commissioners. If applied systematically to the private sector it has the potential to be really transformative.
www.neweconomics.org/gen/newways_socialreturn.aspx

Street markets

Developing and protecting local street markets is a key way of keeping money flowing in local economies, and making places more distinctive. **nef** has specialized in analysing the economic impact of threatened patterns of retailing like street markets, farmers markets and covered markets. **nef** research for the London Development Agency found that London's street markets are increasingly important social hubs and provide a diverse range of food that can be as much as a third cheaper than local supermarkets. They also generate large sums for the surrounding area, with Lewisham market alone generating over £3.6m a year. **nef**'s research into the economic impact of Queens Market in Newham demonstrated that it sustained a third more jobs than the Asda supermarket that was planned to replace it, and was among the factors leading to Asda pulling out of demolition plans.
www.neweconomics.org

Time banks

The thinking behind time banks, developed in the USA by the civil rights lawyer Edgar Cahn, was introduced into the UK by a group including **nef** in 1997. There are now nearly 100 across the UK, many of them embedded in public services. The idea is that people are rewarded for the effort they make helping out in their local neighbourhoods, and – when they need help themselves – that supportive community is there for them too. These are neighbourhood building tools, recognizing that without the 'core economy' of families and neighbours, other economic infrastructure rapidly becomes unsustainable.
www.timebanking.org

Well-being

The new economics suggests that well-being is a better objective for economic policy than narrow measures of money – the data show that, while economic output in the UK has nearly doubled in the last 30 years, happiness levels have remained flat. Focusing on well-being means redefining 'progress' and asking the fundamental question: do our systems and economies really shape the world as we want it?
www.neweconomics.org

Index

absolute poverty 81, 81–2
advertising 46–7
agriculture 26, 34, 119, 138
aid 34, 113, 136
AIDS 70, 111, 135, 148
altruism 65, 72
Annan, Kofi 110–11
anti-trust action 89–90, 116, 133
Argentina 26, 57, 58, 139
assets 15, 60, 105, 136–7, 153
    of African-Americans 141, 142
    people as 15, 57–8, 128–9, 130, 131
Audi 101
authenticity 2, 73, 74, 74–5

bancor (currency) 61
Bangladesh 3, 112, 141, 143–4
banking system 6, 7, 58–9, 147
    see also banks
bankruptcy 147
banks 6, 120, 139, 142, 146, 153
    breaking up 57, 90, 146
    money creation by 56, 58–9, 84, 90, 138,
        147
    see also financial crises
barriers to development 138–43
barter 58, 59, 60, 154
behaviour 15, 29, 35, 67–8, 71
Belloc, Hilaire 19–20, 21
berkshares 57, 151–2
Beveridge, Sir William 19, 127
Bhutan 43

big currencies 53, 54, 55–6, 58, 59
biocapacity 12, 114, 158
Black Hawk (Colorado) 14, 15, 152
'black money' 81
Blair administration 9, 41
Blake, William 18
blood donation 65, 70
Boesky, Ivan 135, 142
borrowing
    by governments 49–50, 58, 62, 141
    see also debt
Bowling Alone (Putnam, 2001) 126–7
Breed, Colin 125
Bretton Woods 148
Buddhist economics 18, 21, 22
Buffett, Warren 7
built-in obsolescence 98, 100, 101
Bush, George W. 28, 96, 154
business 74, 156
Butler, R. A. (Richard Austen, 'Rab') 36, 38,
    40

Cahn, Edgar 54, 58, 88, 123, 127, 131
Campaign for Real Ale 118
Canada 51–2, 57
capital 89
capitalism 20, 155
carbon emission entitlements 45, 90,
    117–18, 148
carbon emissions 114, 117, 148
carbon taxes 117
caring 86–7, 89, 91, 92, 132

Carville, James 27
casinos 14–15
cathedrals 79, 81
CDOs (collateralized debt obligations) 5–6
Central America 32–3
charities 13, 58, 129
Charles, Prince of Wales 23, 100
Chesterton, G.K. (Gilbert Keith) 18, 20, 21, 81
Chicago (Illinois) 87, 127, 131
chief executives 19, 141, 142
children 4, 46–7, 82, 86, 87
Chile 51
China 28, 50, 60, 82, 100, 116, 154
CHP (combined heat and power) plants 102, 103
cities 3, 61, 75, 80, 105–6, 110, 116
  and energy 102, 103
  traffic speeds 65–6
citizen's incomes 45, 58, 73, 91–2, 148
Clarke, Otto 21
classical economics 28–9, 34–5, 44, 67, 89, 123
  assumptions 71, 72, 85
Cleveland (Ohio) 6
climate change 3–4, 40, 96, 112, 115
  tackling 45, 90, 155, 157
Clinton, Bill 27, 52, 145
co-generation of energy 102, 103
co-production 88–9, 127–31, 132, 158, 159
Cobb, Clifford 39, 40–1
Cobb, John 22, 40–1
collateralized debt obligations (CDOs) 5–6
Colombia 33, 51
Columbus, Christopher 139
combined heat and power see CHP
commodities 11, 57, 139
  currencies based on 60, 90, 120
commons 79, 82, 113, 148
communications technologies 58, 59, 78, 158
communities 2, 27, 42, 43, 89, 92
  assets 57–8, 106
  investing in 118

money in 103–5, 107, 124, 151–2
  Wal-mart and 124–5
community 32, 33, 54, 89, 158
community banks 26, 145
community land trusts 46, 73, 151
Community Way model 58
community-supported agriculture 26, 119
companies 74–5, 84, 137–8, 142–3
  see also corporations
comparative advantage 26, 75, 109, 116
competition 90
  regulation 85, 113, 125, 126, 133
complementary currencies 26, 57–8, 59, 62, 154
consumerism 20, 44, 132
consumers 44, 67–8
consumption 11, 34, 39–40, 100, 158
  'defensive' 37
contributing, need for 128–9
conventional economics 10–12, 82, 97, 127
cooperatives 20, 26, 153
'core economy' 54–5, 88, 89, 127, 158
corporate debt 84, 142–3
corporate power 20, 28, 85
corporate raiders 84, 142
corporate responsibility 26, 153–4
corporations 4, 8, 13, 82, 90, 116, 142, 158
  tax gap 52, 137, 157
Costa Rica 99
Country Party 18
crashes 1, 51, 91
  2008–9 crash 2, 3, 5, 6–7, 8, 15, 84, 85, 154–5
creativity 38, 46, 75, 79, 91
credit 91, 145–6
  see also debt
credit cards 84
credit crunch 3, 91, 144, 157
credit unions 26, 144, 145, 146
crime 10, 35, 37, 38, 87, 127, 128
crises, fundamental 3–5
Cuba 95–7, 101, 105
culture 43, 44, 111, 115, 127, 158

currencies 26, 55, 56–8, 81
  barter currencies 58, 59
  based on commodities 60, 90, 120
  based on emissions rights 90, 148
  big 53, 54, 55–6, 58, 59
  complementary 26, 57–8, 59, 62, 154
  global 56, 61, 120, 147–8
  local 26, 27, 56, 57, 58, 60, 151–2, 153
  multiple 58, 59–60, 60, 90
  regional 58, 59, 60

Daly, Herman 22, 23, 40–1, 43, 97
Dawnay, Emma 71
debt 4, 7, 11–12, 81, 83–4
  cancellation 137, 148
  corporate 84, 142–3
  and development 138–43
  GM crops and 91, 119, 140
  Malawi 135–6
  medieval freedom from 79, 80–1
  money creation 7, 8, 11, 56, 60, 84, 90,
    138
  national 49–50, 83, 84, 139, 141
  personal 7, 36, 83–4, 91, 140, 141
  repayments 90, 137
  small-scale 143–4
  see also sub-prime loans
decentralized energy generation 102–3, 106,
    114, 155
decision making 67–8, 71, 158
'defensive consumption' 37
democracy 31, 55, 91, 141, 158
demurrage 57
depression 4, 10, 11, 35, 38, 68, 75, 83
deregulation 8, 12, 22, 28
developing countries 11, 81, 136–8, 143
development 24, 27, 116, 138–43
development projects 82
Dickens, Charles 36
Diggers 18
Disney 141
Distributism 19–21, 29
District of Columbia School of Law 131
diversity 82, 90, 152

domestic tradeable quotas (DTQs) 117–18
Douthwaite, Richard 56–7, 148
Downs-Thomson Paradox 66
downshifting 2, 4–5, 11, 35, 69, 73
Drexel Burnham Lambert 142
drugs, generic 113, 116, 117
DTQs (domestic tradeable quotas) 117–18
Dublin (Ireland) 52, 106
DuPont 85
dynamic equilibrium 43, 44

Earth, Apollo pictures of 101–2
EBCU (emissions-backed currency unit) 148
ecological debt 113–14
ecological footprints 31, 33, 34, 112
ecological issues 3–4, 12, 25
economic activity 25, 148
economic development 24, 27, 116, 138–43
economic growth *see* growth
economic indicators, alternative 26
economic institutions 29, 82, 153, 154
economic processes 97–8, 99
economic system 2, 11, 21–2, 23, 29, 112,
    138
  and poverty 13–14, 18, 29, 81–2, 154
economics 10–12, 18, 19, 29, 72–3, 98
  assumptions 10, 25, 28, 29, 69, 71, 72,
    82, 85, 97, 99, 115
  medieval 78–80, 80–1
  post-autistic 9–10, 71–2
  and psychology 67–8, 71, 72–3
  as a science 15, 34–5, 98, 152
  and sustainability 24
  see also classical economics; conventional
    economics; new economics
economy 12, 26, 84–5, 158
  creating poverty 13–14, 18, 29, 81, 154
ecosystems 99, 112, 114
Edison, Thomas 58, 90, 147
education 13, 33, 35, 46, 113
efficiency 4, 13, 99, 100, 123, 126, 131–2
E.F. Schumacher Society 151
Eisner, Michael 141
Ekins, Paul 1, 22, 23, 24, 24–5

Elgin, Duane 69
elites 23, 59, 153, 156, 158
emissions *see* carbon emissions; greenhouse
    gas emissions
emissions entitlements 45, 90, 117–18, 148
emissions-backed currency unit (EBCU) 148
employment 25, 44, 84
energy 3, 13, 29, 74, 106
    costs 114–15, 145–6, 156, 157
    decentralized generation 102–3, 106, 114,
        155
    prices 3, 82, 112, 116, 117, 155
    re-using 101–3
    renewable 97, 102, 102–3, 114, 156, 157
energy poverty 45, 157
energy service companies (Escos) 103
energy taxation 26
energy-backed currency unit 56–7
environment 19, 26, 43, 98–9, 112, 157,
    158
environmental auditing 153–4
environmental capital 89
environmental costs 114–15, 117
environmental destruction 10, 11, 23, 35,
    37, 115
environmental economics 26, 29, 98–9,
    100–1, 115
environmental impacts 32, 40, 56–7
environmental stewardship 34
Escos (energy service companies) 103
ethical consumerism 69–70
ethical investment 26, 69–70, 74, 154
ethical products 2, 26
ethical trade 26, 119, 145, 153
ethics 11, 19, 22, 35, 69–70, 72, 73
Etzioni, Amitai 127–8
EU (European Union) 26, 55, 98, 100, 101,
    117, 118
euro 55, 56, 59, 120
exchange 25, 34, 111
externalities 10, 35, 45, 87, 115, 155

Fabians 19, 20
Fair Finance 145

fair trade 26, 119, 145, 153
families 4, 35, 73, 92, 132
family 32, 35, 54, 89, 158
farmers, supermarkets and 125–6
Federal Reserve 49–50, 147
'feel-good factor' 39
feudal system 79, 80–1
Field of Dreams (film, Robinson, 1989) 65
financial crashes *see* crashes
Financial Inclusion Fund 145
financial institutions 13, 58, 85, 91, 157
financial interdependence 135–8
financial markets 1–2, 52, 53, 55, 138,
    154–5
financial services 53, 54, 84, 85, 86, 120,
    138, 143, 158
financial system 7, 28, 145, 157
first world debt 141–2
Fleming, David 117–18
food 2, 26, 82, 115–16, 118–20
    GM 91, 117, 119, 140–1
    local 2, 118, 119–20, 151
    production 96, 105, 114, 118, 155
Ford, Henry 58, 90, 147
foreign direct investment 137–8
foreign exchange 7, 8, 50–1, 51–2
fossil fuels 3, 22, 56–7, 96, 113, 114, 117,
    148
    prices 157
France 8–9, 50, 51–2, 71–2
fuel poverty 45, 157
full employment 86–7, 87–8

G7 countries 22, 22–3
Galbraith, J.K. (John Kenneth) 41, 51
gambling 14–15, 152
Gandhi, Mohandas (Mahatma) 18, 19, 21,
    110, 112
Gates, Bill 141
Gates, Jeff 141–2
GDP (gross domestic product) 10, 32,
    36–40, 42, 43, 54, 79
    alternatives to 40–2, 43
    bad measure of success 10, 37, 55, 78

global 141
UK 4
see also growth
genetically modified crops *see* GM crops
Germany 33, 50, 58
Gladwell, Malcolm 68
Global Barter Clubs 57, 58
global commons 113, 148
global currencies 56, 61, 120, 147–8
global greenback 61
global warming 3, 3–4, 115, 155
see also climate change
globalization 8, 28, 143, 153
see also interdependence
GM (genetically modified) crops 91, 117,
119, 140–1
Goetz, Stephan 124
gold standard 8, 143
Good Life, The (BBC sitcom) 69
goods, local 19, 109, 110
Goodwin, Fred 142
government borrowing 37–8, 49–50, 58, 62,
141
governments 2, 28, 116, 129, 158
creating money 58–9, 62, 90
propping up banking system 6, 7
Graham, Benjamin 120
Grameen Bank 26, 143–4, 153
Great Barrington (Massachusetts) 57,
151–2, 153
Great Depression 3, 36, 57
green bonds 157
green collar jobs 106, 157
Green Consumer Guide, The (Elkington and
Hailes, 1988) 26, 69, 72
green economics 23, 100, 117
green energy 26, 97, 102–3, 114, 156, 157
Green New Deal 156–8
green taxation 153
greenhouse gas emissions 3–4, 115, 148
gross domestic product *see* GDP
Gross National Happiness 43
growth 2, 11, 12–13, 23, 36–7, 38–40, 42,
43

bad measure of success 10, 158
maximizing 25
and poverty 4, 39–40, 81–2
and progress 39, 78
wealth defined in terms of 32
and well-being 4–5
see also GDP
guilds 80, 80–1

happiness 12, 18, 29, 41, 43, 45–6
Happy Planet Index 32–3, 34, 43
Hard Times (Dickens, 1854) 36
HBOS 7
health 46, 72, 78, 96, 115, 129
health costs 117
healthcare 13, 33, 44
hedge funds 5, 7, 97, 120
Helsinki (Finland) 102
HIV/AIDS 70, 111, 135, 148
Honduras 139, 141
house prices 36, 46, 79, 83, 91, 126–7, 151
London 53, 54, 91
see also mortgages
Howard, Ebenezer 105, 158
HSBC 5
human interaction 67–8, 74
human needs 20, 24, 67, 86
human rights 110–11, 116, 147

ill-health 35, 38, 46
'illth' 29, 35
IMF (International Monetary Fund) 27, 82,
91, 135–6, 139, 143, 147, 147–8
incomes 24, 37, 43, 44, 78, 79, 81
and happiness 45–6
inequalities 37, 81, 82, 142
of poorest 4, 81, 82, 112, 142
Index of Sustainable Economic Welfare *see*
ISEW
India 82, 91, 110, 119, 136, 139–40, 153
indigenous knowledge 82, 117
inequality 4, 81–2, 96, 112–13, 116
inflation 8, 22, 58, 90
information technology 58, 59, 115

intellectual property 82, 91, 110, 113, 116, 117
interdependence 111–20, 135–8
    Keynes on 19, 109, 110, 115, 143
    see also globalization
interest 8, 11, 11–12, 58, 77, 157
interest rates 144, 144–5
interest-free money 43, 73, 84, 90
intergenerational equity 25, 117
international bankruptcy 147
International Monetary Fund *see* IMF
investment 14, 45, 53, 60, 104, 118, 137–8
    ethical 26, 69–70, 74, 154
involvement 71, 75, 128–30
Iraq 49, 60, 136
ISEW (Index of Sustainable Economic
    Welfare) 40–1, 43, 78
Islamic banking 58, 90, 146
islands, small 31–2, 33–4
Italy 33, 119–20, 138
Ithaca hours currency 57, 58
It's a Wonderful Life (film, Capra, 1946) 38

Jacobs, Jane 56, 110, 126
Jaffe, Bernie 126
Japan 26, 50, 91, 113, 119, 128
Jefferson, Thomas 18, 20
Jersey 52, 53
Jones, Allan 103
Jubilee Debt campaign 137
junk bonds 1, 142–3
just-in-time 123–4, 155

Keynes, John Maynard 2, 13–14, 15, 17, 21,
    37, 55
    on interdependence 19, 109, 110, 115,
    143
    international currency 61, 120
    on local production 19, 109, 110
    on 'practical men' as 'slaves of some
    defunct economist' 10, 35, 67, 87, 159
Keynesian economics 8, 18, 22, 27, 28
Kinney, Jill 130
Knowsley (Merseyside) 104

Kropotkin, Peter 18
Krugman, Paul 52

land 19, 82, 96
land tax 43
landfill 97, 98, 100, 107
Layard, Richard 41
Lehigh Hospital (Pennsylvania) 129
Letchworth Garden City (Hertfordshire) 105
lets (local exchange and trading systems) 57
liberalism 18, 19, 27
Lietaer, Bernard 56, 61, 120
life 19, 29, 55, 69, 86, 91
    need for meaning 42, 75
life expectancy 31, 32–3, 82
life poverty 82–3
life satisfaction 31, 33, 41, 42
Lima (Peru) 130–1
Linton, Michael 57, 58
Living Economy, The (Ekins, 1986) 24–5
LM3 (Local Money 3) 60, 104–5
loans *see* debt
Local Alchemy programme 152–3
local circulation of money 103–5, 107, 124,
    151–2
local currencies 26, 56, 57, 58, 59, 60,
    151–2, 153
local economies 26, 81, 85, 86, 105–7, 118,
    124, 133
local exchange and trading systems (lets) 57
local food 2, 118, 119–20, 151
local governments 6, 44, 60
local life 4, 81, 158
Local Money 3 *see* LM3
local production 109, 116, 118
local savings schemes 61
local shops 75, 82–3, 104, 124, 124–5, 126,
    151
    supermarkets and 80, 105, 125
local wealth 14, 53–4
localization 155–6, 159
London 52, 53, 61, 97, 102, 103
    house prices 53, 54, 91
    traffic speed 65–6

London Underground 147
Lutzenberger, Jose 26

Macmillan Cancer Care 88–9
McRobie, George 22, 24
mainstream 4–5, 26, 154, 159–60
  see also economics
Malawi 135–6, 137
Malaysia 51
Manchester United 155
manipulated debt 139–41
markets 10, 12, 51, 70, 158
  financial 1–2, 52, 53, 55, 138, 154–5
  free 22, 85, 112–13
  new economics and 67, 72–5, 85
Marsh Farm estate (Luton) 104–5, 152–3
Maslow, Abraham 67
materialism 12, 46–7
Max-Neef, Manfred 24
Maxwell, Robert 143
MDGs (Millennium Development Goals) 39,
  136
Mead, Margaret 129
meaning, need for 42, 75
measurement problem 36–40
measuring 12, 42, 55, 85
  success 2, 8, 10, 43, 44, 55, 154, 156, 158
  value 10, 15, 29, 53, 59, 115
  wealth 32, 37–40, 53–4
  well-being 4, 18, 32–3, 34, 43
mechanics, Cuban 95–6, 97
medieval economics 78–80, 80–1
mega-rich 120, 141, 142
mental health 4, 35, 36, 46, 68, 83
Merck 99
micro-credit 26, 143–4, 145, 146, 151, 153
Milkin, Michael 142
Millennium Development Goals see MDGs
minimum wage 92
misery, of UK young people 35–6
Mishan, E.J. 40
Mogridge, Martin 65–6, 74
Mondragon (Spain), cooperatives 153
money 8, 11, 13, 18, 27, 29, 36, 95
  as a bad measure 10, 15, 18, 53, 59, 90,
    143, 154
  creating 7, 56–7, 58–9, 84, 90, 120, 138,
    147
  designed for money markets 53
  economics and 25, 127
  externalities 35
  and life 55, 86, 154, 159
  local circulation 103–5, 107, 124, 151–2
  means to an end 15
  new economics view 15, 59–60, 89
  new ways of organizing 56–60
  re-using 103–5
  replacing with well-being 42
  slowing down 51–2, 60
  too little 57
  types of 14–15, 57, 59, 120
  and value 10, 15, 53, 59
  and wealth 15, 19, 32, 38, 78
  and well-being 18, 21, 81
  see also GDP; growth; price; trickle down
money flows 26, 50–2, 60, 103–5, 107, 124,
  136–8
money markets 1–2, 52, 53, 55, 138, 154–5
money poverty 81–2
money system 7–8, 50–6, 60
monopolies 8, 20, 83, 84–6, 89–90, 125–6,
  133, 146
Monsanto 85, 140
moral philosophy 12, 19, 72–3
morality 8, 18, 28, 74, 115
  economics and 12, 19, 22
Morris, William 18, 78, 151
mortgages 1, 4, 5–6, 6, 7, 46, 91
  working to pay 46, 68, 73, 77–8, 79, 81,
    83, 84, 89, 126–7, 140
  see also house prices
motivations 4–5, 11, 67–9, 70, 71, 72, 73,
  75
multinationals 14, 61, 84–5, 90, 137–8, 139,
  143
multiple currencies 58, 59–60, 60, 90
multiplier effect 103–5
Murdoch, Rupert 52

Myers, Norman 117

Nanumaea (Tuvalu) 34
national accounting 37–8, 38–9
national debt 49–50, 83, 84, 139, 141
national grid 102, 106
National Health Service *see* NHS
natural capital 3, 99
natural resources 22, 40, 43, 84, 97–8
needs 20, 24, 25, 67, 75, 86
  basic 25, 89, 91–2, 115
nef (the new economics foundation) 24, 26,
    45, 71, 104, 131–2, 145
  Local Alchemy programme 152–3
  see also Happy Planet Index; LM3
'neo-liberal' policies 8, 27–8
Nether Wallop (Hampshire) 80, 81
The Netherlands 58, 106, 138
New Century 5
New Deal for Communities 152
New Deal (US) 157
new economics 2–3, 9–10, 18–19, 28–9, 59,
    153–4, 159–60
  Cuba as object lesson 96–7
  history of 9–10, 18–19, 21–7
  and the mainstream 26
  as new definition of wealth 15
  principles 35, 157–8
new economics foundation *see* **nef**
New York City 52, 128
News Corporation 52
NHS (National Health Service) 87, 114, 131
Northern Rock 6
Nottingham 35
Nu-Spaarpas experiment 106

Obama, Barack 154, 157
obsolescence, built-in 98, 100, 101
odious debt 146
offshore assets 136–7
offshore financial centres 52–3, 61
oil 3, 96, 115, 117, 155
Oil Legacy Fund 157
orchards 111, 112, 115, 124

organic food 26
Ostrom, Elinor 127
out-of-town retailing 75, 80, 123, 132
overconsumption 32, 40, 44, 113
Owen, Robert 57
ownership 11, 46, 60, 91, 118, 156

paid work 87–9, 92
palm oil 112
Partners in Health 130–1
peak oil 3, 96, 117, 155
Pearce, David 25–6, 98, 115
Peasants' Revolt (1381) 18
pensions 7, 44, 61, 73, 155
people, as assets 15, 57–8, 128–9, 130, 131
permit trading 45, 117–18, 148
personal carbon allowances 45, 117–18
personal debt 7, 36, 83–4, 91, 140, 141
Petrini, Carlo 119–20
Pettifor, Ann 135, 137
philanthropy 130, 133
policy makers 28, 35, 73, 87, 90
  assumptions of 67, 68, 73, 128
  Keynes on 10, 35, 67, 87, 159
political agenda 42–7
politicians 11, 54, 159
politics, new 159
pollution 10, 35, 37, 40, 98, 112, 114
  by GM genes 91, 117, 119
poor 29, 145–6
Porritt, Jonathon 23
post-autistic economics 9–10, 71–2
poverty 4, 23, 35, 79–80, 81–2, 127
  economic system and 13–14, 18, 29, 81–2,
    154
  interdependence leading to 111–15
  reduction 39–40, 51–2, 61, 116, 124–5
poverty gap 4, 52–3, 78, 82
power 10, 12, 25, 28, 53, 141–2
  corporate 20, 28, 85
  monopoly power 83, 89–90, 125–6, 146
power relationships 29, 114
price 10, 67, 72, 73, 115, 153
Price, Andrew 132

prices 80, 156, 158
Pritchard, Alison 23
product life cycle 97–8, 101
professionals 130, 132, 133, 159
profits 12, 13, 99
progress 36, 37–8, 39, 43, 44, 77–8, 81–2, 84
Proudhon, Pierre-Joseph 120
psychology, economics and 67–8, 71, 72–3
public goods 148
public sector commissioning 131–2, 133
public services 45, 74, 127–32, 158
public transport 66, 74
'purchasing power parity' 81
Putnam, Robert 126–7, 127–8

qoin system 58

rainforests 4, 10, 111, 112
'rational man' assumption 10, 71
RBS 142
re-use 97, 99, 100–5
Reagan, Ronald 22, 27
real money, generating 120
'real' wealth 2, 32, 36–40
reciprocity 44, 128, 128–30, 133
    see also co-production
recycling 97, 98, 100–1, 105–6, 106–7
redistribution 19, 27, 52, 96
regeneration 27, 104, 105, 107, 116, 124, 128
regional currencies 58, 59, 60
regulation 129, 156
    competition 85, 113, 125, 126, 133
    financial sector 53, 85, 157
relationships 4, 69, 83, 128–30
remittances 137
Rendell, Matt 33
renewable energy 26, 97, 102, 102–3, 114, 156, 157
repair 97, 98, 101, 105, 107
resources 32, 43, 97–8, 99, 100–1, 114, 158
    local 25, 115
    natural 22, 40, 43, 84, 97–8

retirement 46, 73
    see also pensions
rewarded work 88
rewards 7, 8, 11, 25, 92, 141, 142
roads 66, 115
Robertson, James 17, 22, 23, 55, 145
Rockefeller, John D. 28
Roman Catholic church 19, 21, 117
Roosevelt, Eleanor 96
Roosevelt, Franklin Delano 157
Rotterdam (The Netherlands) 106
rubbish 97–105
Rupasingha, Anil 124
Rushey Green surgery (London) 131
Ruskin, John 17–18, 18, 29, 35, 78, 81
Russia 110

St Louis (Missouri) 131
Samoa 34
Sane (South African New Economics) 58
saving seeds 91, 117, 119, 141
savings 7, 46, 73, 90, 157
schools 131
Schor, Juliet 83
Schumacher, E.F. (Ernst Friedrich, 'Fritz') 1, 18, 21–2, 27, 114, 117
SDRs (special drawing rights) 147–8
Seattle (Washington) 41
seeds 91, 117, 119, 140, 141
seigniorage 58–9
Sen, Amartya 12
SERs (special emission rights) 148
set prices 80
sharing 34, 44, 91, 119, 140
shopping 26, 80, 82–3, 104, 105, 125, 133
shops 20
    local 75, 80, 82–3, 104, 105, 124, 124–5, 126, 151
    see also out-of-town retailing; supermarkets
short-termism 11, 13, 14–15
SIVs (structured investment vehicles) 1, 5–6, 6
skills 13, 60, 98, 100, 101, 105, 132

Slow Food 118, 119–20
Small is Beautiful (Schumacher, 1977) 1, 21
small islands 31–2, 33–4
small-scale banks 146
Smith, Adam 89
social auditing 26, 45, 153–4
social banks 144, 146
social capital 19, 33, 54–5, 86–7, 89, 126–7, 132
  Wal-mart and 124–5
social credit 19, 58, 59, 90
social networks 36, 127, 132
social norms 67–8, 71
social relationships 34, 45
social return on investment (SROI) 45
Soros, George 51, 148
South Africa 136
South African New Economics (Sane) 58
South Shore Bank (Chicago) 144
sovereignty 55, 113
special drawing rights (SDRs) 147–8
special emission rights (SERs) 148
speculation 22, 53, 81, 82, 84, 146, 158
  deterring 51–2, 60, 61
  financial 7, 15, 50–1, 51–2, 61
spirituality 4–5, 18, 21–2, 75, 79, 81
SROI (social return on investment) 45
Stamp Out Poverty 61
Starkey, Richard 118
state 12–13, 28, 155
  see also governments
steady-state economy 43, 44
Stern Report (Stern, 2006) 155
Stiglitz, Joseph 61
stress 4, 35, 37, 83
structured investment vehicles *see* SIVs
sub-prime loans 1, 5–7, 144
sub-Saharan Africa 82
'subsidiarity' 117
subsidies 11, 82, 112, 113, 117, 119, 123–4
success 79–80, 89
  measuring 2, 8, 10, 43, 44, 55, 154, 156, 158
suicides 83, 91, 140

super rich 120, 141, 142
supermarkets 80, 85, 90, 104, 105, 123–6, 129
sustainability 24, 73, 89, 113, 114, 116, 117
sustainable development 51–2, 61
Swann, Bob 120, 151
Sweden 102
Swift, Jonathan 18
Switzerland 52, 62

T-bills (Treasury bills) 49–50, 58
takeovers 84, 142, 143
talent system 58
targets 9, 41, 129
tariffs 113
tax havens 15, 52–3, 53, 61, 136, 157
Tax Justice Network 136–7
taxation 73, 92, 116
taxes 10, 15, 27, 32, 43, 62, 136–7
  paid by corporations 52, 61, 137, 157
TB (tuberculosis) 130, 148
TEQs (tradeable energy quotas) 117–18
terra (currency) 56, 61, 120
Tesco 85, 116, 125
Thatcher, Margaret 21, 22, 23, 27
The Other Economic Summit *see* TOES
Thoreau, Henry David 69
time 44, 45–6, 60, 103, 132
time banks 58, 59, 60, 89, 92, 123, 131, 132
Titmuss, Richard 65, 70
Tobin, James 51–2
Tobin Levy 51–2, 61
TOES (The Other Economic Summit) 23–5
Toffler, Alvin 88
trade 25, 81, 109–10, 111–15, 116, 148, 158
  fair trade 26, 119, 145, 153
Trade-Related Aspects of Intellectual Property *see* TRIPS
tradeable energy quotas (TEQs) 117–18
traffic speed 65–6, 74
transport 67, 74, 112, 115
  see also public transport
Treasury bills (T-bills) 49–50, 58

trickle down 27–8, 39–40, 138
  'doesn't work' 27, 52, 104
TRIPS (Trade-Related Aspects of Intellectual
  Property) agreement (1995) 113, 117
tuberculosis (TB) 130, 148
Turning Point network 23

UK (United Kingdom) 4, 39, 55, 61, 70, 85,
  119, 145
  aid from 136
  corporation tax gap 137
  cultural enrichment 111
  debt 83, 141
  Ecological Debt Day 114
  energy 102, 114
  food production 96, 114
  Happy Planet Index 32
  'illth' 4, 35
  interest rates 144–5
  local savings schemes 61
  money deposits 136
  orchard loss 111, 112, 115, 124
  poverty 82
  real costs of road transport 115
  super-casinos 14
  trade 112, 113
  well-being 4, 35–6, 41, 68
  working hours 68
  young people in 35–6
  see also house prices
Ukraine 110
UN (United Nations) 39, 51–2, 60, 91,
  110–11, 157
unemployment 44, 46, 55–6, 91–2, 157
unpaid work 87–9
Unto This Last (Ruskin, 1860) 18, 29
USA (United States) 39, 57, 61, 82, 113,
  119, 127, 157
  and Cuba 95
  debt 49–50, 84, 141
  Happy Planet Index 32
  invasion of Iraq (2003) 49, 60
  subsidies 11, 113
  trade deficit 50

unemployment 55
  well-being deteriorating 41, 68
usury 80, 81, 144–5

value 44, 98, 99
  measuring 10, 15, 29, 53, 59, 115
values 11, 71, 115, 127
Vanuatu 31–2, 35, 42
Vaxjo (Sweden) 102
vegetable box schemes 104
'victory gardening movement' 96
Virgil, *Eclogues* 110
voluntary sector 13, 87, 132, 145
voting 124–5, 127

Wal-mart 104, 123, 124–5
Wall Street Crash (1929) 1, 51, 90
Waring, Marilyn 38–9
Washington Consensus 27–8
waste 97, 100–1, 158
Waste Electrical and Electronic Equipment
  directive *see* WEEE directive
wealth 18, 28, 38, 41–2, 52, 89, 141–2, 152
  defining 18–19, 32, 34, 35, 38
  and 'illth' 29, 35–6
  local 14, 53–4
  measuring 32, 36–40, 53–4, 143
  money and 19, 32, 38, 78, 143
  new economics and 3, 15, 35, 37
  real 2, 32, 37–40
  see also Happy Planet Index
WEDGE project 23
WEEE (Waste Electrical and Electronic
  Equipment) directive 98, 100, 101
welfare 25, 28, 44, 127, 129, 153
Welfare State 19, 129
well-being 4–5, 25, 45–6, 99, 158
  demand for 4–5, 11, 68–9
  falls in 4, 37, 41, 68, 78
  GDP and 4, 36, 37
  measuring 4, 18, 32–3, 34, 43
  money and 18, 21, 81
  as motivation 4–5, 11, 68–9, 72
  new economics and 41–7, 68–9

origins of 43
willingness to pay 99
Willington, Sally 23
Wir currency 62
Witt, Susan 151
Woking (Surrey) 102–3
women 38–9, 77–8, 79, 83, 144
work 24, 45, 81, 84–5, 86–7, 92
 concept of 25, 83, 86, 87–9
 to pay mortgages 46, 68, 73, 77–8, 79, 81,
  83, 84, 89, 126–7, 140
 of women 38–9, 77–8, 83

working hours 45–6, 78, 79, 83, 92
World Bank 27, 81, 82, 91, 137, 139, 143,
 147

Yank Tanks (film, Schendel, 2002) 95
young people, UK 35–6
youth courts 129, 132
Yunus, Mohammed 143–4

Zimbabwe 32
Zurich (Switzerland) 66